FAITH   AFTER   ATHEISM

by

Michael M. Winter

Dedicated

to

Ben   and   Max

Contents

ACKNOWLEDGEMENTS

I wish to express my gratitude to Dr. William Ahearne, to Anthony Faulkner, to Canon John McNamara, and to Jason Squires for reading the manuscript, for offering practical advice and many helpful suggestions.

Quotations from the bible are taken from the Revised Standard Version.

Quotations from the Second Vatican Council are taken from *THE DOCUMENTS OF VATICAN II* (1966) trans. Walter M. Abbott, New York: Guild Press.

Quotations from other General Councils are taken from *ENCHIRIDION SYMBOLORUM DEFINITIONUM ET DECLARATIONUM*, Edition 33, (1965), eds. Denziger, H. & Schönmetzer, A. Freiburg, Herder.

The cover picture of the Magi is reproduced by kind permission of Sonia Halliday Photos, being a reproduction of a stained glass window detail from Canterbury Cathedral. The cover was designed by Sue Longbottom.

1

PREFACE

Is belief in God and its practical expression in religion important or even relevant in the 21st century? My answer is emphatically Yes, because it is the only adequate remedy for evil. I realise that this is a gigantic claim, and its justification will occupy the whole of this book. Yet the core of the argumentation can be set out in one sentence, thus: Religion provides a powerful motive for the individual to lead an honest life, which in turn gives me moral strength to withstand oppression without being dehumanised, and finally it gives me the energy to sustain daunting campaigns to eradicate institutionalised evil, (like the abolition of the slave trade).

Having spoken of evil and oppression, let me be clear about their concrete manifestations. They can be summarised as greed, violence and deception. Or to spell it out more clearly, human selfishness craves more of the world's good things than we need for a contented life. If this greed is frustrated we turn to warfare or economic exploitation, followed up by massive propaganda, lies, and concealment of the real motives of the actual beneficiaries. The twentieth century had all too many examples of warfare, exploitation and deception. The events are still in the collective memory, so I will not spell them out in detail for the moment. In the 21 st century a new peril has become inescapably clear, namely global warming and the reckless exploitation of the planet's limited and diminishing resources. The usual mechanisms have come into play again. Rich nations feel entitled to a disproportionate share of the minerals, go to war to grab them, and then tell lies about the real motive. The scramble for oil which motivated the invasion of Iraq in 2003 is a classic example.

The possible remedies for these gigantic evils can be classified into roughly four categories. First is the hope that education and the progress of science can cure everything. Secondly the values of the Enlightenment are put forward. That is to say the values which have given rise, in the modern world to concepts like the equality of all people before the law, equality of the sexes, free speech, and democracy in politics. This set of values chimes in with a great deal of common sense and ordinary decency. Thirdly there is Marxism which has its own perspective and programme for the creation of a better society. Fourthly there is religion, in which vast field I must limit myself mainly to Christianity and particularly to Catholicism which is the largest Christian Church, which I know well having been a been a member for more than sixty years.

The potential and the limitations of those four categories of possible cures for human woes will be examined throughout the book. At this stage I offer a very brief summary as a taster of what is to come.

Although education and science have eradicated many diseases and improved the comfort of our lives in some countries, the same processes have made warfare incomparably more cruel and destructive , and have paved the way for economic exploitation on a scale that the sixteenth century merchant adventurers could never have dreamed of.

The values of the Enlightenment have indeed yielded great benefits in such areas as the concept of human rights, enshrined in documents like the United Nations Charter, and its Declaration on Human Rights. It does not belittle those achievements if I point out two caveats. Firstly the majority of the human race do not possess the intellectual capacity or the education to plan their lives on those laudable principles. It remains something of a theoretical programme. Secondly we should bear in mind how much it owes to Christianity. Although the classical proponents of that way of life were avowed atheists like Voltaire, Rousseau, Diderot and others, like many revolutionaries they retained more than they realised of the values of the older regime which they attacked. This can been seen by reference to seventeenth century England. During the Civil War Cromwell's soldiers were discussing basically the same issues in their famous debates in Putney parish church, namely the equality of all men, and the source of political authority. The difference between them and the scholars of the Enlightenment was that Cromwell's Puritans based their principles on the bible. The Christian origin of these concepts has been largely ignored and deserves much more research.

Marxism as a cure for human sufferings has an almost self imposed limitation in that it deals mainly with economic forces at the national level. It has little to say about individual conduct. Moreover in its short history it has been its own worst enemy. Its record in the twentieth century was a terrible disincentive to would-be imitators. It has been implemented by extreme violence, particularly in Russia and China. It proved inefficient economically, crushed human freedom , and was rejected decisively when the oppressed peoples had the opportunity to throw off the compulsions of the police states.

Theoretically religion (especially Christianity) has the best chance of aiding humanity. Confining my attention for the moment to the most ancient and most recent mission statements, I have no hesitation in claiming that the New Testament and the documents of the Second Vatican Council contain, in germ, an adequate programme for the proper living of human life at the individual and collective levels. If any reader should think that this is an outrageous claim I would simply invite them to read those two collections with an open mind. The basic thrust of the Christian message is a moral one, which confronts the human evils at their crucial interface. The remedy for warfare, economic exploitation and systematic deception cannot be found in education or better bureaucratic organisation. These are basically moral failings for which a moral remedy alone will suffice.

The most recent problem on the scene, global warming is in even greater need of a moral solution. It is caused by the excessive use of the world's diminishing minerals, principally carbon fuels, and this is driven by the insatiable appetites of the rich countries of the West. Cheap holiday flights are a typical example. The planet does not have enough oil to maintain this luxury. To curtail this extravagance collective asceticism is the only answer. This will require religious motivation. Political considerations are not strong enough, nor is the rational consideration that there will be no oil left for our grandchildren.

Is Christianity capable of inspiring the human race to this level of self denial and generosity ? Despite its long history, Christianity has rarely been tried as a radical remedy for mankind's evils: for the most part it has been used like an inoffensive source of comfort.

In the twentieth century the Second Vatican Council hammered out a programme for the spiritual renewal of the Catholic Church, to prepare it for the service of the modern world. Since then the task of institutional reform to implement the theology of that council has been started, but for the most part it has been blocked by the Roman Curia.

In the course of his book I will not hesitate to criticise the shortcomings of Church policies which frustrate the true message of the gospel. If non - believers are to be encouraged towards Christianity they are entitled to be shown the true face of the Church and not its abuses.

Finally I must say a word about atheism, which will be the background to all the subsequent chapters. As it is impossible to prove the non-existence of God , as a matter of logic, the usual argument is to suggest that the deity is no longer necessary, by a train of thought like this :- Primitive people did not know the cause of events like storms, earthquakes, and famines, so they attributed them to gods , and sought to control the outcomes by methods which worked among humans like requests, bribes, bargaining and the like. It is alleged that as science explains the true causes of all natural phenomena the need for gods or a God, simply vanishes. In reality scientific progress while explaining a great deal in the natural world, has merely moved back the framework of causes. The workings of the universe can be explained scientifically until we get back to the biggest cause of all, which itself demands a gigantic cause, namely the Big Bang. Where did that stupendous initial mass and unimaginable energy originate from ? Science has no answer. Towards the end of the 20th century scientists who are believers saw in that event a confirmation of their belief in a Creator.

The framework which I have outlined in these few pages will be filled out in detail in the subsequent chapters of this book.

CHAPTER ONE : DEEP ROOTED EVIL NEEDS RELIGION AS A REMEDY

In the Preface I claimed that religion is the only comprehensive cure of humanity's evils. Many people may find it difficult to agree with that contention. For readers in that dilemma I offer two preliminary reflections.

First of all, life in Britain within living memory has been for many people so secure and comfortable that we can scarcely appreciate the power of evil and its repercussions in human suffering. Secondly it seems likely that the progress of science is helping humanity better than the efforts of religion.

To these difficulties I offer the following reflections. It is undeniable that the progress of science in the last two centuries has provided cures for countless illnesses and hardships, but by the same token it has created just as many victims thanks to atomic bombs and other more powerful weapons of war. Whether the achievements of science will benefit the human race and not subject it to worse afflictions, depends almost entirely on how its achievements are deployed, this in turn entails moral choices, and for the majority of people this means religion.

The concentrated message of the preceding paragraph needs to be spelt out in more detail for the sake of clarity . The basic sciences like physics and biology have transformed our lives in the last two centuries. Thanks to surgery and other medical advances most of the life threatening illnesses of past history have been brought under control. Scientific agriculture has massively increased food production, which has been further augmented by better irrigation and pest control. Thanks to the social sciences like economics, sociology, and geography we can understand the causes of poverty, and take the appropriate remedies, by education, and legislation in the form of re-distributive taxation , unemployment benefit , the national health service etc. Finally the refinement of radio, TV and other communication technologies means that most of the human race knows what is happening in other parts of the world. Our failure to eradicate suffering and injustice cannot now be excused by the plea of ignorance.

Granted that there is now so much ability to cure humanity's diseases and injustices what are the barriers which prevent the improvement from happening ? Quite simply they are the obstacles created by our free choices which can be summarised as variations on selfishness, violence, and deception. Irrational self interest is the basic motor driving us to seize more of the world's goods than we need. If we are frustrated in this enterprise we turn to violence to secure what we crave, and then because of an almost instinctive shame, we conceal our badness as best we can. If this seems a fanciful scenario, then I invite the reader to reflect on the American and British invasion of Iraq in 2003. In order to secure more than our fair share of Iraq's oil supplies the country was invaded, and the whole operation was justified by excuses about the threat or terrorism, weapons of mass destruction and our duty to depose a tyrannical dictator. All of these were subsequently exposed as falsehoods.

Contrary to what many people assume, religion supplies the remedy as I stated in the Preface. Namely it enables individuals to overcome their own tendency to selfishness, violence, and their concomitants, secondly by giving the victims the moral strength to endure suffering without being psychologically crushed by it, and thirdly by providing a strong enough motive to inspire people to change the structures of institutional injustice and violence. In the absence of religious motivation, and the other spiritual strengths which I will discuss further on in this book, enlightened policies of democracy, education, and rational self interest are not strong enough to prevail against human wickedness; and of that history has all too many examples.

To some readers the statements which I have made about human badness and religion's ability to cure it will seem far fetched. Most individuals do not perceive themselves as wicked still less in need of repentance and religion. That may be the perception when life is comfortable, but if the delicate balance of tranquility is disturbed, a far more brutal animal soon manifests itself. The Second World War had all too many examples. For the present I will cite just one. The Nazi policy of exterminating the Jewish people required the active collaboration of thousands of ordinary German citizens, which was indeed forthcoming. The pattern of that kind of collaboration was evident in one group whose conduct reads like a sociological experiment. It was the conduct of a police reserve unit exposed by the researches of C.R. Browning[1]. His book describes how literally average citizens very easily became brutal executioners who would callously shoot Jewish citizens whom they had rounded up, including children. It is the most chilling reminder of just how shallow is the veneer of civilised behaviour. All of us have the potential to perform the most depraved acts of cruelty, depending largely on the circumstances of our lives. Those of us who have not perpetrated crimes of that kind should be very humble about it, and grateful that we have not been put to the test.

The human propensity to evil can be backed up with more examples than this book could contain, but before presenting a few of them there are two factors which must be born in mind, concerning our perception and evaluation of suffering and wickedness . The first is a combination of habit and ignorance. For example in the centuries before scientific medicine transformed our lives, infant mortality was so widespread that people regarded it as normal . Across the whole social spectrum it was not uncommon for half of all children to die as infants. The parents grieved their deaths as we would today, but having no idea as to how such deaths might be prevented, they seem to have regarded it as inevitable, and hence part of the normal course of life. The same applies to present day attitudes to crime and warfare. Most people regard them as regrettable but normal . It is only when the possibility of eradication is realised that people in general perceive just how inexcusable are these aberrations from the standards by which human beings ought to live.

The second factor which distorts our perception of badness is the comfortable indifference bred by a lack of immediate experience. In Great Britain, people who have grown up after the Second World War will have had little first hand experience of violence, fear, destruction, hunger, poverty, and disease. Admittedly there have been wars elsewhere and unemployment at home, but the air raids have not been directed to our own towns, and the basic securities of the welfare state have ensured that the families of unemployed workers do not go hungry. Obviously the media have informed us about wars like that in Vietnam and elsewhere. The famines in Ethiopia and many other countries have featured on our TV screens. None of this information can have the same effect on us as direct experience, like bombs falling in our own streets in the 1940's or entering the work house in the 1840's, when husbands ,wives and children were all separated. In short, Britain since the Second World War has been a

[1] Browning, C.R. (1993), *Ordinary Men: Police Reserve Battalion 101 and the Final Solution in Poland.* passim.

remarkably comfortable place in relation to the long perspectives of history , and this has dulled our sensitivity to moral badness and physical suffering.

In an attempt to remedy this lacuna in experience I will cite a few examples of just how wicked human beings can become, and just how powerful is the force of religion to bring about the remedy.

As an example of collective greed , I will start with the generally acknowledged factors of climate change due to global warming, and the depletion of the planet's resources. Both of these are caused by greed which is the simple motivation for the excessive use of limited supplies of minerals or energy. The situation is further aggravated by over-population. Only the most dishonest or obtuse politicians deny the existence of the problems. It is appreciated most keenly by the generation born before the Second World War, because in our lifetime we have witnessed the doubling (at least) of the world's population. This is the context in which other problems must be evaluated. Land which is suitable for farming is a finite quantity, and most of it is already under cultivation. Fresh water too is a finite quantity. The sources of energy, coal, oil and gas have finite limits. Coal is the first to show signs of being exhausted. It was significant that in 2005 the last coal mine in France was closed down. In England the most rewarding seams have already been exhausted. Experts debate the quantity of oil still left underground. It is suggested that production may decline after 2010. Some suggest that the peak has already been passed. Supplies of natural gas are still great, but they are not unlimited, and as the other fossil fuels decline the demand for gas will increase dramatically. In spite of all these known facts, the demand for fossil fuels continues to rise. Airlines compete with one another to promote cheap flights. Governments sanction the expansion of airports, knowing that any curtailment of the budget holiday market would be politically unpopular, as would a realistic tax on aviation fuel. Governments, business, and the population in general are united in a thoughtless conspiracy of greed which seeks to satisfy present desires, without any thought to the future. When I say future, I do not mean some remote date beyond the next century, but the adult lives of children who are now at school.

These facts have been widely recognised for some years. They were summarised in an important international report drawn up by the collaborative efforts of 1360 scientists from 95 countries under the chairmanship of Robert Watson, the British born chief scientist at the World Bank, and presented to the public in London at the Royal Society on 30th March 2005.[2] The principal conclusions of that report can be summarised as follows. Almost two thirds of the natural machinery that supports life on Earth is being degraded by human pressure. Because of population increase, more land has been claimed for agriculture in the last 60 years, than in the whole of the 18th and 19th centuries together. As a result an estimated 24% of the Earth's land surface is now cultivated. That figure is deceptive. It does not imply that a further 76% is still available for farming. Within that 76% we have to take account of enormous hot and cold deserts as well as mountains where agriculture is impossible. The same applies to the area taken up by towns and cities, industrial sites, roads, motorways and airports. As a result there is very little land left which could be claimed for farming. The use of water is perhaps the most dramatic feature. Withdrawal of fresh water from lakes and rivers has doubled in the last 40 years. Humans now use between 40% and 50% of all available freshwater running off the land. The flow of rivers has been reduced

---

[2] Reported in *The Guardian,* 30th March, 2005.

dramatically. For parts of the year, the Yellow River in China, the Nile in Africa, and the Colorado in North America dry up before they reach the sea. Underground aquifers are also seriously depleted. In many cases it is literally a matter of living on borrowed time. By using up supplies of fresh ground water faster than they can be re-charged , we are depleting assets at the expense of our children. In short, the whole picture is one of collective greed on an unimaginably large scale. Such findings have been confirmed by every subsequenet scientific report published on the matter.

The next area of human activity which I will illustrate is that of violence, and I will begin with some examples of individual violence , because these incidents are more easily envisaged, and their impact on us is more powerful. (We just cannot realistically imagine the impact of one million violent deaths). As with the examples of greed, the potential list is endless, so I will limit myself to three cases to illustrate my contention about human moral badness.

In February 2006, during a football match between Liverpool and Manchester United , the Manchester striker Alan Smith suffered a broken leg. Some Liverpool fans started jeering at him, but worse was to follow. When he was being driven to hospital after the match, the ambulance was attacked by a group of Liverpool fans. The ambulance was pelted with bottles, stones and glasses, and then the fans tried to overturn it as it was stuck in a traffic jam.[3]

My final example comes from the persecution of the Jews during the Second World War. I have selected one incident because it has a peculiarly tragic aspect. The Italian writer Primo Levi, himself a prisoner but who had the good fortune to survive till the end of the war, and who chronicled the life of the prisoners. He described a fellow Jew who had been appointed to control the Lodz ghetto for the Nazis. He said of him " He's not a monster, but he isn't like other men either; he is like many, like the many frustrated men who taste power and are intoxicated by it."[4] That individual's activities reveal the potential for depraved cruelty which is latent in so many human personalities, and what is really disturbing is the fact that it only requires a certain combination of circumstances to activate it.

Slavery too was once regarded as normal.To the modern mind it is inconceivable that this institution should ever have been tolerated. From the dawn of recorded history it existed in all the societies of the Mediterranean and Near East, from which Europe has derived its culture. Many people are shocked when they discover that Aristotle, one of the greatest philosophers of all time, regarded slavery as natural to human society. The discovery of America gave it an additional boost, and from the sixteenth century until its abolition in the nineteenth, it has been calculated that eleven million human beings were transported from Africa to the New World.[5]

Collective violence in the form of warfare is so endemic in human history that it is difficult to know how to select representative examples. I repeat here, what I stated above, namely that

---

[3] *The Guardian* , 23rd February 2006.

[4] Levi, Primo, (1987), *Moments of Reprieve,* London: Abacus p. 171.

[5] Thomas, H. (1966), *The Slave Trade,* London: Picador, p. 805.

people have come to regard it as a normal feature of human life. At the outset it is important to bear in mind that it is not normal and could be eliminated. An instructive parallel is the similar history of blood feuds. About one thousand years before Christ they were dying out from really civilised societies. Early Greek drama and the earliest books of the Old Testament bear witness to the transitional period when blood feuds were yielding place to the rule of law, which meant that disputes were settled before judges and not by brute force. The tragic element in those Greek dramas indicates that the older generation regarded the vendettas as normal, whereas the establishment of the rule of law was unfamiliar and to some extent unsettling. The same transition could be made in the abandonment of warfare if the human race had enough courage and imagination.

For the sake of brevity I will confine my observations on warfare to the first half of the twentieth century, because the conflicts are still vividly remembered by so many people still alive. In the description of the three wars which I have chosen, I will not dwell too long on the factual details, which have been published in countless books, but in each case I wish to draw attention to specific moral considerations revealed by those tragic conflicts.

It is paradoxical that warfare should have been so vicious at that time, and initiated by the Europeans of all people. In the previous half century incredible advances has been made thanks to science, technology, and education. The leading nations of Europe had by that time introduced democratic government with a reasonably wide franchise, destined eventually to be extended to all adults. Universal elementary education was provided out of public finances. Free speech and freedom of the press had been achieved. Medicine and public health measures, such as the rudimentary separation of drinking water from drainage, had effected dramatic improvements in health. A combination of strong trade unions and some enlightened legislation had improved wages and working conditions . The situation was not ideal, but it was a vast improvement on the situation of manual workers in the middle of the nineteenth century described so vividly in the novels of Dickens and Zola. Yet in spite of all these advantages most of which had been achieved within living memory, the early twentieth century saw wars in which whole new dimensions of cruelty and moral depravity were experienced.

My first specific example is the Boer War. Admittedly it did not take place in Europe, but its principal actor was Great Britain, at that time the most powerful nation in Europe and the world. The details of the conflict need not detain us at this point, but one element requires special mention, namely the invention of an entirely new measure in warfare, the concentration camp. After the Boers had been defeated (with great difficulty) in formal campaigns, their surviving soldiers scattered into the countryside and conducted an extremely successful guerilla warfare against the British army. After various ineffectual attempts to defeat them, the British authorities decided to cut off their food supplies. This entailed removing all the civilian population from the farms over large tracts of land. The vast majority of those who were rounded up were women and children. They were taken to prison camps established on the open veldt, and there behind barbed wire they were accommodated in tents, with inadequate sanitation, poor food and minimal clean water. The combination of a poor diet, harsh climate and unhygienic conditions soon produced disease, which decimated the inmates. Literally thousands died, of whom a disproportionately large number were children.

The second example is the First World War. Once again I will not dwell upon the facts which have been recorded in countless books about that conflict . Practically everyone is now aware of the millions of young men who were slaughtered, and the new forms of cruelty which science had made possible with weapons like poison gas. What I am at pains to emphasise here are the moral characteristics of the conflict. Stemming from nations which had become industrialised within living memory, it is almost as if the conduct of war was organised as if it were an industrial operation. Conscription meant that millions of men were enlisted, far more than in any previous wars, and they were deployed by methods which seem to have borne an uncanny resemblance to the process of mass production in factories. At the risk of some over simplification, one can perhaps epitomise the worst aspects of that war, as the sending of wave after wave of infantrymen across deep mud in the face of uncut barbed wire against well protected machine guns. The result was the swift and massive slaughter of thousands of seemingly disposable men.

The first World War also saw the first example of modern genocide. During and immediately after the war the Ottoman Turks systematically killed hundreds of thousands of Armenians living within their borders. The figure may be as high as one million. The slaughter undoubtedly influenced Hitler in his systematic killing of Jews in Europe a generation later. It is a matter about which the modern Turkish government displays extraordinary embarrassment and secrecy. Many writers and journalists have been imprisoned merely for mentioning the fact. Such frankness is defined in their legal system as an insult to the Turkish State, which is a criminal offence.

The Second World War is sufficiently close to the memories of many people living, so that it is not necessary to go into too much detail about its cruelties. I merely mention the worst aspects, namely the indiscriminate bombing of civilian targets by the British and American air forces. It culminated in the dropping of two Atomic bombs on Japan, but German cities had suffered almost as badly. In one night in 1943 approximately 40,000 civilians were killed in a raid on Hamburg. In the course of that war the Nazis' treatment of the Jews is so well known as to require no further comment.

These examples from the wars of the first half of the twentieth century are tragic evidence of just how much wickedness human beings are capable of. Sadly it seems that the lessons of history have not been learned. In the year 2006 the nations of the world had 19, 954,934 soldiers in their standing armies, not counting reserves and paramilitary police. The annual international budget spent on weapons, troops, and military equipment in general is the staggering sum (in U.S. dollars) so large that I cannot formulate its correct name, so I must write out the plain figures $ 1,097,115,610,000. [6] If that sum of money were directed to other objectives all the world's population could be accommodated in decent housing, all children could have schools, and pure drinking water could be provided for everyone.

After briefly describing greed and violenc, the third element in the basic paradigm of human badness which merits examination is deceit. Every human being has a conscience, and though for many it is smothered by self interest, the majority of people preserve some vestige of morality, which paradoxically drives them into another channel of evil, namely the concealment of their wickedness. This course is pursued by individuals, and also by groups

---

[6] *The Guardian,* 25 th May, 2006.

like governments, Churches and commercial organisations. As with the previous examples of badness, I will limit myself to a small number of examples for fear of burdening the text with too many instances.

The first case follows directly from the policy of carpet bombing described above. When the War Cabinet's decision had been communicated to Bomber Command, another measure was agreed upon at the same time, namely to keep the matter secret. At a later date, the Secretary of State for Air, Sir Archibald Sinclair stated that only by claiming that the bombers kept to military targets " could he satisfy the enquiries of the Archbishop of Canterbury, the Moderator of the Church of Scotland and other significant religious leaders , whose moral condemnation of the bombing offensive might disturb the morale of Bomber Command aircrews". [7] Thereafter the public were fed with official but deceptive news releases which routinely claimed that military targets had been successfully attacked.

It is consistent with the motive of greed, that industrial corporations will conceal immoral practices which conflict with their quest for profit, even when their misdemeanours threaten safety of the environment, their clients , and above all, their workers. For many years it has been known that working with asbestos exposes the human lungs to the incurable disease mesothelioma. Although the causation was known as far back as the 1950's , it was concealed and workers were consistently denied compensation until it was forced upon their employers, late in the 20th century as a result of numerous legal cases.

It is a matter of inexcusable immorality that the Catholic Church as an institution has been guilty of this kind of concealment. Among the various instances which could be considered, the example which I will cite is the widespread scandal of child sex abuse by the clergy. The details have been so widely publicised in the media for the last decade that I will simply draw attention to the main lines of the problem. If a priest had been accused, credibly, of having sexually abused a child he was not suspended or defrocked permanently, but transferred to another part of the country to give him the opportunity to make a new start. It would have remained concealed indefinitely (because of the Church's obsession with secrecy) but for the exposure of the crimes by erstwhile victims at the end of the twentieth century. The sequel is too well known to require further comment.

Having described a few examples of humanity's three main areas of badness (greed, violence and deceit), the time has come to present religion as the most effective remedy to all three. It is an audacious claim, but I stake it out with full confidence.

In the first instance I make a claim to history in the broadest context. For nearly all societies , in the past, religion has been the foundation of public and private morality, and has provided the rationale for legal systems, social customs, and all the conventions which promote justice and honesty in our interactions with other people. This applies to family life, education, business, government, and even military affairs. This has been the case with other world faiths like Islam , Hinduism and many others, but I confine my analysis to Christianity. Although this influence was strong in the past I am well aware that in Europe certainly, when the effects of the Enlightenment percolated through to the majority of citizens, vast numbers

---

[7] *The Guardian,* 24 th July 1993.

of people have abandoned religious convictions.[8] This has brought its own problems in the regulation of public morality (like M.P.'s deceiving parliament). However in the creative period of our culture, from roughly 600 AD to the 19th century, Christianity was the ideology which shaped the morality, customs and laws of this country and the rest of Europe. I do not discount the influence of the ideas which flowered as a result of the Enlightenment, but as I stated earlier, they owe more to the Christian roots of Europe than their propagandists were aware of. Admittedly medieval Christianity had its own share of violence and cruelty, but the creative forces of its civilising influence never ceased to operate. As far as Great Britain is concerned the last great flowering of this influence on public morality was the beneficent and pervasive effect of the so called non-conformist conscience in public life. Sadly its effectiveness has declined in proportion to the relative eclipse of the free Churches, but nothing comparable has replaced it in the moral vacuum which has ensued. Deceit and dishonesty in business and politics are the consequences.

The decline in public morality in England for example in recent years has gone hand in hand with the abandonment of religion. Of the countless examples that one could cite, I will limit myself to a few. Years go I knew an elderly woman who had trained as a midwife at the London Hospital in Whitechapel in the 1920's. It was located in an exceptionally deprived area of London, and the local population lived in what is now unimaginable poverty. New-born babies were frequently wrapped in newspaper to keep them warm because the parents could not afford to buy even a small blanket. In spite of the poverty and deprivation the people maintained a high standard public morality. In particular the midwives (some of them in their early twenties) would go out alone, on foot, to their patients' homes to deliver babies. Even at night they were confident that provided they were in uniform they would never be attacked or harassed. In the same city, at the end of the twentieth century, street violence, car theft, mugging and other forms of crime are too well known to need further comment.

The decline of religion and the corresponding erosion of its influence in the nation's private and public life has left an ideological vacuum. A minority of intelligent agnostics create their own systems of morality, on the basis of which some of them lead genuinely edifying lives. High minded people can construct a system of personal morality based on considerations such as the cultivation of creative relationships with other people, rather than exploitative ones. However the fact is that very few people have the intelligence, and the time to work out an adequate rational system of morality for themselves.

At the start of the First World War so many men volunteered to enlist that the military apparatus could scarcely cope with the vast numbers offering their services. Another example of irrational enthusiasm for the war was the attitude of Winston Churchill, who at that time was First Lord of the Admiralty. In a conversation with Violet Asquith (the daughter of the Prime Minister) on 20th February 1915, Churchill stated "I think a curse should rest on me - because I love this war. I know it's smashing and shattering the lives of thousands every moment and yet - I can't help it - I enjoy every second of it".[9] The enthusiasm of the working class to join in the war, and the implied willingness to kill their opposite numbers in the

---

[8] The matter has been described admirably in Prof. O. Chadwick's indispensable study *The Secularisation of the European Mind in the Nineteenth Century.* (1975) Cambridge: Cambridge University Press.
[9] Quoted in Clifford, C. (2002), *The Asquiths,* London: John Murray, p. 247.

12

German working class was a severe blos to international socialism as a remedy for evil.

Examples like this can be multiplied so frequently, that one is tempted to agree with Aldous Huxley's famous judgement, after a journey to the Eastern Mediterranean :- "I have never had such a sense of the tragic nature of the human situation; the horror of a history in which the great works of art, the philosophies and the religions, are no more than islands in an endless stream of war, poverty, frustration, squalor and disease."[1] In the pre-scientific age, the philosopher David Hume observed that the lives of most people were short, brutish and nasty.

Having stated above that religion could and should be the remedy for the basic evils of the human race, I am aware that such a claim must face a number of serious objections. The opposition from the atheists can be summarised roughly into two main areas. The first of these concerns the basic competence of Christianity in general, and specifically Catholicism to deliver a programme for such an audacious undertaking in the modern world whose scientific culture is totally different from the era up to the nineteenth century when religion held sway. The second is more fundamental, and concerns the very existence of God.

What I say about Catholicism can be applied to other Christian Churches up to a point, but to simplify a potentially unlimited field I must draw the line somewhere, and from the practical point of view Catholicism is the Church of which I have been a member for more than half a century, and I could not speak with insider experience about any other Church. The method which I will use to vindicate my contention is to analyse the foundational documents of the Church to see if they could support the claim (at the theoretical level) to remedy all the world's evils, and to illustrate that competence at the practical level by examples of institutional success and individual heroism from a variety of periods in the Church's long history.

The foundational documents which I have in mind are those in which the Church deliberately proclaims its self identity, operational goals, and the means to achieve them. The reader must judge if the claims are reasonable or outrageous. It will cause no surprise if the first such document (effectively The Constitution) is the New Testament, whose central message is the love of God and neighbour. When Jesus was asked what was the greatest commandment in the Law, he replied that it was the injunction to love God and our neighbour (Matthew, 22: 34 - 40). The same question is recorded in slightly different words in Luke's gospel, where the answer is illustrated by the well known parable of the good Samaritan (Luke 10: 29 - 32), which emphasises that the neighbour is not a person of one's own race, but a stranger who in this case would have been thought of as an enemy. These examples also indicate by their implications that the message of Jesus was an organic development of Jewish faith; the Law in question being the Law of Moses. Throughout the book I will supply further examples of the love of neighbour, as it is the key stone of the Church's policy.

The whole corpus of St. Paul's letters illustrate the immense task of putting those ideals into practice, particularly among the recent converts of non-Jewish peoples around the Eastern Mediterranean. It is difficult to make a selection from so many edifying statements exhortations but one passage from the last part of the letter to the community in Philippi has the attraction that it urges his readers to embrace every authentic human value and turn it to

---

[1] Murray, N. (2002), *Aldous Huxley: An English Intellectual.* London: Abacus, p. 405.

the service of God. His exact words are as follows :- " Finally brothers, fill your minds with everything that is true , everything that is noble, everything that is good and pure, everything that we love and honour, everything that can be thought virtuous or worthy of praise. Keep doing all the things that you have learnt from me and have been taught by me and have heard and seen that I do. Then the God of peace will be with you." (Philippians, 4: 8 & 9).

The second foundational document is the most recent up - dating of the programme, namely the decisionss of the Second Vatican Council held in the 1960's. Like other general councils, it provided the opportunity for the Church to take account of its self-identity, and to express its mission in relation to the circumstances of the modern world. For the Catholic Church general councils, being international assemblies, provide the most effective method of clarifying the principles, and legislating for their implementation. Although the Church now comprises about one billion members world-wide, the structure of a general council is a fairly efficient organ for ascertaining the opinions and experiences of Catholics across the globe since all territorial bishops are obliged to attend. In the case of the Second Vatican Council its deliberations included considerable input of talent from theologians and individuals (clerical and lay) with experience in the Church's work. All things considered it was a remarkably successful exercise in clarifying the Church's collective self awareness.

In the difficult task of selecting from seven hundred pages of documents a few extracts which will convey the authentic ethos of the Council, I will start with one paragraph from the document explaining the nature of The Church. "The Church like a pilgrim in a foreign land presses forward amid the persecutions of the world and the consolations of God , announcing the cross and death of the Lord until He comes. By the power of the risen Lord she is given strength to overcome patiently and lovingly the afflictions and hardships which assail her from within and without, and to show forth in the world the mystery of the Lord in a faithful though shadowed way, until at the last it will be revealed in total splendour."[2]

The Council's programme for improving the quality of life for the world's peoples is too long and complex to be summarised within the confines of this chapter. Further on in the book examples will appear, but for the moment I must limit myself to stating that the Council adopted positive attitudes and policies towards the strengthening of human rights, the freedom of scientific research, free speech, the equality of all races and both sexes, and a more equitable distribution of the world's wealth. Further than that, I must invite the reader to study the individual documents of the Council.

In assessing the significance of the New Testament and the programme contained in the Second Vatican Council in relation to my claim that Christianity has the capability to remedy humanity's evils, I suggest that one should compare them with other documents which have set out similar objectives for the human race. The United Nations Universal Declaration on Human Rights is an obvious parallel. The vision of humanity's dignity is practically the same as in the two sources which I have chosen, but the Declaration is, by its own terms of reference, limited, it does not cover the whole field of human affairs, nor does it propose a practical scheme to implement those rights. Another document which made similar claims was the Communist Manifesto. This document , which was published in the latter part of the

---

[2] Vatican II, *Lumen Gentium,* section 8, English translation, W.M. Abbott, (1966)*The Documents of Vatican II* , New York: Guild Press, p.24.

nineteenth century set out a comprehensive programme for the improvement of the human race, based on a fairer distribution of wealth, which in turn was dependent upon revolution. This I think is a fair epitome of that well known text. [3] Comparing the Communist Manifesto with is Christian counterpart (the New Testament and the Documents of the Second Vatican Council) I think it is fair to characterise the latter as an invitation to human betterment based on generosity, whereas the former is a programme for clawing back economic equality by force.

Apart from the comparison of the theoretical values of the two programmes for the human race, the practical implementation speaks for itself. Communism has been its own worst enemy. It is paradoxical that the first published writings of Karl Marx (when he was a journalist writing for the Deutsche Jahrbucher and the Rheinische Zeitung) were essays attacking the evils of press censorship. [4] Wherever Marxism has gained political power the press has been censored totally. Since the collapse of the system in the Soviet Union and Eastern Europe, scholars have had access to hitherto secret documents in the official archives in Russia. The results are devastating. Communist regimes in Russia, Eastern Europe and China were only established by force of the most brutal kind. Any restraints like human rights, democratic freedoms and an uncensored press were suppressed. Writing about the Russian revolution, Orlando Figes has commented: "Nobody knows the full human cost of the revolution. By any calculation it was catastrophic. Counting only the deaths from civil war, the terror, famine and disease, it was something in the region of ten million people". [5] The establishment of a communist government and economic programme in China was even worse. In their remarkable biography of Mao Tse-tung, Jung Chan and Jon Halliday have calculated that " well over seventy million people perished in peacetime as a result of his misrule". [6]

Having given a brief indication of Christianity's theoretical claim to be the remedy for mankind's many problems, the reader is now entitled to some practical vindication of such a momentous claim. So I will illustrate the realisation of those hopes in recent and past history. Once again the field is so vast , that within the limits of this chapter, I must confine myself to just a few representative examples, to show that the hopes which I hold out are not unreasonable, and ask the readers' patience until more detailed justification is presented at later stages in the book.

After the collapse of the Roman empire in western Europe, against all likelihood the Church survived as a coherent well functioning international organisation. Over a period of some centuries all the newly emerging nations of that region were converted to Christianity.

Within that overall movement of evangelisation and civilising , the monastic orders, and later on other religious orders, made an incalculable contribution to human betterment. The

---

[3]   Marx, K. and . Engels,F.(1967), *Manifesto of the Communist Party* , Moscow: Progress Publishers.

[4]   cf. Hitchens, C. writing in *The Guardian (Saturday Review)* 16 June 2007

[5]   Figes, O.(1996), *A People's Tragedy.* London: Pimlico, p.773.

[6]   Chung, J. & Halliday, J. (2006) *Mao: The Unknown Story.* London: Vintage Books, p.651.

educational role of the monasteries is too well known to need repeating, but the other aspects of what would now be described as social services are less well appreciated. In mediaeval Europe all hospitals were religious foundations. Incredibly some of them are still standing to this day, like the vast hospital of the Order of St. John in Valetta on the island of Malta.

In the sixteenth and seventeenth centuries Spain was opening the New World to commerce, colonialism, and Catholicism. The overall movement was a mixed blessing, but the Church made many creative contributions. The first universities on that continent were founded in Mexico, and Peru in 1553 and 1557.[7] The first realistic protests against slavery were launched by the Dominican friar Bartolomé de las Casas. The most innovative experiment in social organisation was created by the Jesuits in Paraguay in the 17th century, which for a number of years produced a just and efficiently working society for the indigenous peoples. Similar examples could be multiplied indefinitely.

Back in Europe St. Vincent de Paul organised a massive operation of hospitals, almshouses, and orphanages thought the whole of France. At the same period other Christian Churches were making similar contributions to human betterment, like the Quakers in England, and later the Salvation Army, which in the 20th century emerged as the second largest provider of social services after the government.

Admittedly there have been many abuses and failures to live up to the high ideals of the New Testament, and I will devote much space to them in the course of this book. For the present though, I wish to draw attention to my claim that both at the theoretical level and in the realm of institutional organisation, Christianity has proved itself to be capable of remedying mankind's badness, when it is operating normally. This is an important consideration because all organisations must be judged by their normal performance and not by their abuses.

To complete the picture, I would like to draw the reader's attention to a number of heroic Christians who lived and worked within living memory, and whose lives illustrate just how powerful is the influence of the gospel when it is lived in accordance with its proper aims. The lives of Franz Jagerstatter and Mother Teresa of Calcutta are too well known to need elaboration. He was executed for refusing military service under the Nazis, she devoted her life to nursing the very poorest people in the slums of India, and latterly in other countries. Other equally heroic persons are less well known.

In February 2005 a 73 year old American nun Sister Dorothy Stang was shot dead in a remote part of Brazil. Her religious order had sent her to that country as a missionary in 1966. In 1982 she started working for the Pastoral Land Commission, which had been set up by the Brazilian bishops in 1957, in response to the growing violence in the Amazon region as wealthy landowners employed gunmen to clear peasant farmers from disputed land. In spite of the dangers Sister Dorothy lived and worked in the region for 23 years. In 2004 she travelled to the capital to give evidence to a congressional committee of enquiry into illegal deforestation. She knew that she was putting her life at risk, in a contentious matter where it is estimated that 90% of the timber is cut down illegally. On her return from Brasilia she started to receive death threats, but she continued her work undeterred. On February 14 th, 2005 she

---

[7] Cristiani , L. (1948) *L'Église a l 'Époque du Concile de Trente,* Paris: Bloud & Gay, p.469. (Being volume 17 in *Histoire de L' Église ,* eds Fliche, A. & Martin , V. Paris 1946, onwards.

was walking alone to a meeting of local peasant farmers when two gunmen approached her. She must have known exactly what to expect; she opened her bible and started reading it to them. They shot her six times. Her assassination caused widespread outrage in Brazil.[8]

The power of religion to motivate altruism has been stated quite simply by Jenni Russell, a well known journalist of avowedly humanist convictions. Writing about her non-religious, humanist upbringing she stated "For most of my life I have unconsciously shared this assumption that there is something desirable about a secular, rather than a religious, approach to existence.- - - - The trouble with this belief is that it takes for granted that people can be as powerfully motivated by humanism as they are by faith. That is not borne out by the evidence. Statistically it is believers, not secularists, who are most likely to be engaged in charitable and voluntary work, and who participate most in the organisations that bridge the gaps between rich and poor. They are more generous with both money and time."[9]

For the present I have said enough about the first defence of religion as the cure for human badness. The second major objection against religion in general is at a deeper level and concerns the very existence of God, which I will deal with in Chapter Three.

At this point the logical path should be to proceed to the existence of God, and then take the reader step by step through God's different stages of his self disclosure to the human race, and thence to the individual's response to this revelation.

However I have decided to adopt another approach because the great problem of the Christian Churches is not the existence of God, but their failure to introduce him realistically to potential believers. Accordingly I will proceed immediately to explain the all important process by which the average man or woman comes to belief in God, because it is the understanding of this personal encounter which has been effectively lost in the long and complex history of Christianity in Europe. After that I will return to the more logical path in Chapter Three, and fill out the picture of God, and his self disclosure to the human race.

---

[8] *The Guardian*, 21st February 2005.

[9] *The Guardian*, 24 th December 2005.

CHAPTER TWO: RESPONSE TO JESUS IN FAITH

SECTION 1 :   THE PRACTICAL STARTING POINT

The Church as community announces the life and work of Jesus to the enquirers, and invites them to respond to him in faith. This is a decision of personal commitment somewhat similar to marriage, in which the neophyte accepts the person and message of Jesus and undertakes to live henceforward according to the ideals contained in the New Testament. It presupposes a certain amount of knowledge about Jesus, his Church, and his teaching, but the decision is less an acceptance of truths, than the start of an interpersonal relationship. Aquinas had stated this centuries ago with the succinct declaration that "the act of faith homes in on the reality, not on the proposition"[1] . In other words faith centres on the person of Jesus, rather than on statements which convey knowledge about him, and his heavenly Father.

The decision of faith also entails the components of hope and charity, which are no less important in the conduct of the Christian life, but are less complicated than the cognitive part of the process of personal commitment, because it is this intellectual area which has been so much distorted by the accidents of history and their impact on the life and profile of the Church. In fact a large part of this chapter will be devoted to unravelling the distortions of true Christianity in which the Church has become entangled in the course of a long and complicated history. This process is absolutely necessary if we are to penetrate through all that has obscured the true message of Christ, and appreciate just how powerful are the disincentives which currently it carries with it, and which must be put right.

The manner in which the simple communication is made has varied greatly over the course of history, depending upon the circumstances in which the Church finds itself. The purest initiative is to be seen in the first three centuries when the Christians were few in number, when their communities were small but close knit, when the Church had no special buildings (their meetings were in private houses[2]), and above all there was no official liaison with the state. The rank and file, ordinary laymen and women shared their religious convictions with their neighbours initially in a homely and informal manner.[3]

As is well known, the Roman government's attitude became one of hostility and persecution as early as the latter part of the first century. Despite official hostility, the social background was generally favourable to the Christian missionary expansion. Society as a whole was thoroughly religious, and although the portrayal of the gods of Greece and Rome could scarcely be described as edifying , the cultural climate took for granted the existence of some kind of supra-mortal beings, and in that context serious minded seekers could not fail to be

---

[1] Aquinas, Summa Theologica ,II - II q.1, art. 2, ad 2.

[2] cf Acts of the Apostles, 18:7, 19: 7 - 10, 20:7 & 8, Romans 16:5 & 23, I Corinthians 16:9, Colossians 4:15.

[3] Lampe, P.(2003), *Christians at Rome in the First Two Centuries.* trans. M. Steinhauser, London: Continuum, p.103.

impressed by the dignified monotheism of the deity proclaimed by the Christians and Jews.

The Jewish contribution must not be overlooked. In the first century there were Jewish communities in every important city of the Roman empire. They were known to be monotheists , and they provided a point of contact, and a springboard for the first Christian missions.

Evidence of the daily life of Christians is scarce in that period, but what has survived is informative . An unlikely source is the Letter of Pliny the Younger to the emperor Trajan (c.107 A.D.), where he gives the latter information about apostate Christians: - " They also declared that the sum total of their guilt or error amounted to no more than this : they had met regularly before dawn on a fixed day to chant verses alternately amongst themselves in honour of Christ as if to a god, and also to bind themselves by oath , not for any criminal purpose , but to abstain from theft , robbery, and adultery, to commit no breach of trust and not to deny a deposit when called upon to restore it. After this ceremony it had been their custom to disperse and reassemble later to take food of an ordinary harmless kind; but they had in fact given up this practice since my edict issued on your instructions , which banned all political societies" . [4]

A generation later we have a beautiful description of the Sunday liturgy in the *First Apologia* of St. Justin, written in Rome between the years 148 - 161, which was addressed to the Emperor Antoninus Pius (138 - 161). He was destined to prove his sincerity a few years later when he suffered a martyr's death. "On the day which is called Sunday , all who live in the cities or in the country gather together to one place and the memoirs of the apostles and the writings of the prophets are read as long as time permits. Then the reader concludes, and the president verbally instructs and exhorts us to the imitation of those excellent things, then we all rise together and offer up our prayers; and as I said before when we have ended our prayer, bread is brought and wine and water; and the president in like manner offers up prayers and thanksgivings according to his ability and the people give their assent by saying 'Amen'; and there is a distribution and a partaking by everyone of the Eucharist and to those who are absent a portion is brought by the deacons. And those who are well-to-do and willing give as they choose, each as he himself purposes; the collection is then deposited with the president who supports orphans, widows, those who are in want owing to sickness of any other cause, those who are in prison and strangers who are on a journey and in a word takes care of all who are in need. But Sunday is the day on which we hold our common assembly because it is the first day on which God, when he changed darkness and matter, made the world, and Jesus Christ our Saviour on the same day rose from the dead."[5] A century later a famous remark of Tertullian, has survived, apparently repeating a popular sentiment, " See how those Christians love one another".[6]

---

[4] Pliny the Younger, Letter 96 ed. Betty Radice, (1963), *The Letters of Pliny the Younger.* Harmsworth, Penguin, pp.293-4.

[5] St. Justin, *First Apologia* chap. 67. (1966) trans. H. Musurillo, in *The Fathers of the Primitive Church* ,London, New English Library, p.134.

[6] Tertullian, *Apologeticum* 39:7.

The above descriptions of Christian life in   the period of the Roman empire should not mislead us into thinking that they enjoyed tranquillity in their religious practices. Although the penal

laws were not always enforced at full pressure, the possibility of arrest and execution was always present in the background. Severe penalties had been enacted against Christians from the time of Nero in the first century, with a view to deterring pagans from converting, and exterminating those who were already believers. To achieve both objectives the executions were carried out with the maximum publicity in the amphitheatres which existed in all important cities, most notably in the Colosseum in Rome. The emperors calculated that the cruel deaths should be seen by as many people as possible, so as to maximise the deterrent effect. Actually the plan backfired seriously, since it was the example of heroism which provided the most powerful motive for people to become Christians. In the Colosseum and other arenas, literally thousands of spectators saw simple and sincere people (not fanatics) endure unbelievable cruelties with dignity and courage. It was an extremely effective advertisement for Christianity.[7] Commenting on those persecutions some centuries later, St. Augustine remarked rather ruefully that more women than men were to be found among the martyrs. [8] The scenario of Calvary had been repeated.

In the modern world, in most countries , the invitation to belief is transmitted in less dramatic circumstances. Whereas the average Christian in the Roman empire might have been putting his life at risk by talking about his religion to an acquaintance, the English Catholic of the twenty first century is in no such danger. Yet the simple unsophisticated contact of lay people with their neighbours is still the basic interface at which the Christian message passes to a potential convert. Homely examples abound. Not many years ago the wife of a distinguished Cambridge scholar was contemplating entry into the Catholic Church. After a considerable time she started attending mass. One Sunday she noticed that the man beside her in the pew was not singing the hymns. She pushed the hymn book in his direction and pointed to the place. His reaction surprised her. In a courteous whisper he said " Thanks all the same luv, but I can't read". That proved to be decisive. The fact that the illiterate man was quite at home and felt accepted in the liturgy impressed her more than any theological arguments could have done .

In addition to the homely examples of simple sincerity, it is also reassuring to remember that real heroism still exists in some areas of the Church's mission, I mentioned Sister Dorothy Stang in Chapter One. Two more such heroes come to mind. Brazil is also the scene of the next tale of heroism. It is recorded by the journalist George Monbiot, who prefaces it by quoting Roy Hattersley who had stated " good works are most likely to be performed by people who believe that heaven exists ." George Monbiot adds his comment on this :- "The only two heroes I have met are both Catholic missionaries. --- Frei Adolfo, the German I met in the savannahs of north - eastern Brazil, thought when I first knocked on his door, that I was a gunman the ranchers had sent for him. Yet he still opened it. With other liberation theologists (sic) in the Catholic Church, he offered the only consistent support to the peasants

[7] Chadwick, Henry (2001), 'The Early Church', in Harries, Richard & Mayr - Harting, Henry (eds), *Christianity : Two Thousand Years.* Oxford, Oxford University Press, p. 5.

[8] Augustine, *Tractatus on the Gospel of St. John,* section 51, quoted in Chadwick, H. op.cit. p. 12.

being attacked by landowners and the government. - - - - -Joe Hass an Austrian I stayed with in the swamp forests of West Papua, had spent his life acting as a human shield for the indigenous people of Indonesia; every few months soldiers threatened to kill him when he prevented them from murdering his parishioners and grabbing their land.-----If they did not

believe in God , these men would never have taken such risks for other people."[9]

Parents who are themselves believers will have countless opportunities to speak of God and religion to their children. Also within the family it is not uncommon for a non-religous partner to adopt the Church of his or her spouse after years of marriage in which the neophyte has had ample opportunity to perceive the conviction and integrity of the believer.

Although the immediate point of contact for a non-believer will probably be his encounter with an individual member of the Church, his final acceptance of Catholicism is not limited to the life of the one individual with whom he had the first contact. At some point he has to judge of the credibility of the Church as a whole, that is to say, a world wide community of approximately one billion believers, organised into an identifiable institution of parishes and dioceses in which the teaching of Jesus is proclaimed, the reliability of the traditional doctrines is safeguarded, the sacraments are celebrated, and a life of prayer is sustained . In short he will see a community which does its best to live out the ideals of the New Testament, admittedly within the parameters of heroism or lassitude which have varied greatly over the course of history. To express the matter in other words, the Church itself is an object of faith in the overview of the prospective enquirer. This evaluation of the status of the Church as being itself an object of faith is frequently overlooked, but it is of crucial importance.

In the ordinary circumstances of life we are totally dependent on the Church for access to God, by the preservation and transmission of the Bible, by the traditional doctrinal teaching which confirms the written message and supplies the gaps on matters where the Scriptures are silent, in the bestowal of the sacraments, as well as the invisible sharing of grace (which the creeds call the Communion of Saints). To some readers it may seem strange that I have not accorded a larger place to the bible. Basically it is because one cannot make a personal commitment to a book, but only to a person or a community.

In addition to all these rather formal considerations one must not overlook the more humane and indefinable ethos of the community. By that I mean the quality of life which is apparent when the Church is living as it should, and the elements of sincerity, moral beauty, joy and fulfilment are apparent in the unselfconscious lives of sincere believers. These qualities are self authenticating and constitute the most powerful recommendation for the Christian life.

All of this has been stated since the earliest centuries in the words of the official proclamations of faith which we call the Creeds. Every Sunday at mass we affirm this belief when we recite the Creed. The wording which we use is that which was promulgated by the Council of Constantinople in the year 381. The Greek original begins with the words " We believe in one God , the Father the Almighty-- - - - -", and that initial verb governs the whole of the subsequent statement. For the sake of clarity the English translators have repeated it at the start of the subsequent paragraphs proclaiming faith in the three persons of the Trinity.

---

[9] *The Guardian,* 11 October 2005.

Thus , " We believe in one Lord Jesus Christ,   - - - - -We believe in the Holy Spirit- - -. And then, significantly "We believe in one holy catholic and apostolic Church". In other words our attitude of trust towards the Church is basically the same as our trust in God. It is perhaps a startling statement, but it has been the constant conviction of Christians, as can been seen

from the fact that it was present in all the earliest forms of the Creed. The earliest form from the community in the city of Rome, now known as the Apostles' Creed, states the basic principles in fewer words than that of Constantinople, namely " I believe in the Holy Spirit, the holy Catholic Church, the communion of saints - - - -"[10]   Although this aspect of our relationship with the Church is not spoken of very frequently, it is eminently reasonable. A neophyte could hardly commit himself to God unless he could repose a similar trust in the vehicle which brings him to that God.

The path to God and the Church underwent a perilous mutation early in the fourth century. At the risk of some oversimplification one can say that the emperor Constantine realised that Christianity could not be stamped out by force, so he tolerated it. Moving with some caution he then extended further legal securities to the Christians. He had perceived that the new religion could serve the unity of the empire by ensuring that all its citizens had the same moral vision of life, thereby underpinning the moral basis of the legal system.

With the abrogation of the laws persecuting the Church, and the evident signs of imperial favour many thousands of people flocked to join the Christians. Undoubtedly many did so for social and political advantage. The Church authorities at the time were aware of the danger of insincere conversions and reacted accordingly. The catechumenate was strengthened and applicants had to go through a rigourous training before admission to baptism. Nevertheless it was difficult to counterbalance the impetus given by the imperial favour. Numbers increased and the liturgies could no longer be held in private houses. The solution to this problem was the use of the public buildings known as basilicas for religious assemblies. These buildings were a cross between a modern town hall and a law court. Their size suited the large numbers then coming to the Sunday eucharist, and the format which evolved in those larger buildings was the context in which the remarkable development of the liturgy took place in the fourth and fifth centuries. For instance choirs and processions became not only possible but desirable in the evolution of a liturgy of great beauty and dignity. That epoch was the truly creative period for the Church's liturgy, and in its essentials we still have it today. Over many centuries it was inevitable that formalisation and distortions would creep in, but thanks to a century of scholarly study and the work of the Second Vatican Council the theological structure of that remarkable achievement has been restored to us.

In spite of all that the Church authorities did to try and ensure sincerity in the new converts, it was almost inevitable that with the passage of time, more and more people were to be found in the Church whose allegiance depended on what could generically be described as cultural reasons rather than a deep personal commitment. As one generation succeeded another there was a danger that children grew up accepting Christianity rather like the way in which they inherited their parents' nationality and family name. It had become the accepted outlook of

---

[10] The original texts of these credal formulate, together with much relevant information, can be found in *Enchiridion Symbolorum* , ed. Denziger, Henry. 33rd edition,(1965), ed. Schönmetzer, Adolf, Barcelona and Freiburg: Herder. Numbers 1 - 76, 125, and 150.

society as a whole. The increasing practice of   infant baptism had the unforeseen effect of reinforcing this tendency. The state benefited from the moral consensus given to society by the Church, and the Church's life was helped by the protection and benevolence of the government. It was an uneasy alliance whose inherent contradictions would create severe problems in the future.

SECTION 2 :   OBSTACLES TO A PERSONAL ACT OF FAITH :
                          THE HISTORICAL PERSPECTIVE.

Having stated above that the Church as a community is an object of faith, and a path to faith in Jesus, we must now face up to the fact that in many respects the policies and structures of the Church in the 21st century are also a barrier to belief. This deterrent factor is due to the retention of many policies and other accidents of history which have accrued to the community over its history which has endured for many centuries and during which it has mingled with many different cultures. The institutional Church is so large in numbers, so dispersed all over the world, and so ancient that its cultural momentum makes reform extremely difficult. The Second Vatican Council in the 1960's laid the theological foundations for a modernising reform of the structures and institutions, but at the beginning of the 21 st century we have yet to see these insights being translated satisfactorily into practice. For the present, an earnest seeker will have to penetrate patiently through many irrelevancies and worse, if he is to perceive the authentic message and the person of Jesus.

The root cause of all these problems can be traced back to the uneasy alliance referred to already of Church and State in the reign of the emperor Constantine during the fourth century. It established a pattern which had taken hold firmly by the time that the imperial power collapsed in Western Europe in the fifth century.

To appreciate he significance of that situation a brief digression into the history of the Church in Western Europe is necessary, for which I beg the reader's patience. Paradoxically a proper understanding of the Church's problem with evangelism in the 21 st century requires some appreciation of what happened to it in the fifth century and beyond. Basically the theology of evangelisation was put on hold in that period. Moreover the holding operation was reflected in the community structures which evolved then, and which are still with us today.

First of all something extremely positive must be kept in mind. The spiritual vitality of the early Church showed itself by the speed in which the invaders of the Roman Empire were themselves converted to Christianity. In what are now the nations of Spain, France, Germany and England Christianity was victorious. The process was confused, and at times chaotic. One constantly recurring factor was the importance attached to the conversion of the kings or other powerful military leaders.

In 496 in northern France Clovis the leader of the Franks was baptised by St. Remigius, and the 3000 soldiers of his personal guard were also baptised at the same time. Almost exactly a century later (597) in England King Ethelbert of Kent was converted to Christianity in the famous mission of St. Augustine, and his subjects did the same. Similar conversions of kings took place all over western Europe. The process in England is almost a textbook case. The tiny kingdoms whose populations were miniscule by modern standards, one by one adopted Christianity following the lead of their kings, until eventually the whole country became

Christian, in name at least. The process was neither tidy nor uniform. There is no doubt that ancient pagan practices continued alongside the official Christianity. There were reversals too, as when St. Mellitus the first bishop of London was forced to take refuge in Gaul after the king of Essex (Ethelbert's son) relapsed into paganism after his father's death. The same process continued for centuries, and it is significant that when King Alfred made the

definitive settlement with the Danes they were obliged to accept Christianity as their religion. Admittedly these conversions were accompanied by genuine theological preaching given by missionaries and local bishops of heroic stature. Obviously St. Augustine of Canterbury comes to mind, and in France the mission benefited from the labours of heroic bishops like St. Martin of Tours and St. Germanus.

In the melting pot of political and cultural change which characterised the emergence of the nations of western Europe after the Roman period, the success of the Christian mission is the most remarkable phenomenon, and within that context the conversion of the kings is the most difficult for the modern mind to appreciate. It may help us to understand the events when we realise that the newcomers were not simply plunderers, but they intended to establish stable societies, and with that end in view the Church had a great deal to offer. It was the one organisation which survived coherently amid the ruins of the empire with its own internal organisation still functioning. The network of local churches and dioceses whose bishops were in regular communication with one another and with the pope, provided a framework for the exercise of some kind of authority, discipline and order. The pastors preached a moral code whose observance was all the more important for justice and order in public life after the disappearance of the Roman legal framework. As is well known education and culture in the widest sense were preserved by the organs of the Church, particularly the monasteries. These civilising influences were appreciated by the erstwhile pagan leaders, and in addition there was one more unforeseeable benefit which the Church could convey on these rulers, namely the concept of the king as the anointed representative of God.

This principle comes straight out of the Old Testament, and the religious status of the kings of Israel was bestowed upon the newly converted Christian kings of western Europe. The rite of anointing was a symbolic gesture of great significance since it proclaimed that their authority derived from God. The enhancing of their status was considerable and its advantages were not lost upon those early monarchs whose love of power was no less than that of political leaders of all times and places. With the passage of time the rite of coronation became more and more sophisticated, and by the high middle ages the ceremony closely resembled the celebration of a sacrament. (It is one of the anomalies of history that in its essentials this ceremony is still in use with the English monarchy, and anyone who has seen the TV film of Queen Elizabeth's coronation in 1953 cannot have failed to observe the intensely religious character of the whole ceremony).

A simple reading of the New Testament could hardly have prepared anyone to anticipate such an anomalous missionary movement. In its essence the newly converted kings needed the moral authority and civilising influence of the Church. The Church in its turn benefited greatly from the protection which was provided by the military power of the kings. It was a marriage of convenience which produced spectacular success in the later development of European culture. But it contained intrinsic flaws. Theologically, the most serious of these was the presence of military power to back   up the spiritual message, of which I will have more to say later in this chapter. The second major flaw was the absence of a personal act of faith in those who followed their kings into Christianity. Admittedly it is difficult in the 21 st century to appreciate the sociological situation of sixth century Europe and an individual's sense of loyalty to his overlord, but one cannot help feeling uneasy about the apparent absence of a clearly motivated personal decision. We should also remember that in the past, personal autonomy was much less than it is today. Often it was taken for granted that young

men would follow the trades and careers of their fathers . Marriages were frequently arranged by parents for their children. The complete autonomy which we take for granted in western society in the modern period is a comparatively new phenomenon in the perspectives of history.

Before pursuing the negative aspects of the missionary movement, one should not forget the spiritual power of the pure message of the gospel. In that confused period one has glimpses of true religious sincerity. As with the Roman empire this society too was fundamentally religious in its culture, and to people of intelligence and sensitivity the monotheism proclaimed by the Christians could not have failed to impress them in contrast to the polytheistic and animistic deities of their erstwhile pagan religions.

As is well known the whole of this missionary enterprise and the alliance of royalty and Church found its most powerful embodiment in the life and work of Charlemagne. [11] His dramatic coronation in Rome by Pope Leo III in the course of the Christmas mass in 800, formalised the status of the Frankish kings as protectors of the Church , which had operated in practice since 732 when Charles Martel defeated the Muslim invasion of France at the battle of Poitiers. Charlemagne's particular contribution to the process (apart from his unusually long reign) was the spiritual conviction and cultural creativity which he brought to the partnership. He gathered to his royal court distinguished ecclesiastics and scholars from many parts of Europe, and personally underwent education at their hands. Bishops were taken into the administration of the empire, and they accompanied the royal counts on their tours of duty, enforcing the royal decrees. Charlemagne realised that he needed the cultural and spiritual resources of the Church if he was to establish a truly civilised empire embodying culture, rather than simply holding society together by force. Ultimately his policy was successful, and it laid the foundations of the immensely rich culture of mediaeval Europe.

The alliance of Church and State which was creative in the hands of enlightened kings like Charlemagne and King Alfred, ensured that Christianity as a powerful spiritual force prospered in Europe and shaped its subsequent culture for centuries to come. However as I indicated above, there were inherent disadvantages whose shortcomings would undermine the Church's spiritual vigour at a much later date. The first of these was the virtual disappearance of a fully deliberate decision of faith when the individuals accepted baptism.

---

[11] A considerable literature exists dealing with Charlemagne and the Church, among which one could single out :- Bullough, D. *The Age of Charlemagne,* (2nd ed. 1973); Fichtenau, H. *The Carolingian Empire ,* (1968); McKitterick , R.. *The Frankish Kingdoms under the Carolingians* (1983). A useful summary is to be found in Mayr-Harting , Henry, (2001), 'The Early Middle Ages' , in Meyr-Harting, Henry & Harries, Richard (eds), *Christianity : Two Thousand Years,* Oxford: Oxford University Press, pp. 45 - 59..

The traditional catechumenate was severely weakened, infant baptism became the norm and as the children of Christian parents grew up they received the sacraments and became subject to the rules of the Church in a process which was as uncomplicated as their accepting the laws of the land. It was only in the twentieth century that the weakness of that situation became truly apparent. In the secular culture of nations like Great Britain, where the intellectual
climate is also intensely critical in all its activities, the absence of a personal individual decision about belief is literally devastating to religion. I cannot over emphasise the seriousness of that lacuna. It amounts to the non-existence of the foundation of religion in an individual's life.

The next presupposition of the Carolingian settlement which is theologically questionable is the implied presupposition that all the citizens in the kingdom of a Christian king should themselves be Christians. There is no warrant for this in the New Testament. The Apostles and their followers were instructed to announce the gospel to all nations, but there is no guarantee that everyone who heard it would be converted. It is a sobering thought to reflect that just the opposite is implied in several of the sayings of Jesus, such as "Many are called but few are chosen." (Matthew 22:14).

A further departure from the ideals of the New Testament was the way in which the clergy became a separate class. To some extent it was practically unavoidable . Since they were virtually the only people who were educated it was almost inevitable that they would come to fulfil the roles which in modern society are undertaken by teachers, social workers and civil servants. For hundreds of years the clergy's discharge of those roles was genuinely creative. Even as late as the 20th century it was taken for granted that unmarried monks were the natural educators of school boys. The creative side of that role was gradually undermined as the modern world developed its own administrators, teachers and social workers, and as their status as a separate class gradually became that of a a highly privileged class. In the modern world that has really diminished their spiritual effectiveness.

The time has come to return to the Carolingian period and analyse other factors which arose out of the alliance with the Crown, and which distorted the Church's authentic mission. Basically they flow from the unconscious imitation of the State, whose influence entered the Church's ways of acting by a sort of osmosis of secular political principles.Charlemagne's soldiers protected the Church, and for that the ecclesiastics were grateful, but his armies also propagated Christianity at the point of the sword, and the bishops seemed to have been too inhibited to protest. The most serious crime in Charlemagne's long reign was his treatment of the Saxons. Between 772 and 785 he engaged in repeated wars to subjugate them and incorporate them into his empire. Several revolts were put down savagely, and on one occasion as many as four thousand of them were executed in his presence. Ultimately his military power prevailed, the Saxons became part of this empire and Christians at the same time , since baptism was compulsory.

The origin of the Papal States antedates Charlemagne, but they became securely established under his protection. It lies outside the limits of this book to trace the origin and development of this curious anomaly on the European stage. It must suffice to say that from the early middle ages, as is well known, the pope was the secular ruler of a substantial region of central Italy. On the one hand it served to protect his spiritual independence, but on the other hand in the ruling of it he was drawn into the power   politics of the European secular scene. Having entered the secular field it was inevitable that the Papal States would have to imitate the conduct of other nations, eventually developing a civil service, army, taxation and legal systems.

The papal army is the element most obviously at variance with the teaching of Jesus. Nevertheless its ethos was so powerful that religious orders were created precisely to enlist combat soldiers (like the Teutonic Knights and the Knights Templar), and the greatest military undertaking of the middle ages (the Crusades) was launched on the initiative of the Church.

However the legal system was perhaps the most subversive of the gospel values. A well known biblical scholar, Fr. Jerome Murphy-O'Connor, has declared that law has no place in the Church.[12] Unfortunately, due to the accidents of history it has all too large a place. The Code of Canon Law of 1919 had 2414 of them , and the revised Code of 1983 has 1752. Today we speak about the Code of Canon Law, usually oblivious of the fact that over the centuries the vocabulary has changed its meaning. In the third century local councils of the Church were making decisions about ecclesiastical policy and promulgating rules for the Christians to follow. The technical term chosen for those rules was the Greek word *kanon* which in modern English means literally a rule, not a law. The difference is important. The former applies to the business of a voluntary society (like a university or a football club), the latter is exclusively the preserve of the state. After Constantine's official toleration of Christianity the Church continued to hold councils in which they promulgated not laws, but rules, which were still designated by the established technical term *kanon*. Even the most sympathetic Christian emperors would not have tolerated a second law-making organisation within the Empire. Yet over the centuries as the Church and the Papal States became more powerful the meaning of the word *kanon* changed to being that of Law. An alternative society had come into existence making its own laws which have been studied as a separate branch of learning, known as Canon Law since the early middle ages.

Eventually the laws of the Church were enforced just like the laws of the State, and for serious offences there was the death penalty. In other words dissenters from Christian doctrine were treated in just the same way as traitors guilty of high treason within the State. The punishment was execution. A legal fiction was created by which the condemned heretic was handed over the civil power for the actual killing, but it was a totally artificial subterfuge. In reality the Church authorities effected the executions of doctrinal dissenters. It is superfluous to point out how far this differs from the teaching of the New Testament.

Granted the nature of the alliance between Church and State which came into being most obviously in the policies of Constantine and Charlemagne, it should not surprise us if one of its effects was the creation of the habit of obedience of citizens towards their rulers. It suited the secular rulers admirably to have really obedient citizens. It was also a moral attitude which the Church encouraged in its own sphere, and indeed demanded in lay peoples' relationship to the clergy. In spite of any superficial advantages to Church and State the habit of obedience is of such limited value morally (as I will show in a later chapter), that it has not

---

[12] He made this remarkable statement in a public lecture in Westminster Cathedral Hall, presided over by his cousin the Cardinal of the same name, on 19th June 2008.

engendered authentic virtue. Very briefly one can say that it has not notably promoted the goodness of the average Christian in a positive sense, and negatively it has weakened his or her ability to defy wicked authorities in all walks of life .

The more sinister outcome of creating loyal and obedient citizens has been their willingness to obey whatever the governments have told them to do. The worst realisation of this habit has come about in warfare, where Christian soldiers of different nations have displayed virtually blind obedience in killing anyone whom their rulers have ordered them to kill, even children. This widespread occurrence of that so called patriotism in all nations and over many centuries must rank as one of the worst failings of institutionalised Christianity and

constitutes perhaps the most powerful barrier to the Church's ability to invite people to belief in Jesus. If Christianity has been so ineffectual in ameliorating the most obvious and basest form of human wickedness one might well ask what is its value, and what is the point of joining a Church? Before Constantine tamed the Church there had been many martyrs in the early centuries who were put to death because they refused military service. After the pragmatic alliance of Church and State became an established fact there have been few protesters. In the second world War the heroic protests of Franz Jagerstatter, Dietrich Bonhoeffer and the White Rose group are well known , but it is difficult to think of any others. Although he was beatified in November 2007, it is significant that the Catholic Church has so far refused to canonise Jägerstatter, more than sixty years after his execution although in the pontificate of John Paul II hundreds of other individuals were granted that accolade.

The Nazi period was a time when religion was most urgently needed as an ideological counter weight to Hitler's form of fascism. From the 1930's onwards it was rendered ineffectual by the extreme form of the Church State alliance. The Catholic and Protestant Churches were supported financially by the state, because every taxpayer had to indicate his Church allegiance, on the basis of which a proportion of his tax was repaid to his Church. (For atheists the same proportion went to philanthropic causes). The Lutheran Church was the established religion of the nation, but the Catholics tied themselves into an equally debilitating situation by ratifying a Concordat (official treaty) with the Nazi government. It is tragic to reflect that in the 1940's the Catholic Church had signed Concordats with four fascist dictatorships right across Europe. They were in force with Portugal, Spain, Germany and Italy. There can be no doubt that this extreme strengthening of the Church State alliance effectively undermined any possibility of an effective protest against the horrors of warfare by the Catholic Church. When Mussolini's army set off for the invasion of Ethiopia in 1935 Pope Pius XI was present at the embarkation ceremony and blessed the regimental flags. Worse was to come in the summer of 1940. When the French were obviously on the point of military collapse Mussolini declared war on them. None of the conditions for a just war could be advanced in justification of his decision, yet not one Italian bishop protested. From the Pope downwards the Catholic authorities were silent , and therefore complicit in the enterprise. The same was true of the Italian invasion of Greece, and the earlier German invasion of Poland in September 1939. In neither case were there justifying causes according to the theology of a just war. These first moral surrenders probably explain the subsequent silence when the darkest evils of that war came to light, namely the systematic extermination of Jews, gypsies, and others at the command of the Nazis.

I have devoted considerable space to the damage done to the Church's apostolate by its close alliance with the State, because it is this partnership which has atrophied the real missionary capabilities of Christianity . In addition to these institutional weaknesses which act as a deterrent against sincere atheists joining us, there is a whole raft of badly directed moral programmes, like denying condoms to Aids victims, which are equally damaging to the Church's moral credibility. I will deal with the moral deterrents in a subsequent chapter. In this present chapter I am focussing attention on the institutional and structural shortcomings because they are more deeply rooted in the Church's life, and could have been eradicated in the wake of the Second Vatican Council in the 1960's.

To sum up, it is fair to maintain that over the centuries the alliance with the civil govern-

ments of Europe had given misguided support to the Church directing all citizens into membership of that organisation, in a way that rendered personal commitment superfluous. All the cultural and psychological pressures of society combined to make people nominally Christian. The traditional organs which could have engendered personal faith simply atrophied. The catechumenate vanished, infant baptism became universal, and children grew up in Christianity accepting its values in almost the same way as they accepted their parents family name, nationality, language, and obedience to the law of the land. Undeniably there were sincere committed Christians in every age and nation. What proportion of any society was sincere in its religious commitment, and how many were cultural passengers is impossible to say. What is clear is that the ecclesiastical institutions did little to engender an authentic act of faith. Both the Church and State presumed that the adults at any rate were fully convinced Christians.

In the latter part of the 20th century all factors described in the preceding pages led to the exposure of the crucial pastoral problem which became inescapable (to those who had eyes to see it) namely that in the whole of the Church's programme there was no point at which the child of a Catholic family was formally invited to make an act of faith in Jesus. It had been presupposed in the whole of his religious formation at home and school. On reflection this realisation is quite simply devastating. Since the time of Constantine and Charlemagne religion had been handed down from one generation to another on roughly the same basis as the transmission of nationality and family surname. The Catholic Church had no ceremony, sacrament or custom to invite a deeply reflected decision about personal belief. Baptism had been given in infancy and all the obligations following from it had been imposed in childhood with only the most token gestures about freedom. The most constricting form of this process was the linkage of sacraments to school. " Class three will be making first communion on June 4th". In those circumstances it is morally impossible for one child to say that he wishes more time to think about it.

SECTION 3 : OBSTACLES TO FAITH AT THE ORGANISATIONAL LEVEL

In the preceding pages I have dealt at length with the historical factors which removed a personal act of faith from the lives of the average child born into a Christian family. In this section I will develop the theme in relation to the community which ought to nourish, sustain, and encourage the life of faith in the neophyte, whether he be a newly arrived adult convert or an adolescent who has felt that it was the right time in his life to make his personal commitment to Christ and the Church. This problem was understood fully by a distinguished

Anglican patristic scholar, the late Professor Geoffrey Lampe. Writing about the local parish as a community of believers, he stated:- "The most searching test is probably that which the Christian community, represented by the local congregation, ought to apply to itself : can it undertake to care for new members, children especially, in such a way as to communicate the Christ-Spirit to them, and is it a recognisably Spirit-inspired body ? Is it, in other words, worth joining ?"[13] The short answer to that question is a further question: is it a real community or just an agglomeration of people. After that we must ask, does it embody specific Christian characteristics. Every authentic Christian community, be it diocese, monastery, parish, or chaplaincy, should embody four characteristics. It should be a

community of worship, witness, charity and apostolate.

Whatever may have been the case in the past, by the nineteenth and twentieth centuries the only Christian community which was on offer to the laity was the ancient, time honoured and familiar structure of the territorial parish. In the modern period it had become basically an administrative unit not unlike a borough council in the sphere of civil administration. It is neither a missionary community nor a support group.

The erosion of this sustaining role from the life of the average parish, was brought about over many centuries by basically the same historical causes which allowed the element of personal decision to drop out of the lives of many Christians. In other words personal Christian conviction was assumed, largely because the whole of society was presumed to be Christian. With the passage of time the basic Christian community became the parish: there was nothing smaller or more intimate. Mass and the sacraments were not available at any more informal level. The longevity of the familiar institution which we call the parish is remarkable. Administratively and legally it was put into its present form all over Europe in the early middle ages and has not changed essentially since them. [14] In England the parish became established in the eighth century. Hitherto the typical ecclesiastical unit was the minster. This was not always a monastery, but a community of clerics for whom it provided a base from which to direct their missionary journeys. When the conversion of the population was substantially achieved these communities gave way to the parishes, which were originally founded by local landowners for their tenants and servants.[15]

As far as modern Catholics are concerned, it is defined in Canon Law, then and now, as an institution in which the people are presumed to be believing Catholics. As late as 1919, when the first Code of Canon Law appeared, there is a passing reference to non-Catholics. In the section on preaching the word of God, canon 1350 enjoins that bishops and parish priests should regard non-Catholics residing in their dioceses or parishes as being commended to them in the Lord. In other words their presence is an anomaly in institutions whose populations are presumed to be totally Catholic. The priest's duties are basically to provide mass, the sacraments, and the rites of passage to the faithful when they require them.

---

[13] Reported in *The Tablet* , 8 March 2008.

[14] Stutz ,U. (1895), *Die Eigenkirche als Element des mittelalterischgermanischen Kirchenrechtes,* Basel: Eng. trans. Barraclough,G.(1938) *Mediaeval Germany ,* Oxford, Basil Blackwell, Vol. II, pp. 35 - 70.

[15] Pounds, N.J.G. (2000), *A History of the English Parish,* Cambridge: C.U.P. p. 22.

In certain circumstances parishes appeared to function quite well as communities , such as mediaeval rural villages. However on closer inspection it becomes clear that the administrative apparatus of the parish was merely sharing space with some other structure whose inner dynamics were the real source of the cohesion of the community, such as the economic interdependence of the people in an agricultural community. The same uneasy tandem was to be seen in the Irish ghettos of British industrial cities in the latter part of the nineteenth century. It was their sense of being Irish exiles in a hostile environment that held them together, the parishes whose frontiers were somewhat arbitrarily drawn around them made use of that sense of community but did not create it. This became devastatingly clear after the First World War when the third or fourth generation of the immigrants had become

culturally assimilated to the English working class, and the community life of those parishes dissolved .

Quite simply the parish is a holding operation within whose structure valid sacraments are dispensed to those who seek them, and the rites of passage are conducted with dignity and a sense of spiritual purpose. Masses are celebrated and sermons are delivered on the Scriptures. The preaching is perhaps the most paradoxical indicator that the gathering cannot sustain the faith of neophytes. As a method of teaching , the sermon is the most impractical exercise that could be imagined. The preacher is faced with an audience of possibly three hundred listeners of every age from infancy to 80 plus. Their intelligence also varies, from almost illiterates to the very bright and well educated. It is humanly impossible to address any message which will be relevant to more than a small section of such an audience.

The worst aspect of the parish structure , and the most debilitating for its attempt to sustain belief, is its sheer anonymity. Anyone who has moved house to another town, and sought out a new church at which to attend mass, will have been struck by this impersonal quality of the building and its clientele. Simply entering the building before mass and finding a place to sit, is as impersonal as going to the theatre. In the vast majority of parishes there is no one at the door to give a word of greeting to those coming in, and more importantly spotting a newcomer and addressing to him or her sincere welcome to the community .

After the Second World War all these defects in the parish system became more pronounced and debilitating. The cause was the steep increase in the Catholic population in England. In the first few years after the war, when immigration restrictions were lifted, it has been calculated that about one million Irish people came into this country.[16] At that time Catholic families usually had significantly more children than non-Catholics , because then most of them did not use contraception.

While the numbers of lay people were increasing, the number of priests was not . At best it remained more or less static. The solution to that problem was unbelievably short sighted (if indeed there was any conscious planning behind it), namely small churches were pulled down and replaced with larger ones, and most priests were given permission to celebrate three masses on each Sunday. In relation to the spiritual quality of the liturgy the latter permission

---

[16] Hickey, J. V. (1960) *The Irish Rural Immigrant and British Urban Society,* London: Newman Demographic Survey Publications. (passim).

was thoroughly undesirable. The character of the mass is so sacred that it simply must not be celebrated too frequently. Once a day is the maximum , and in the infant Church it was once a week. For the priests, particularly in rural areas, the distracting nature of the measure is compounded by the necessity of driving from one village to another, and arriving at the place of the third mass with virtually no sense of recollection at all.

In short the parish presents itself as a large administrative unit, which is too big to function as a community, whose most obvious characteristic is anonymity and whose members are so diverse in age and intelligence that the sensitive nourishing and sustaining of delicate matters like an adolescent's nascent faith (for example) is virtually impossible.

This is the inescapable conclusion to an examination of the second component of the Church's main pastoral problem in the twenty first century. Hence we are saddled with the twofold crisis: no structured opportunity to elicit a personal decision of faith, and no adequate community to nourish such a decision if it should be made. It is impossible to over-emphasise the seriousness of that double problem. It is undoubtedly the cause why so many young people abandon religion in the adolescent years, yet the Church authorities have not perceived that it was the root cause of the widespread relinquishing of Christian allegiance in the latter part of the twentieth century .

The time has come to look for possible remedies to this twofold problem.

SECTION 4 : POSSIBLE REMEDIES FOR THE CRUCIAL PASTORAL PROBLEMS

Having shown in the previous sections the limitations of the traditional parish, it is urgently incumbent on us to seek other structures and forms of social engineering to achieve that kind of commitment in the future.

The distant history of our Church offers alternative models which have been employed successfully, and although they fell into disuse in the early middle ages, they could be revived. The most obvious of these is the ancient institution of the adult catechumenate. It was a training programme for adult converts from paganism. They were instructed in Catholic doctrine , tested morally, and gradually admitted to the instructional part of the Sunday mass, but excluded from the offertory onwards, because they were not initially ready for the deeper mysteries like the eucharist. It is worth remembering that the children of Christian parents were not always baptised in infancy, they could enter the catechumenate and accept baptism as adults. Indeed two of the best known personalities of the Latin Church were catechumens in their adult years, namely Saints Ambrose and Augustine. It seems as if the ancient Church regarded religion as a commitment for adult years.

In England there has been in operation for a number of years a programme for the systematic formation of adult converts to Catholicism. They are instructed as a group, in contrast to the older practice of individual instruction. This programme suffers from the fact that the conventional parish does not serve as an adequate support community once the neophytes have been baptised. Nor is there any specific provision for entry by the children of Catholic parents which was an integral component of the ancient catechumenate.

If the catechumenate were to be revived on the lines of its ancient counterpart, there would be some difficulties in relation to the Catholic schools system. The complete system of schools from age 5 to 18 has been constructed on the assumption that all the children of Catholic families will attend the Church schools. The reintroduction of the catechumenate would not undermine the Church schools, but there would be a conflict of interests. The catechumenate would receive its members at a time of their choosing. The Catholic schools require the children to enter them at the age of five, (as laid down by the law of the land). There would be a considerable potential for discord.

Another model from the past which is the most likely serve us well is the Jewish Passover supper. That meal is celebrated at home in the family, and significantly not in the synagogue. The parents preside, and not the rabbi. The atmosphere is informal, emotionally warm and

intimate. Every year at a certain point in the ceremony the youngest son is directed to ask the question . "Why is this night different from all other nights?" The parents explain that it commemorates their ancestors' liberation from Egypt, which was the effective beginning of their religion. The Passover supper was also the beginning of Christianity. Jesus performed the foundational act of establishing the Church at the Last Supper, which was the Passover. At the same time it was the institution of the Eucharist. For that reason the first Christian communities celebrated the Eucharist in the context of a domestic supper and not in any "official building". It seems probable that the primitive pattern continued until the epoch of Constantine when Christian communities were offered the use of the official basilicas.

If Catholics were to return to the simple domestic setting for the regular Eucharist something special could be arranged on the night of Holy Saturday. The answer to the great question would be then be "On this night Jesus rose from the dead". That could serve as the starting point for an explanation of the whole of Christianity, not on one evening of course, but the information could be imparted year by year in accordance with the childrens' ability to understand it, and appreciate its relevance. Such an arrangement is rich in possibilities. As the solemn supper liturgy would be repeated year by year, each child could consider the invitation at a time appropriate in his or her life when they were really ready to take up the offer. The same small group would be ideal for sustaining the faith of the newly committed Christian.

In addition to setting the scene for a young people to commit themselves to Jesus in faith, the long term success of the process also demands a community which will support that decision, and this is the second part of the crucial pastoral problem facing the Church at the start of the twenty first century. Experience makes it clear that the present large sized parishes simply cannot function as communities in any practical sense. They are the gatherings where people assist at Mass and receive the sacraments. These activities can be done in virtual anonymity, as we all know from attending church while on holiday. What is really distressing is that the same anonymity can operate in the regular attendance at our home parish too, where presence at Mass is about as personal as a visit to the theatre. The total cause of this disfunction is size . A building holding five hundred people, living in an urban parish of perhaps two thousand Catholics simply cannot engender any sense of community. For an enriching community experience, such as could sustain a young persons nascent faith, we must search for a group which is structured differently, and above all which is smaller.

In recent years this question has been studied extensively by the Irish theologian Dr. Thomas

O'Loughlin, who has examined the New Testament information about the eucharist from a new perspective, and the results are impressive.[17] A sensitive reading of the New Testament accounts of the eucharist (I Corinthians 10:17 & 11:26) indicates that the participants shared literally one cup and one loaf which was divided between them in the course of the celebration. At the risk of stating the obvious one must insist that they did not share one jug, nor did they use the modern small hosts (which resemble circular pieces cardboard rather than bread). Without attempting too much mathematical precision, one can infer that the numbers involved in that scale of sharing must have been about seventy at the most.

This order of magnitude is confirmed by the architecture of church buildings from the Saxon period to the late middle ages. It seems surprising to the modern mind that mediaeval cities had so many parish churches. It has been suggested that Canterbury had forty parishes in Saxon times, and Norwich had so many churches that one street (now called King Street) had no fewer than eight churches in the late mediaeval period. Since mediaeval cities were small by modern standards, all the citizens were within easy walking distance of the cathedrals, which were large enough to contain the whole population of the city. The provision of so many parish churches must have been an expression of policy which was to them so obvious that it did not need to be spelt out. Clearly they understood that their eucharistic celebrations had to be authentic community experiences, and for that relatively small numbers were imperative. Those ancient parish churches indicate a capacity for about 70 to 100 people. The large urban parish churches with which we are now familiar were largely a phenomenon of the industrial revolution and the massive expansion of cities occasioned by the migrations of rural populations to the new centres of industry. Admittedly there are exceptions, such as the large churches of the friars in mediaeval Italian cities, but those buildings, like the cathedrals, had a different function from the normal parish churches which were the ordinary setting for the communities' regular liturgies.

Size is also perfectly clear from the various references in the New Testament to private houses as the meeting places of Christians. The sources do not say how large the houses were, and they could have ranged from buildings which could hold only about a dozen, to dwellings of the well to do where perhaps one hundred could have stood. The sophisticated liturgies in Rome described in the third century Apostolic Tradition of Hippolytus would have required an assembly of about one hundred.

This pattern of activity is confirmed by yet another indicator from the traditional practice of the Church, namely that the priest should celebrate mass only once on a Sunday (or any other day for that matter). This too confirms the idea that the whole community should be present at the same celebration. The rule that a priest should celebrate no more than one mass on a Sunday is enshrined in he present Code of Canon Law (canon 905). The practice of celebrating several (perhaps private) masses every day in the late mediaeval period is recognised as an abuse.

---

[17] In this chapter I am relying principally on two articles, " How Many Priests Do We Need?" in *New Blackfriars* Nov. 2005, pp 642 -657, and " The Eucharist as 'The Meal that Should Be' "in *Worship* January 2006, pp 30 - 45.

All the above considerations point to the need for a group of about 70 to 100 people as the normal community for Christian liturgy, and that size of gathering would be of a human scale in which all the members would know one another, and in which the faith of a neophyte could be encouraged and sustained.

In case the above mentioned scenario seems somewhat theoretical or fanciful , I would like to draw attention to an example which I have witnessed over the years. It concerns the life of a university chaplaincy which I knew well in the 1970's . The university's colleges , and the students' halls of residence were scattered around the city. The chaplains had established a network of small communities in most of them. These communities met once a week in a seminar room or something similar, not a chapel. The meeting comprised mass, business discussion and a sandwich lunch. The territorial base of the chaplaincy was a student house, which did have a chapel, in which Sunday mass was celebrated. That liturgy began with an invitation from the priest for each person to turn to his or her neighbour and say their name and their college. That was a real ice-breaker. The liturgies were enjoyable and effective.

Admittedly the circumstances were favourable. Preaching was relatively simple because all the people were of roughly the same age and intelligence. A informal supper followed the main (evening) mass, as was the case in St. Paul's days. A genuine sense of community was engendered, and this was helped by the fact that the meeting took place not in a church but in a students' hall of residence.

The examples described in the preceding paragraphs indicate that there is no "one size fits all" group for the basic Christian community. Flexibility is essential to tailor the dimensions of the community to the living situation of the people. For example the number of Catholics in a village in rural Wales might easily fit into a cottage whereas in the suburbs of a city a larger meeting place would be needed . One could envisage a progression from a dozen people in an average house to fifty or so in a community centre, both of which sizes would retain their self identity under the umbrella organisation of a conventional parish, which could enjoy a co-ordinating role.

To sum up, it seems clear to me that in the totally secularised society of 21 st century Britain, the best hope for eliciting real faith and sustaining it, is for the whole practice of religion to be anchored to small domestic sized communities. It accords well with the vision of the Church given in Vatican II, placing the emphasis on the laity who are the People of God. Structures have to be organised round the laity to facilitate their spiritual life. It is theologically counterproductive to do it the other way round, i.e. to start with a prearranged structure (the parish) and fit the laity into its dimensions and functions.

At the risk of great oversimplification one can say that a group small enough to meet in an average size house is the answer. In addition to its regular eucharists, such a group could conduct a special annual supper (to invite the act of faith) such as I have described above. It would be a true community, because anonymity could not survive in such a context. If the group were permanent it could serve to sustain the belief of the youngsters, or neophytes and indeed of the adult believers too. If such groups existed then the present administrative parishes could act as umbrella organisations ensuring for them a wider context of extended unity with other such groups in the neighbourhood. In fact the parish structure could still serve a useful purpose at that level, provided that it is based on a network of domestic communities. There are some authentically   Christian tasks which the house groups could not really perform , such as issues of social justice. If the local M.P. is being contacted about the government's policy on asylum seekers for example, it would probably be best for the parish or diocese to be the immediate agency. In carrying out that kind of role, both parish and diocese would fulfil the fourfold vocation of a true Christian community namely worship, witness, charity and apostolate.

Needless to say, the scheme would entail considerably more eucharistic celebrations and therefore more priests than have have today. Present legal restriction on who is admitted to ordination would have to be lifted, but I will deal with that question in Chapter Sevenon the sacraments and in the immediate context of the sacrament of Holy Order. The whole process for the necessary structural reforms, in whose context these changes would have to be made, will be dealt with at length in Chapter Five on the nature of the Church.

SECTION 5 : THE OTHER COMPONENTS OF THE ACT OF FAITH

Whereas faith effects the basic religious commitment because it entails knowledge of the God to whom we are committing ourselves. It is accompanied also by hope and charity in the overall dedicating of one's life to God in the fundamental existential relationship.

Charity is a word which has been over exposed and debased in other contexts. It means the generous love of God and our neighbour. The neighbour is not a person whom we find naturally attractive , to whom it would be easy to show kindness, but it extends to all and sundry, particularly those who need our help, and who may be total strangers to us, as for example starving people on the other side of the world. The extent of this generous love, and its practical ramifications are spelt out in many places in the New Testament. The 25 th chapter of St. Matthew is perhaps the most explicit, where Christ tells us that practical kindness done to the homeless and starving is an act of love done to him.

The exercise of charity is not easy, and to sustain a lifelong commitment to helping the victims of illness and injustices requires strong psychological support. This comes from the third theological virtue, hope. It must not be confused with the vague optimism based on the possibility that things will work out for the best (like the possibility of winning the lottery). True Christian hope differs from that rather shallow optimism, because it is not based on a possibility of success, but on the realisation that the victory of good over evil has already been achieved, by the liberating work of Christ. Hope is based on the fact that the basic evils facing the human race have already received their remedy, what remains is to apply that remedy to individual human circumstances. Such a multifarious task is not easy. It is motivated by the resurrection of Jesus which is the tangible evidence of the triumph of goodness. That consideration keeps us motivated to persevere in working against all injustices and sufferings until the ultimate manifestation of the victory over evil which will be the second coming of Christ in glory.

The detailed working out of charity and hope in the life of the Christian are more conveniently dealt with in the context of the moral life , which I will develop in Chapter

Eight. It was necessary to make a brief mention of them in this chapter, since they will be present in a Christian's life if his or her initial act of faith has been authentic. In fact they are the sure indicators of the sincerity of that basic commitment.

CHAPTER THREE: THE LONG MARCH TO MONOTHEISM

SECTION 1 : WHERE IT STARTED.

Many books on the subject of religion, and even those presenting it to the uncommitted, speak about God as if the reader is familiar with that fundamental idea. In the present climate of opinion no such knowledge can be presumed. However, we have to start somewhere and an initial description of God is perfectly reasonable, because at this stage it does not prejudge the argument as to whether or not he exists. I use the word 'description' advisedly. If God exists he must be infinite, and hence the attempt to encapsulate him in anything so limiting as a definition must be impossible.

I take for my starting point the description provided originally by Richard Swinburne and subsequently employed by other writers. " God is a person without a body (i.e. a spirit), present everywhere, the creator and sustainer of the universe, able to do everything (i.e. omnipotent), knowing all things, perfectly good, a source of moral obligation, immutable, eternal, a necessary being, holy, and worthy of worship".[1]

How did the human race come to the knowledge of such a being ? And how did we come to formulate our perception in such terms? An oversimplified answer is that he disclosed himself to certain privileged individuals who conveyed their insights to their contemporaries. Their contemporaries were convinced of their sincerity, and transmitted the message to subsequent generations. How many people have been thus favoured is impossible to say. Although I will concentrate on the revelation to Abraham and the subsequent Judaeo-Christian tradition, I do not deny authentic revelations to spiritual geniuses of other religions.

At the risk of some oversimplification one can say that Abraham (who lived about 1900 B.C.) was given communications and visions of the deity who would subsequently be recognised as the one true God. However at that period of history he was perceived as one among many deities, but recognised by Abraham as a personal protector to whom he gave total and exclusive allegiance. The slow path to the elevated monotheism which we see in the last books of the Old Testament took nearly two thousand years. It was a history in which God patiently educated the Israelite people in a process which was not a linear intellectual development. It was an uneven historical drama of divine favours, protection, and punishment where necessary, accepted with gratitude, fidelity or backsliding. The people had to be weaned from false gods and encouraged to give their total allegiance to an awesome divinity who could not be represented in pictures or statues, and whose nature was ultimately inscrutable.

It lies outside the scope of this book to elucidate the details of early Israelite history, on which countless books have been written. Yet one or two salient points must be noted. The first is the realisation that in those primitive times, the true faith would have to be nurtured in a society where all the members shared the same religion. Religious pluralism was impossible

---

[1] Swinburne, R. (1977), *The Coherence of Theism,* Oxford: Clarendon Press, p. 2. quoted by Flew, A. (2006), in *God and Philosophy,* Amherst, New York: Prometheus Books, p. 9.

in the primitive state of societies nearly four thousand years ago. So the true faith which had taken root in the family of Abraham was nurtured among his descendants initially in Egypt, where they lived as a separate community isolated from the mainstream of the nation as slaves, and thus spared the dilution of their faith by Egyptian religion.

The formative event of the Egyptian period was the departure as a group, ever since known as the Exodus, recorded in chapters 13 and 14 in the book which bears that name. The accounts of the exodus have been extensively edited, but there is evidence of at least two departures, one being an escape, and the other an expulsion. The whole incident of the mass departure of a large group by night might seem improbable, but for the fact that in the nineteenth century an almost identical event occurred which was well documented historically. At the beginning of the nineteenth century, Mohammed Ali of Egypt settled various Bedouin tribes from the Nejd and Mesopotamia in the wadi Tumilat (where Israelites had settled long before). They were industrious, cultivated mulberry trees, propagated silk worms, and produced silk cloth. They were exempt from taxes and from military service. After Mohammed Ali's death, attempts were made to impose taxation and conscription on them. They refused, but their protests were of no avail with the new government. One night the whole Bedouin population fled, with their flocks, leaving their houses empty and the doors open.[2]

The date of the exodus has to be conjectured since it is not mentioned in the Egyptian chronicles. Probably the only relevant historical source is the stele of Mernephtah of 1200 BC which names Israel as being one of the groups whom he claimed to have defeated in a campaign in Palestine. So if Israel was to some extent established in Palestine at that date, it is safe to assume that they departed from Egypt earlier in that century.

The number of the group which departed is even harder to conjecture. Exodus 12:37 speaks of about six hundred thousand men besides women and children. This figure cannot be taken literally because the oases of the Sinai desert simply could not support such a large population, plus their animals. A total of some hundreds would seem to be more reasonable, and this would explain the absence of the event from the Egyptian chronicles. The numbers were not sufficient to warrant a mention. In this context it is important to keep in mind the historian's prudent principle, that absence of evidence cannot be taken as evidence of absence.

The next significant stage in the development of Israel's fidelity to the one true God was the covenant which was given at Mount Sinai shortly after the exodus. The important episode is recorded in the book of Exodus (chapters 19 - 24). The technical word in Hebrew *Berith* which is translated as 'covenant', was the usual term to describe several types of agreements ranging from political alliances to ordinary business contracts. In the context of the people's faith it is extremely important, because it gave them a sense of security. God promised them his protection and guidance, and they knew exactly how to serve him. For their part they pledged loyalty and obedience. All of this was sealed not by mutual pledges as if the parties were equals but on the assurance of the fidelity of God. This gave the people the all-important psychological security of knowing just where they stood with their God, but it was achieved

---

[2] Recorded in de Vaux, R. (1978), *The Early History of Israel*. London: Darton Longman and Todd, Vol.1, p.374.

without any compromise with what later Christian theologians would call the gratuity of grace.

Their monotheistic education was advanced by the prohibition (in the Decalogue) against worshipping any other gods, or making any image of the true God, either in a statue or picture. This was to remind them that he was too great to be depicted in any representation, and it would set them on the path of learning ultimately that he was a transcendent , infinite, spirit. It also regulated their dealings with him, in contrast to the pagans who had statues of their deities in the temples. This led to an attitude of bargaining with the deity, whose benevolence they sought to canalise. Israelite worship was lifted to a higher plane, which included seeking favours which were not asked for as of right, but whose bestowal was perceived to be gratuitous.

The moral obligations laid on the Israelites included the well known ten commandments, and a lot more besides, like the prohibitions against eating shell fish and ham, together with the property regulations suitable for an agricultural society. The books of Exodus, Leviticus and Deuteronomy list dozens of regulations concerning liturgy, private morality , and what we would describe as civil and criminal law. Clearly not all of these were given on the same day on Mount Sinai. Comparison with the law codes of adjacent nations indicates remarkable similarities. It is reasonable to infer that the Israelites lived by similar laws and customs before the period in Egypt. No society can live without laws, customs and private morality to regulate the conduct of individuals and the community. Israelites before the Egyptian period could not have lived in a moral vacuum. After the exodus, those same customs and laws were then taken up into the Covenant, and received a new status. They became part of the code of conduct in which they served the true God, and these rules now had the enhanced dignity as enshrining his authority.

The settlement of the Israelites in Palestine and the final securing of political independence under king David was a complicated process whose ramifications lie outside the scope of this book. Once the land had been occupied and a reasonable measure of political stability was achieved the education of the people towards an elevated monotheism was effected principally by the prophets. This is one of the most distinctive characteristics of Hebrew religion. Prophecy can be defined as human utterance believed to be inspired by a divine or transcendent source.[3] Unlike the priests who acquired their role by birth in the tribe of Levi, or the Scribes of a later period whose competence in the law came simply via education, the prophets were chosen by an individual vocation from God. There was no human preparation for it. In most cases it seems to have come as a surprise and appears to have been psychologically almost irresistible. Occasionally the prophets foretold the future, but most of their messages were concerned with the present, namely holding the people true to the God of Abraham, and reminding them of the moral responsibilities which went with this faith. Frequently they concerned themselves with issues which we would classify as social justice.

more than a century. The first part of the book (up to chapter 44) contains the utterances of the prophet who was born about 765 B.C. and is famous for the foretelling of the future

[3]   Murray, R.P.R.(1983), art. "Prophecy",in *A New Dictionary of Christian Theology* , ed. Alan Richardson & John Bowden, London: S.C.M. Press, p.473.

It is clear from the accounts of their lives and work that the prophets were not speaking to gullible audiences. Their mission was never one of smooth acceptance. Ultimately, and sometimes after their deaths, the reliability of their teaching was acknowledged, occasionally on account of miracles with which they substantiated it, but most of all it seems that their sincerity and integrity were recognised intuitively and unmistakably. Yet before the final acceptance of their messages some of them were subjected to scepticism, hostility, persecution, and dramatic purification by God in the form of sufferings. This was the fate of two prophets of the exilic period.

Jeremiah, who was born at about 646 B.C . had the unenviable task of persuading the people that God willed the destruction of the city which had been saved miraculously a century earlier. Needless to say in the context of the Babylonian invasion of the seventh century he was regarded as a traitor. He was punished by being imprisoned in the bottom of a well shaft, where he nearly died. Nevertheless his oracles were recorded by faithful followers, and one cannot read them without being moved by their noble and tragic pathos. During his lifetime the city was captured and destroyed together with its temple. A significant section of the population (the natural leaders) were deported to Babylon to endure years of exile from their homeland.

During the exile itself (587 - 538 B.C.) the prophet Ezekiel had the unenviable task of teaching his fellow exiles the divine purpose which lay behind their calamities. which the nation was enduring.While in exile in Babylon his wife died, but the prophet was commanded to show no emotion, nor was he to display the customary signs of mourning. Through his own personal tragedy, he had to teach the people that the loss of the city and temple was not a matter for sadness, but at a deeper level God was purifying their religion. In the years of the exile the people went through an extraordinary maturing of their religion. Being deprived of political independence, seeing the extinction of the monarchy , and having endured the destruction of the holy city and the unique temple, they based their faith solely on their trust in God and the testimony of his enduring love as recorded in the Scriptures. At an earlier stage in their history they had been forbidden statues and images : now all created visible supports had gone. The result was a profound, mature, and tested loyalty to their God.

It was in this period that the earliest dateable and unambiguous statement of pure monotheism is to be found in the bible. It occurs in Deutero Isaiah chapter 45, from verse 5 onwards :- " I am the Lord, and there is no other, besides me there is no god; I gird you though you do not know me, that men may know, from the rising of the sun and from the west, that there is none besides me; I am the Lord and there is no other." Although the exact date of the composition of that statement cannot be determined, it is to be found in Deutero Isaiah, which was composed during the exile, namely between the years 587 and 538 B.C.

As the ancient Israelites came to understand that there was no other God, apart from the one to whom they gave their allegiance, their understanding of his nature and power also advanced. In particular they came to understand the greatness of his power as the maker of the world. Their concept was not the later notion of creation out of nothing, but during the exilic period they realised that he alone was the maker of the universe, there was no helper divine or otherwise , and they judged his power in relation to the greatness and beauty of the universe which they observed. Deutero Isaiah contains several noteworthy passages in which the power of God is described in relation to his being the maker of the universe, as for

40

example in 40: 10 - 15 :- "Behold the Lord God comes with might, and his arm rules for him ; - - - - - - - -Who has measured the waters in the hollow of his hand and marked off the heavens with a span, enclosed the dust of the earth in a measure and weighed the mountains in scales and   the hills in a balance ? Who has directed the Spirit of the Lord, or as his counsellor has instructed him.? - - - - - - - -Behold the nations are like a drop from a bucket , and are accounted as the dust on the scales; behold , he takes up the isles like fine dust."

One other aspect of God's nature which is difficult for the modern mind to appreciate is the gradual perception of the holiness of God. We have lived with the concept for so long that we take it for granted. Among the ancients it was not so. For the Israelites it seems that their appreciation of his power might have led to and unhealthy sense of fear, but for one factor . The prophets, and especially Isaiah, introduced the notion of holiness which ensured that fear in the negative sense would not dominate their attitude. God's holiness was presented as an aspect of his transcendence, as a contrast to the   smallness and moral frailty of men, and above all as supreme moral goodness. As I noted above, we Christians have lived with the idea for so long that its significance is sometimes overlooked. It is instructive to reflect upon the sheer silliness and malicious behaviour of the gods of the ancient Greeks, as described in Homer, so that we can grasp the importance of the prophets' vision of an awe inspiring and morally perfect deity.

The next window on the development of Jewish monotheism, which I will examine, is supplied by the Book of Ben Sira (sometimes referred to as Ecclesiasticus) whose composition can be dated reliably to a few years before 170 B.C. This lengthy book supplies a great deal of information about Jewish piety in the last period of tranquillity before the Seluecid persecutions, the Maccabean revolt, and the advent of the Romans. It is no surprise that Ben Sira proclaims absolute monotheism (36:5). The omnipotence of God is taken even further than in the writings of the prophets. The remarkable passage of 42:18 - 21 deserves to be quoted in full. Referring to God he states:- "He searches out the abyss, and the hearts of men, and considers their crafty devices. For the Most High knows all that may be known, and he looks into the signs of the age. He declares what has been and what is to be, and he reveals the tracks of hidden things. No thought escapes him, and not one word is hidden from him. He has ordained the splendours of his wisdom , and he is from everlasting and to everlasting. Nothing can be added or taken away, and he needs no one to be his counsellor." There are few other passages in the bible which speak so clearly about what we would call God's eternity, immutability, his omnipotence and omniscience. [4]

To this dignified but perhaps rather too austere monotheism the teaching of Jesus supplied the all important qualification, namely the concept of intimacy. The four gospels indicate the constant use by Jesus of the Aramaic word *Abba* which is best translated by something like "My most respected Father", since it carries the overtones of respect as well as intimacy. Without diminishing the purity of traditional monotheism believers are invited into a relationship of intimacy with the transcendent, infinite God . It is an astounding innovation of Christianity into the world's religious ideas. I will have more to say about the relationship

[4] cf. Alexander A. Di Lella, (2002) " God and Wisdom in the Theology of Ben Sira", in *Ben Sira's God: Proceedings of the International Ben Sira Conference, Durham - Ushaw College 2001,* ed. Renate Egger-Wenzel. Berlin & New York: Walter de Gruyter, p.8.

later in this book in the chapter on prayer. For the present it is important to appreciate the profundity of this concept which Christians can all too easily take for granted because of its familiarity for us after centuries of constant use. The Greek speaking world had no preparation for such an idea. Some of their philosophers held that if the Supreme Being really was infinite and eternal, it would be impossible for him (it) to take cognisance of such insignificant individual objects as sticks, stones, and human beings. Either it was beneath his dignity, or psychologically impossible.

The Christian concept of the fatherhood of God is so pervasive of the whole New Testament that it will be unnecessary to cite more than a few illustrations. The opening words of the Lord's prayer supply the most frequently used application of the term Father. The word is also used in the homely assurances about petitionary prayer, as in Matthew 7: 9 - 11 "What man of you , if his son asks him for bread, will give him a stone ? Or if he asks for a fish, will give him a serpent ? If you then who are evil , know how to give gifts to your children , how much more will your Father who is in heaven give good things to those who ask him !" The same idea underlies the statements about divine providence, as for example in the famous speech about the lilies of the field . "Look at the birds of the air; they neither sow nor reap nor gather into barns, yet your heavenly Father feeds them . Are you not of more value than they?" (Matthew 6:26).

In the letters of St. Paul, this concept of fatherhood receives a somewhat more reflective presentation, as is the case with other ideas from the teaching of Jesus. St. Paul informs his readers that the Christians have been given the status of adoptive sonship (Galatians 4:5 - 6, and Ephesians 1:5). It is a technical term which obviously applies to both sexes, but Greek language does not contain a word for "daughtership"; (nor, strictly speaking, does English !).

In the first few centuries of the Christian era Greek philosophy was widely employed to illustrate the content of New Testament thought, which had been mostly within the confines of the Semitic world picture. It is thanks to the Greeks that we have more enriched concepts of the divine attributes like eternity. In the Old Testament that concept was originally presented within the context of history and implied a very long period. Greek philosophy made it clear that it was a state of being , totally outside time and its succession of happenings. Similar enrichment was given to the notions of God's transcendence, omnipotence, and power of creation , whereby he made the universe literally out of nothing.

SECTION 2 : DENIALS AND PROOFS OF GOD'S EXISTENCE.

The magnificent picture of God which is contained in the New Testament does not convince everyone, and in the modern world there have been increasing numbers of people who deny his existence altogether. Although the number of atheists is now larger than in the past, they were not absent in antiquity, and their attitude has prompted a long tradition among believers of presenting a rational justification for their belief in God's existence. It can bee seen in the Old Testament in the Book of Wisdom, (13: 1 - 9) in the New Testament the argument is taken up in the Letter to the Romans (1: 18 - 23). In Christian tradition the five proofs of Aquinas are the best known, but not the only demonstrations of the existence of God. The tradition reached its apogee in the First Vatican Council's declaration that rational knowledge reflecting on the created world could arrive at reliable knowledge of God's existence.[5]

Since the whole tradition of that intellectual approach has originated among believers, it seems best to regard the rational process as a reasoned justification by a believer for his faith in God, which he already enjoys, rather than an independent demonstration commencing from a theoretically neutral starting point and proving rationally that God exists. In other words, the believers are defending themselves against the allegation of basing their religion on inadequate, false or illusory foundations.

In the eighteenth and nineteenth centuries the foundations of modern science were firmly established on the basis of experiments which could be carried out in laboratories. This gave undue prominence to the value of experimental proof in general. Many of life's key decisionsmust be made without it, like marriage. In the twenty first century, in astro-physics for example, experiments are not always possible. Scientists now have to make assumptions which are not unlike the believers act of faith, as was noted by the famous cosmologist George Ellis when he was awarded the Templeton Prize in 2004.[6]

The best known set of proofs for the existence of God are the famous five demonstrations by St. Thomas Aquinas, which are variants on the principle of causality. In other words when a fair minded person looks at the natural world and perceives its structure and functions, he is led to enquire into the causes of such a wonderful and complex entity. The quest for the causes leads back to the ultimate cause who is God. Intellectually it is not unlike modern scientific research, as for example the discovery of radium by Madame Curie and her husband working on the observed effects, and tracing them to their cause. One can summarise the five ways of Aquinas as :- 1) from the occurrence of change to an unchanged changer; 2) from series of causes and effects to an uncaused cause; 3) from the existence of contingent things to that of a necessary being; 4) from imperfect instances to a perfect cause of them ; and 5) from the regularity and function of natural processes to a cosmic designer. [7]

The rational arguments advanced by theologians about God's existence are clearly not like mathematical theorems , nor are they akin to laboratory experiments. They can be compared perhaps with historical / archaeological demonstrations. For example, thanks to the work of archaeologists and historians, there is now almost complete unanimity that the Dead Sea Scrolls were written by the Essene community who lived in a monastery at Qumran up to the time of its its destruction in 70 A.D, by the Romans as part of the subjugation of Judea after the Jewish revolt. Hence biblical scholars are entitled to pursue their researches on that basis

---

[5] First Vatican Council, Dogmatic Constitution , *Dei Filius,* 24 April 1870, Denziger - Schonmetzer, number 3004, "Deum , rerum omnium principium et finem, naturali humanae rationis lumine e rebus creatis certo cognosci posse";

[6] Reported in *The Guardian* 13 th May 2004.

[7] The summary is from John Haldane,(2000) art. ' Natural Theology', in *The Oxford Companion to Christian Thought,* ed. Adrian Hastings, Oxford, O.U.P. p. 466. The sources in Aquinas are, *Summa Theologica,* I, q.2 , art. 3 and *Contra Gentes ,* I, 42.

without being accused of being irresponsible or irrational in their work. Roughly the same

scale of assurance is enjoyed by believers who had already based their lives on belief in God, and subsequently justified their decision in a reasoned fashion.

Having stated a few preliminary ideas about the arguments in favour of God's existence, now is the place to describe the outlines of rational attacks on his existence, before analysing how they are rebutted. At the risk of some oversimplification they can be divided into two broad categories, namely those who deny God's existence because there is so much evil in the world, and those who claim that the progress of science has rendered God superfluous, since we now no longer need such an entity to explain how the universe operates. (From the very nature of logic, non-existence of anything cannot be proved rationally, and this applies to God also).

The argument from evil is the simplest to deal with. David Hume expressed it succinctly centuries ago. The allegation is more or less a complaint that there is so much badness in the world that a good God simply cannot exist. Either he would be powerful enough to obliterate pain , distress, and other forms of badness, or if he tolerates it he cannot claim to be either good or omnipotent. First of all it is necessary to identify what is really evil and what is only apparently bad. Frequently we use the concept of badness in a purely relative sense. If an apple has turned brown and sour I may say that it is bad from the point of view of one who wishes to eat it. In a different perspective it is now a very good agent for nourishing the seeds for the next generation of apple trees. Similarly the argument derived from the cruelty of carnivorous animals needs to be looked at in a wide context. But for the existence of scavengers, the whole earth would be covered by decaying corpses as the slow agency of bacterial and chemical decomposition reduced them to simple elements. The eating pattern of scavengers is essential to clear the corpses quickly enough to enable the earth to function as we know it. Granted that these animals have evolved the ability to derive nourishment from recently living flesh, the next stage of evolution is clear.

Disease and death among humans and animals is a similar process. As living beings come to birth, then develop, mature, and die , we are part of an immensely complex system of interacting biological and chemical forces. The ramifications of this reciprocally inter-dependent system are so numerous and complex that it would not be possible to eliminate just one item, shall we say the influenza virus, without upsetting the equilibrium of the whole complex interacting system. Whatever admirable advances may be made by medicine, they merely postpone the eventual collapse of the organism. All living creatures are destined to die sooner or later.

Ultimately we come to acknowledge that the only true evil is moral evil. This shows itself most acutely when human greed gets out of hand and people exploit one another by violence and deceit in order to seize for themselves more than their reasonable share of the earth's good things. Human aberrant behaviour in greed is far worse than the irrational behaviour of those who are insane. Anyone who lived through the twentieth century and reflected on the nature of that century's wars, revolutions, and campaigns of economic exploitation, can be in no doubt about the moral badness of which human beings are capable. Does this constitute a rational argument against the existence of a good and omnipotent God ? No. It is his highest achievement to have created living creatures who are conscious and free. We are destined to love God and our fellow humans, and if this is to be authentic, we must also be capable of

abusing the freedom and pursuing evil. It is rather like the situation of parents with adolescent children growing towards maturity. If their emotional and psychological development is to be properly achieved they must be given freedom and allowed to make mistakes, which hopefully they will learn from. The alternative in the divine perspective would be to create humans who were perfectly programmed like computer-directed robots so that they never made a mistake or committed a sin. Such totally programmed automatons would not really serve the glory of God , they would be incapable of love, nor could they establish authentic human culture or civilisation.

On the other hand we cannot deny God the freedom on his part to produce creatures who are genuinely free. That is to say, human beings are in no position either to understand God so completely, or to control his activity to the extent that we might pronounce that he was incapable or not allowed to produce an intelligent creature, who was possessed of enough freedom to make deliberate choices and love his maker and other persons authentically. [8] It should not surprise us if a wise God should be prepared for his creatures to spurn him and turn away to sin, because on a smaller scale it is the price that parents are prepared to pay for their childrens' healthy psychological progress to adulthood, entailing various forms of the assertion of independence, sometimes expressing itself in emphatic rebellion.

The second major category of denials of God's existence arose in the period of the Enlightenment. The general thrust of the argumentation is something like this: Primitive people ascribed earthquakes, lightening and other natural forces to deities because they simply could not understand the causes which produced them. Religion was the process of requests, bargaining, bribes and promises by which the same primitives tried to canalise the benevolence of those deities, using roughly the same methods which were employed to solicit favours from powerful humans to whom they were beholden. It is further argued that the advance of science has answered those questions. When scientists discovered the movement of the earth's tectonic plates and the presence of electricity in the atmosphere, the gods of earthquakes and lightening were seen to be no longer necessary. Then as education enriches the human understanding of how the world really works, people will abandon religion and seek human betterment by scientific methods like irrigation, scientific farming, surgery, and economic planning.

This line of argument which with minor variants is common in western culture , owes its intellectual impulse to the eighteenth century Enlightenment. In various forms it was enunciated by Rousseau, Voltaire, Diderot and others. Its classical formulation can perhaps be ascribed to Baron d'Holbach. In his treatise *Le Système de la Nature et des Loix du Monde Physique et du Monde Morale* (1770) he expressed it very succinctly :- " Religious adherence issues from an imagination driven to create gods because it despairs of a natural explanation of the phenomena that terrify it. Belief in the supernatural is a gesture of human despair of the mind's own analytic powers".[9] That line of argument implies that as scientific discoveries

[8] cf. Hawkins,D.J.B.(1949), *The Essentials of Theism,* London: Sheed & Ward, p.134.

[9] Quoted in the indispensable study by Michael J. Buckley, (1987),*At the Origins of Modern Atheism,* New York:Yale University Press, p.289, citing d'Holbach op.cit. pp. 46, 47.

45

push back the frontiers of knowledge all those deities are rendered superfluous. In reality it

creates a bigger problem : the causal explanations are merely pushed back further and not eliminated. [10] As the process of explanation proceeds, the remoter causes are seen to be ever more powerful, until we get back to the Big Bang whose colossal release of energy was so great and complex that we can scarcely comprehend it at all. Atheists have not accounted for the origin of the Big Bang.

In the latter part of the twentieth century biblical fundamentalism acquired a new lease of life, particularly in the U.S.A. They staunchly upheld the individual creation of all species (against Darwin) and incurred the scorn of biologists who were also atheists, who thence extended their hostility to religion in general.

In England the best known of those supporters of Darwin is Professor Richard Dawkins who has written frequently in favour of evolution as the scientific explanation of the world which makes God simply unnecessary .[11] His basic thesis, following Darwin, is that the theory of evolution traces the progress of minute random variants between one generation of living things and the next, which give rise to slight advantages in the struggle for life. Over many years some organisms prove to be more successful in finding food or adapting to the environment etc. , and in competition with the weaker ones it is the better adapted which survive and prosper. He claims that this process can give rise to the illusory notion of intelligent design by a Supreme Intelligent Being.[12]

At this point I would like to make clear that I, along with countless other believers, accept the validity of the theory of evolution for the development of the bodies and functions of living organisms. I am equally persuaded that the said theory does not explain everything. In particular it does not do away with the need for God, as I will show later in this chapter.

To add weight to his argument Dawkins has drawn attention to computer programmes which can be designed to reproduce the evolutionary sequence. By factoring in a number of forces and constants he can reproduce the sequence of evolution for quick inspection, rather like fast forwarding the film in a cine-camera. This he claims invalidates the traditional argument from design.[13] The philosopher Mary Midgley has pointed out the dangers of extrapolating unreasonable conclusions from computerised simulation, precisely because it introduces an intelligent operator into the process, to design the programme. Paradoxically it was to remove any intervention by a conscious and intelligent operator that Dawkins formulated his theory. [14]

---

[10] cf. McGrath,A. (2005), *Dawkins' God,* Oxford: Blackwell, p.59 .

[11] His books include *The Selfish Gene, The Blind Watchmaker, Climbing Mount Improbable* , and in 2007, *The God Delusion.*

[12] for example in Dawkins,R.(1986), *The Blind Watchmaker,* Harmondsworth: Penguin Books, p.xvi.

[13] Dawkins,R.(1997), *Climbing Mount Improbable,* Harmondsworth: Penguin Books, pp. 150, 193, 219.

[14] Midgley, M.(1985), *Evolution as Religion,* London: Routledge, p.150 - 153.

It is instructive to recall that the owners of racing pigeons and livestock farmers have been planning selective breeding for centuries. Their activities are like an accelerated evolutionary

sequence, brought about artificially, by deliberate intelligent intervention. In a sense they have been reproducing a process something like evolution, and their activities have confirmed the need for an intelligent agency, rather than dispensing the need for one. The limitations of evolutionary theory to account for too much have been analysed by the philosopher Anthony Kenny.[15] Basically there are three great unanswered problems which are untouched by evolution, how the universe came into existence, the origin of life, and the origin of speech (which implies too the origin of consciousness). These simple statements imply vast problems whose extensive ramifications simply cannot be accounted for by evolution, which is a convincing explanation of the development of living organisms once they have come into existence. The origin of life itself is intriguing. It was an event which would have to have been achieved across just one generation, and the first progenitor would have had to acquire all the characteristics of living organisms in its own (perhaps very brief) life span. These are principally the ability to assimilate nourishment drawn from outside itself, and the ability to reproduce offspring like itself. Although the theory of evolution has been with us for a century and a half, it shows no sign of being able to bridge that enormous gap from inanimate to living. The origin of speech is extremely complex because it entails not only the ability to produce and understand particular precise sounds, which are very different from animals' inarticulate shrieks of pain or fear. But from the evolutionary point of view, it would offer no evolutionary advantage in isolation. It needed a community who could share the asset.[16] These three problems illustrate what I stated above, namely that scientific progress merely pushes back the causality of the worlds' activities, and far from rendering God superfluous, it provides admirable confirmation of his existence in view of the magnitude of the operations of the fundamental causes of the universe's functions.

A further important area of development which cannot be explained solely by the principles of natural selection is the presence of beauty and mathematical precision in living organisms, as perceived by humans, who emerged upon the evolutionary stage literally millions of years after the complex patterns had been established.[17] One striking example is what is known as the Fibonacci sequence of numbers.[18] In this sequence each term is the sum of the two numbers which preceded it, thus it runs 0+1=1, 1+1=2, 1+2=3, and so on 3, 5, 8, 13, 21 etc. It was discovered by a mediaeval mathematician Leonardo of Pisa (nicknamed Fibonacci) in 1202. In its own right the sequence is interesting and indeed intriguing. What is absolutely staggering is that it occurs naturally in plants and animals. It is to be seen in the spiral patterns of sunflower seeds, and pine cones, and also in the proportions of the expanding shell of the shell fish known as nautilis. If that were not enough to astonish us, it also imposes itself upon the human perceptions as something beautiful. It occurs in music, for instance in Bach's

---

[15]   Kenny, A.(2006), *What I Believe,* London: Continuum Books, esp. pages 25 - 28.

[16]   Kenny, A. op. cit. p.25.

[17]   Polkinghorne,J. op. cit. pp. 2-3.

[18]   For this section I am indebted to an article by Jonathan Jones, entitled *As Easy as 1, 1, 2, 3....*in *The Guardian,* 12 th May 2005.

Art of the Fugue (in the first statement of Contrapunctus One). Whether John Sebastian was consciously aware of the sequence is difficult to say. What cannot be denied is that the sequence in the musical notes is supremely pleasing to the ear.

The same line of thought can also be extended beyond mathematical harmony to the sheer complexity of many aspects of living beings. The DNA helix is a good example. The main outline of the famous discovery by Crick and Watson is too well known to need repeating. What is relevant to the present enquiry is to ask ourselves if a structure of such complexity and practical importance in the transmission of characteristics to the next generation, could have come about as the result of unplanned chance. At this point I think that it is appropriate to invoke a thought which I have not stated in the previous pages, namely at some point in this investigation common sense rises up in a state of exasperation and declares that it is simply absurd to ascribe such complicated and clearly purposeful mechanisms to random happenings. It is more logical and reasonable to see them as the consequences of a stupendously powerful cause or causes.

It may not be without interest to comment on the alteration of one famous scholar's views on science and religion after the significance of the DNA and other discoveries had become apparent. The scholar in question is Professor Anthony Flew. In the 1960's he was one of the foremost philosophers who argued against the existence of God. However in 2004, in a letter to the journal *Philosophy Now* he indicated that the implications of the helix structure of the DNA was producing something of an alteration in his attitudes.[19] In February 2007 at a conference on philosophy and religion Professor Flew indicated that his thinking in this area had progressed to the acceptance of a deity. He described himself as a deist. The path had been via the complexity of the natural world as revealed by modern scientific research. He could no longer accept such notions as purely accidental evolution, the origin of life from nothing, or the randomly accidental development of DNA.[20]

In reality many Christians have found no incompatibility between evolution and belief in God the creator. In the latter part of the nineteenth century, quite soon after the publication of Darwin's *Origin of Species* in 1859, the well know Anglican priest Charles Kingsley pointed out that it enhanced our idea of God to ascribe to him the creation of a world which evolved, in contrast to envisaging his having to intervene to modify it on countless occasions in its long history. By and large that has become the accepted position of the majority of Christians. However in the twentieth century another priest, the French Jesuit Pierre Teilhard de Chardin, took the matter even further. Instead of regarding evolution mainly as the response of living organisms to circumstances and forces outside themselves, Teilhard de Chardin reversed the inference and viewed living things as having an inner dynamic driving them forward, pushing the process of evolution, so to speak, rather than just reacting .[21] A simple illustration would

---

[19] Anthony Flew, in the journal *Philosophy Now* (47) Aug/Sep. 2004, p. 22.

[20] Flew's position as presented at that conference is reported fully by Anthony Towey in his article 'One Flew Out of the Atheist's Nest', in the journal *The Pastoral Review* , Sept/ Oct. 2007, pp.40-46.

[21] These ideas occur in most of his writings, but are enunciated most clearly in *The Phenomenon of Man* , London: Collins, 1959, pp. 146 - 149.

perhaps be the example of a river, let us say the Nile, at its delta. In finding a path to the sea the river splits up into several channels depositing alluvium and conveying the fresh water out into the sea. The impetus for all of this has been the volume of water coming from tributaries in the mountains far away. The force is by no means expended as the river comes close to the

sea, where it diversifies its outlets, some taking more water than others, depending on factors such as the hardness of rocks or subsoil through which it penetrates. This image of a river directing itself to the sea, supplies some sort of comparison with the onward progress of life, ultimately diversifying into different channels in seeking its own objective. Whereas the river's inner dynamic leads it to convey fresh water to the sea, the stream of life is impelled to evolve towards consciousness, so that the beneficiaries of this asset, human beings, can rise to the level of spiritual pursuits in culture and, most importantly, contemplate their Maker. This vision of evolution is perhaps the strongest integration between faith in a creator God and the ultimate destiny of the supreme product of the creative/evolutionary process.

Whereas the biological sciences provide admirable rational confirmation of the existence of God, despite the views of some supporters of evolution, cosmology and astro-physics confer even stronger arguments in support of a purposeful creation. A useful intermediate step between the two branches of science is the anthropic principle.

In 1988 Barrow and Tippler published the book bearing that title, which has since become a quasi technical term.[22] In a detailed study they showed that the whole universe is finely tuned to produce both the conditions and the forces needed to produce life, and indeed carbon based life.[23] Within the limited environment of planet Earth further stringent conditions are necessary to ensure that life can emerge, such as precise margins of gravity and temperature to keep a thin layer of air above the earth's surface, one of whose components is free oxygen which would be antecedently unlikely in view of its being so active chemically. Fresh water is equally important and for it to be available in liquid form requires another narrow margin of temperatures. The list of precise, interacting requirements must be pursued even further, building up to a complicated machine whose complexities are so intricate that one scientist was prompted to declare :- " The universe looks as though it has been tailored for the emergence of intelligent life" .[24]

Another scientist Russell Stannard put forward the ingenious suggestion of a creation game, namely how would one go about constructing a universe which at some time it its life of billions of years would produce humans. It is an interesting intellectual exercise since it forces one to face up to the detailed planning which would have to be done to produce any component of the whole process. It is a healthy antidote to the glib remarks in some quarters about its having happened by chance. For example, the difficulties which would have to be overcome to produce just one component like the aforementioned carbon. Concerning emergence of this one building block of life, it has been observed that "The odds against this happening by chance are so great that the famous astronomer Fred Hoyle declared : a

[22] Barrow,J. & Tippler,J.(1988), *The Anthropic Principle,* Oxford: Oxford University Press.

[23] Barrow & Tippler, op.cit. p. 3.

[24] Timothy Radford, writing in *The Guardian,* 21st March 2006.

common sense interpretation of the fact suggests that a super-intellect has monkeyed with the physics."[25]

Over the last forty years physicists have assembled a widely agreed picture of the structure of the universe. They do not claim to have identified the precise origin, but all the presently observed phenomena can be accounted for by an "early event" namely the vast explosion, known as the Big Bang, which took place 10-15 billion years ago. The massive diffusion of matter and energy has given rise to a universe of some 200 billion galaxies, each of which contains perhaps as many as 200 billion stars. Those stars are thermonuclear reactors whose ash contains the heavier elements which in turn become the basis of planets. On one such planet life emerged about 3.5 billion years ago, although the scientists still do not know how. The universe achieved all this because the fundamental forces which sustain the whole vast system interact successfully. They act in this fashion because they are tuned with exquisite precision. If any of these forces were different even to the slightest degree the whole vast enterprise would have collapsed into chaos long ago.[26]

A more precise description of the forces alluded to in the the preceding paragraphs, and their interaction is now called for. It has been provided recently in accessible form by Professor Sir Martin Rees, a scholar singularly well equipped in this field having been Astronomer Royal, and currently he is the President of the Royal Society. At the risk of some over simplification, one can say that the functioning of the universe depends upon six fundamental numbers of staggering magnitude, yet whose precise interaction and mutual fine tuning keeps the whole universe operating as it is today, and as it has done during the billions of years required for its development of intelligent life on our planet, at least. At this point it is best to allow Professor Rees to speak for himself, and I will reproduce the summary which he has provided at the beginning of his indispensable book, entitled *Just Six Numbers.*[27]

The cosmos is so vast because there is one crucially important huge number N in nature , equal to 1,000,000,000,000,000,000,000,000,000,000,000,000,000. This number measures the strength of the electrical forces that hold atoms together, divided by the force of gravity between them . If N had a few less zeros , only a short lived miniature universe could exist : no creatures would grow larger than insects , and there would be no time for biological evolution.

Another number (epsilon), whose value is 0.007, defines how firmly atomic nuclei bind together and how all atoms on Earth were made. Its value controls the power from the Sun and, more sensitively, how stars transmute hydrogen into all the atoms of the periodic table. Carbon and oxygen are common, whereas gold and uranium are rare, because of what happens in the stars. If epsilon were 0.006 or 0.008 we could not exist.

---

[25] Russell Stannard, writing in *The Tablet* 6 th May, 2000.

[26] cf. Timothy Radford in *The Guardian* 6 th Jan. 2007, reviewing 'The Goldilocks Enigma : Why is the Universe Just Right for Life?' , by Paul Davies.

[27] Rees, M.(2000),*Just Six Numbers,* London : Phoenix, (Paper -back ed, Orion Books), pp. 2,3.

The cosmic number (omega) measures the amount of material in our universe - galaxies , diffuse gas, and 'dark matter' Omega tells us the relative importance of gravity and expansion energy in the universe. If this ratio were too high relative to a particular 'critical' value, the universe would have collapsed long ago; had it been too low, no galaxies or stars would have formed. The initial expansion speed seems to have been finely tuned.

Measuring the fourth number,. (lambda), was the biggest scientific news of 1998. An unsuspected new force - a cosmic 'anti-gravity'- controls the expansion of our universe, even though it has no discernible effect on scales less than a billion light - years. It is destined to become ever more dominant over gravity and other forces as our universe becomes ever darker and emptier. Fortunately for us (and very surprisingly to theorists), lamda is very small. Otherwise its effect would have stopped galaxies and stars from forming, and cosmic evolution would have been stifled before it could even begin.

The seeds for all cosmic structures - stars , galaxies, and clusters of galaxies, were all imprinted in the Big Bang. The fabric of our universe depends on one number, Q , which represents the ratio of two fundamental energies and is about 1 / 100,000 in value. If Q were even smaller, the universe would be inert and structureless; if Q were much larger , it would be a violent place, in which no stars of solar systems could survive, dominated by vast black holes.

The sixth crucial number has been known for centuries, although it's now viewed in a new perspective. It is the number of spatial dimensions in our world, D, and equals three. Life couldn't exist if D were two or four. Time is a fourth dimension, but distinctly different from the others in that it has a built-in arrow: We move only towards the future. Near black holes, space is so warped that light moves in circles, and time can stand still. Furthermore, close to the time of the Big Bang, and also on microscopic scales, space may reveal its deepest underlying structure of all: the vibrations and harmonies of objects called 'superstrings', in a ten dimensional arena.

The preceding paragraphs are a taster. Readers with an interest in mathematics and science are strongly advised to read the whole of the book *Just Six Numbers* by Professor Rees. The implications of this system of perfectly tuned interacting numbers of unimaginable magnitude is summed up by another distinguished scientist who is himself a believing Christian, John Polkinghorne: "The universe is not just any old world, but it's special and finely tuned for life because it is the creation of a Creator who wills that it should be so".[28]

Before leaving the area of science and religion it is worth mentioning two other factors, the first of which is causality. In the scientific area its use is so well known as to require little discussion. For example in the nineteenth century the planet Neptune was discovered by inference from the otherwise unaccounted for variations in the orbit of the planet Uranus. Having done the calculations the astronomers were able to direct their telescopes in the right direction and the newly discovered planet was seen. The whole of scientific progress has been led by similar applications of the principle of causality. Theologians too make use of basically

---

[28] Polkinghorne,J.(1994), *Quarks, Chaos and Christianity* , London :SPCK , quoted in Martin Rees, op.cit. p. 166.

the same principle when presenting the rational case for the existence of God.

The second factor which we take for granted is the reliability of numbers and the coherence of the whole of mathematics. This assumption was brought into prominence at the beginning of the twentieth century when German mathematician asked if that assumption could be proved. At the World Congress of Mathematics in 1900 the German mathematician David Hilbert

proposed a challenge to the mathematicians of the twentieth century ; namely to *prove* that mathematics is both complete and consistent. After 30 years another mathematician proved that Hilbert's quest was unattainable, in principle and forever. The proof astonished the learned world and has implications to this very day.[29] It is a healthy reminder that scientists work on assumptions that cannot receive total rational justification. In this perspective the intellectual journeys of scientists are not totally dissimilar from those of theologians. The latter admit freely that the foundations of their discipline are accepted on faith.

As a post script to this chapter one may well ask why it is that so many intelligent scientists are not convinced about the existence of God. In the previous chapter I indicated the deterrent effect of the behaviour and policies of many Christian Churches. Here I wish to add the consideration of the sheer volume of knowledge. Any given scientist, or scholar in any field, may feel reasonably sure of his or her competence within one speciality, and they will be equally assured that other experts are competent in their own fields. This engenders a habit of limiting one's investigations to one field only, and it can give rise to a sort of relative agnosticism, or unwillingness to enquire into other fields. It received its most extreme expression some years ago in a radio debate between the agnostic philosopher Bertrand Russell and the Jesuit philosopher Frederick Copplestone. The question arose as to why the universe existed. Why is there anything rather than nothing ? Russell asserted that this was a question that could not be posed. The universe was just there. It was the Christian philosopher who insisted that he was giving up thinking too soon.[30]

---

[29] John Cornwell, writing in *The Tablet*, 18 th March 2006.

[30] *The Tablet,* 7 th May 2005.

CHAPTER FOUR : THE PERSON AND MISSION OF JESUS THE MESSIAH

It is not surprising that for Christians the whole of our religion centres upon the person of Jesus. Initially he was recognised as a prophet, later his close associates realised that he was the long awaited Messiah, and last of all they perceived what could not have been foreseen, namely that he was divine. For the sake of simplicity I will divide the matter into two chapters, dealing first with his role as Messiah, and in Chapter Six the more complex question of the recognition of his being divine.

When Jesus appeared as a preacher at about the age of thirty, he was quickly recognised as a prophet. John the Baptist had been identified in the same way. Although the office of prophet was not one of the institutionalised religious functions of Judaism (like the priests), there had been a sufficient number of them in Israelite history for the role to be recognised easily. In popular parlance he seems to have been designated as " the prophet Jesus from Nazareth in Galilee"(cf. Matt. 21:11).

After the lapse of nearly two millennia we have to ask ourselves about the reliability of our knowledge about him. The obvious sources are the four canonical gospels and the information contained in the letters of the New Testament. Although it is not widely known, there are brief references to Jesus in four Roman historians, namely Tacitus, Seutonius, Pliny the Younger, and the Emperor Hadrian. [1] The information amounts to little more than a testimony to his having lived, but it is a useful counter-argument against the extreme critics who denied his very existence.

The textual reliability of the New Testament far exceeds that of any other book from antiquity. It has survived in 2500 miniscule manuscripts (after the ninth century), and more than 250 magiscules of the earlier period. In addition there are more than 80 papyrus fragments of which the oldest dates from about 135 AD, and contains four verses of the 18th chapter of St. John. By contrast the Roman poet Catullus, for example, has survived in only one manuscript, and Josephus's History of the Jews exists in just three manuscripts of which the oldest is from the eleventh century.

However the textual reliability of the New Testament is not the only problem to be faced in the search for the true record of Jesus. It is now generally agreed that a great deal of theological editing took place before the New Testament acquired its final form. It is safe to assume that in the earliest period of the Church's mission, shortly after Pentecost, the sayings and actions of Jesus were transmitted verbally as propaganda, catechetical instructions, sermons etc. At what stage these were preserved in written form is hard to say. It is equally safe to assume that collections of his sayings and doings should have been assembled at an early stage. Since all this material was collected to persuade people to accept his message, it is not surprising that a deliberate presentational slant should appear. The catastrophe of the destruction of Jerusalem by the Romans in 70 AD (in the suppression of a nationwide 0rebellion), coincided with the gradual dying out of the generation of those who had known Jesus in his public life. This seems to have provided the impetus to assemble the known facts

[1] Precise references and an evaluation of their reliability are to be found in Ferdinand Prat, (1953), *Jésus Christ, sa vie, sa doctrine, son oevre.* Paris: Beauchesne, Vol. 1, p.2.

and write them in book form before all the eye-witnesses died out. Thus the canonical gospels came into being as the result of a complex process lasting about forty years, or more in the case of the fourth gospel. It is unlikely that any of the evangelists had sat down in the leisurely setting of a sabbatical term, and composed a biography of Jesus from zero. The gospels should be regarded as compilations more than compositions. All of them bear the marks of deliberate editing and each has its own theological theme. None of this impairs their trustworthiness.

If all of this seems strange to the readers, I would invite them to reflect on a few simple facts. The Lord's prayer is recorded in two versions in the gospels of Matthew and Luke. The gospel of Matthew contains several artificial groupings, such as the collection of parables allegedly spoken on one day , in chapter 13. The famous collection of moral ideals in Matthew chapters 5, 6, and 7, traditionally called the Sermon on the Mount is clearly an artificial grouping. Luke gives a slightly different assemblage of sayings and reports that it took place on the plain (Luke 6:17). The brevity with which the parables are recorded strongly suggest that what we have are summaries. The Hidden Treasure is just one verse in duration (Matthew 13:44), and the Merchant seeking Pearls consists of two verses (Matthew 13: 45, 46). It is almost inconceivable that they could have been so brief when first spoken.[2]

Greater problems arise in trying to fit the incidents of the public life into a consistant chronology. It is exceedingly difficult, and much of it remains conjectural. As a result, it is now generally agreed by conservative and radical scholars that it is impossible to write a chronological biography of Jesus in the modern sense. But it is important to remember that this does not invalidate the truthfulness of any of the individual incidents whose exact chronological sequence eludes us. The writers intended to present the person of Jesus and his message as an invitation to discipleship.

The difficulties inherent in the New Testament presentation of the life and teaching of Jesus, which I have outlined in the preceding paragraphs, do not seem to have troubled our ancestors. They came into prominence roughly in the 150 years which stretched from the early part of the 19th century to the latter part of the 20th. In that period both Old and New Testaments sustained what appeared to be serious attacks on their reliability. The first and most vulnerable targets were the accounts of the origin of the universe in Genesis. With the publication of Darwin's *Origin of Species* in 1859, it became clear that individual species came into being by natural selection, rather than by special creation for each of them. These advances in science posed serious difficulties for believers in all Churches. At that period no clear solutions were forthcoming, and people of faith simply had to suspend judgement on a considerable area of traditional teaching.

However help was at hand. At the turn of the century archaeologists in the near East had laid bare the evidence of the lost civilisations af Assyria, Babylon Egypt and other centres of ancient culture. The most important finds were the written records, and fortunately they

---

[2] Some years ago, when teaching undergraduates, I used to conduct a simple experiment. I would read out those parables, enunciating every word clearly, and ask the students to time the recitation. Over the years the average was constant as being less than one minute, and more surprising, it could be done with just one breath.

succeeded in deciphering them. Of major interest to biblical scholars were the law codes, of which about half a dozen were unearthed. They disclosed remarkable similarities to the laws of the Pentateuch, thus demonstrating that the Israelites shared in the general pattern of the culture of that region in the second millennium B.C. and thereabouts. Of equal value were the discovery of religious myths also bearing some striking similarities to the Old Testament. The details need not detain us here, but it became clear that myth, for example, was a recognised literary category for teaching about the origin of the world and its relationship to divine powers. The way was clear for a satisfactory interpretation of the book of Genesis, which did not have to cling to a naive literalism.

In the 20th century the reliability of the gospels was subjected to serious attacks in the process which is commonly known as the quest for the historical Jesus.[3] Albert Schweizer (1875 - 1965) analysed the previous historical researches into the history of Jesus, and eventually came to the conclusion that little could be established with certainty. The next leader of the movement was Rudolf Butlmann, the professor of New Testament studies at Marburg, who exercised great influence on all non-Catholic theology in the decades before and after the Second World War. He adopted a radically negative attitude to the historical reliability of the records of the career of Jesus. His premise was that Jesus and his followers lived in a totally pre-scientific age, whose world view was of a three tier universe, the sky (realm of the gods), earth (which was flat), being the arena of human activity, and the underworld , ruled by the demons. The interactions of the inhabitants of these realms were recorded in mythological accounts, to which one could not accord historical reliability. The only event in the life of Jesus which could be accepted as plain history was the crucifixion. He reduced the resurrection of Jesus to nothing more than a myth, formulated to convey some idea of the lasting influence of his moral idealism. Although Bultmann did not use the comparison, it reminds me of the American song "John Brown's body lies a moulding in the grave but his soul goes marching on."

It was almost inevitable that such an extremely negative stance would be followed by an opposite reaction. The turn of the tide came in 1953 when one of Bultmann's former students, E. Kasemann published an influential essay on the problem of the historical Jesus. From then onwards there has been an increasing optimism establishing continuity between the sayings of Jesus and their transmission in the gospels, as well as more confidence in the records of events in his life. From about the last two decades of the twentieth century there has been a major return of confidence in the reliability of the gospels and their picture of Jesus.[4]

It is also important to remember that the New Testament writings were composed shortly after the earthly life of Jesus, when many people who had known him then, were still alive.

---

[3] A brief, reliable, and accessible account of this question is to be found in the article by John.A.McGuckin(2000) ' Quest for the Historical Jesus', in Hastings, Adrian (ed.), *The Oxford Companion to Christian Thought,* Oxford: O. U. P. pp 587- 589. A more exhaustive account of the problems can be found in the work of Imre Koncsik, (2005) 'Christologie im 19 und 20 Jahrhundert', being Band III, Faszikel 1e, of *Handbuch der Dogmengeschichte* eds. Michael Schmaus et al. Freiburg: Herder, pp. 24 - 88.

[4] For what follows I am deeply indebted to the important article by Evans, Craig, A. (1993) 'Life-of-Jesus Research and the Eclipse of Mythology', in *Theological Studies,* **54,** pp. 3 - 36.

Although it is not possible to determine the exact dates at which all the various gospels and letters were written, the latter part of the twentieth century saw a broad consensus on the dating of most of them. There is wide agreement on the dates of composition of the following:- I and II Thessalonians in 50 - 52 AD, I Corinthians in 57, Mark's Gospel in 64, Matthew, Luke and Acts between 70 and 80, and John in the last decade of the century. These dates are important because they show that the writings in question are so close to the time of Jesus that legends and myths could not have had time to develop.

The overall reliability of the gospels is also confirmed by a number of general considerations. Negatively the gospels (and the rest of the New Testament writings) are in accord with what is known of the politics, history and geography of those lands from secular writers of the same period. The apostles' moral shortcomings are not concealed. The first generation of the disciples of Jesus gained nothing in the secular sense, from their spreading of his message. They acquired neither wealth, political influence, nor social advancement. On the contrary the same apostles who had fled from Gethsemane endured martyrdom, as did thousands of Christians in the first three centuries, which is the supreme guarantee of the reliability of their message.

In the last analysis we have to ask ourselves the inescapable question: do the gospels constitute an impenetrable barrier through which we cannot pierce to find to the real Jesus, or are they to be regarded as the best possible vehicle for appreciating his life and teaching, from the hands of the people best placed to know him. Personally I advocate the latter course, and I recognise that it is simply a variant on our faith in the Church which I mentioned in Chapter Two. It is consistent too with our total dependence on the infant Church for deciding the canon of Scripture. It is an inescapable factor in our whole religious life that we are totally dependent upon that early community.

On the controversial question of miracles one must keep in mind that hostility to them is not so much on account of the alleged unreliability of the gospel accounts, but the philosophical presuppositions of the writers who dispute them. To some extent their attitude has been preserved by modern sceptics, of whom the most influential has been the philosopher David Hume. His attitude, in summary, was that the invariable behaviour of the material things of the world gave rise to the laws of science. It was not the same as the predictability of mathematics. If there were any apparent deviations from the usual regularity they must be investigated to find an alternative explanations, such as error, ignorance, illusion etc. Even Hume admitted that miracles were not logically impossible.[5] On his own principles it would have been possible to admit a divine intervention when an exception to the usual behaviour of the natural world had been reported, since he conceded that the regularity which he saw in nature was not the same as mathematical necessity. This is the point at which the believer invokes the simple considerations that if God exists he must be omnipotent, and if he is omnipotent he must be capable of miraculous interventions. In summary, many hostile treatments can be exposed as following roughly this line of argumentation : " Miracles are philosophically impossible, but this narrative reports them, so it must be a myth. Because it is

[5] Richard Swinburne, (1997), 'Evidence for the Resurrection', in *The Resurrection*, eds. Davis, Stephen. Kendall, Daniel. & O'Collins, Gerald. Oxford: Oxford University Press. p.197.

56

a myth its content is not to be accepted literally". It is a simple example of arguing in a circle.

Opponents of miracles have also suggested that the conception of Jesus was simply the employment of a myth, copied from similar stories in Greek culture, to enhance his reputation.[6] One of the best documented cases of the overlaying of myth on a normal human being is the life of Pythagoras. He was born in 569 B.C. the son of Mnesarchus and his mother's name was Parthenis (sometimes called Pythias). His father was probably a native of Tyre on the coast of Syria and his mother came from the island of Samos, which was where Pythagoras was born. The surviving biographies (by Porphyry, Iamblichus , and Diogenes Laertes) were all written in the second or third centuries A.D., a gap of nearly eight hundred years since the life of their subject. This fact alone should suggest caution. As a child and youth he received a good education, and subsequently displayed great ability in mathematics, which he applied to weights, measures, and music. In adult years he migrated to Italy and lived in the south Italian town of Crotona. He gathered round himself a large number of followers and guided them in an ascetical form of life. The inhabitants of Crotona became hostile to Pythagoras and his followers, and one day they set fire to the building in which they were assembled. Probably Pythagoras died in that conflagration, but another tradition holds that he escaped to Metapontum where he starved himself to death.

It is clear that in his life time he was famous and that reputation carried on after his death. At some later stage , which is hard to determine, the plain facts of his life were embellished by mythological elements, to enhance his reputation for posterity. The literary equipment was well known in the Greek speaking world, namely the accounts of gods disguising themselves as men and having sex with beautiful women, who then gave birth to heroes. The birth of Hercules is one of the best known. His mother was Alcmene who was married to Amphitryon. When Amphytrion was absent on military service against the Taphians, Zeus who had taken note of Alcmene's beauty, disguised himself as her husband, presented himself at home and enjoyed a very long night of sexual passion with her. The child of that union was Hercules. However the incident had not gone un-noticed by the other gods and goddesses. Herea (Juno) was insanely jealous and sent two serpents to kill the baby in his cradle. The infant Hercules strangled them with his bare hands.

In the case of Pythagoras, the godly insemination theme alleged that the god Apollo had sex with his mother, to produce the talented son. The time and occasion of that literary invention is not clear. One modern scholar suggests that it may have been an elaboration of a couplet , whose author was perhaps Apollonius of Tyana, who lived in Asia Minor and who was an almost exact contemporary of Jesus. The words are :-
    "And Pythagoras whom Pythias bore for her beloved, the divine Apollo,
       Pythias who was the most beautiful Samian of all."[7]
It is possible that the alternative version of his mother's name may had had something to do with it . Parthenis closely resembles *parthenos* the Greek word for 'virgin', which could have

---

[6] There is a vast literature on the subject. Two important studies are: Moses Hadas & Morton Smith, (1965),*Heroes and Gods: Spiritual Biographies in Antiquity,* London: Routledge & Keegan Paul, .
Marina Warner,(1976), *Alone of All Her Sex,* London : Picador.

[7] quoted in Peter Gorman, *Pythagoras : A Life* . London, Routledge & Keegan Paul, 1979, p.19.

suggested an idea to a creative writer.

Other legendary details in his life are the report that he spoke to an ox telling it to stop eating beans, and it obeyed. He is credited with having commanded earthquakes and storm winds to stop. It is reported that once some of his followers walked upon air to cross a river. The most extreme claim is that he came to life again after dying, but according to the same narrative he faked it by hiding in an underground chamber and coming out again some days later.[8]

What are we to make of these alleged similarities with the gospel narratives, and their value as evidence against the Christian tradition of the virginal conception of Jesus? There are two considerations which simply invalidate the claims. The first is the long passage of time between the life of Pythagoras and the written records of the legends, contrasted with the gospels which were composed in their present form within the life time of many eye witnesses of the public life of Jesus. Secondly the literary form of the Greek legends is clearly sensational (salacious) fiction , which contrasts all to clearly with the sober reports of the gospels, which from the literary point of view are unique in their genre. In the Greek myths the women are convinced that they are having sex with a man. The only difference from their normal sex life was that they were deceived about the man's identity. On serious reflection one is justified in rejecting the allegations that the Greek sex myths are damaging to the credibility of the gospel accounts of the conception of Jesus.

Of all the miracles of the life of Jesus it is not surprising that the Resurrection should have occasioned the greatest amount of controversy. It has received more attention than any other happening in his life from both opponents and supporters.[9] At the outset it is useful to bear in mind the intellectual climate in which the New Testament writers presented their accounts of the event. The majority of Jews of that epoch believed in bodily resurrection at the end of time. The Greek - speaking world did not. Their opposition was based on philosophical notions on the nature of material beings, and they were as much opposed to resurrection as would be a modern biologist reflecting on the mortality of all living bodies.

In spite of the Jewish acceptance of the doctrine of resurrection, the immediate followers of Jesus were not prepared for his resurrection three days after the crucifixion. Their scepticism is recorded honestly although it was reprehensible and they were reprimanded for it by the risen Lord. Later generations of Christians are entirely dependent upon the testimony of the first generation who saw the risen Lord. No one actually witnessed the event of his rising from death, but the people who saw him subsequently reported the fact by saying that he had "appeared" and that he "had risen". The New Testament as a whole contains more than fifty references to the risen Christ in more than half a dozen literary genres. There are straightforward narratives like that of Luke 24: 32 - 41. Secondly it is contained within moral exhortations, such as Colossians 3:2. Thirdly it occurs in stylised catechesis as in I Corinthians 15: 3 - 5. Fourthly there are plain statements of the facts, as in Acts 10:40. The fifth category are theological reflections as in Romans 6: 6 - 8. The sixth type is polemics,

---

[8] Leonard Mlodinov,*Euclid's Widow,* London, Allen Lane ,Penguin Press, 2002, p.24.

[9] A useful modern assessment of the state of contemporary scholarship on the subject of the Resurrection is to be found in *Resurrection Re-Considered,* d'Costa, Gavin, (ed.) (1996), Oxford: One World .

i.e. answers to disputes or doubts, as in Acts 13: 30 - 31. Finally it features in prayers and hymns such as Philippians 2: 6 - 11. Among those literary genres myth is absent. Admittedly

there are references to angels, but that was a recognised Jewish literary device for the author to explain to his readers the theological significance of what is being described.

It has often been remarked that there are discrepancies between the various accounts which are not easy to harmonise. This is perfectly true, but it should not worry us. Almost the same sort of differences of detail and emphasis are to be seen in the four eye-witness accounts of the murder of Thomas Becket in Canterbury cathedral in 1170. No one has accused his biographers of inventing the murder as a political gesture against the king, for instance.

In the last analysis the Christians' acceptance of the resurrection follows a simple logical path, namely that the event was testified to by witnesses who were judged to be reliable, and that conviction was passed on in the New Testament and the Church's tradition by witnesses who were equally reliable. The event, though stupendous, was not inherently impossible, and no convincing alternative has been demonstrated satisfactorily. The account in Matthew of the bribing of the guards to say that his body was stolen at night by his disciples does not warrant serious consideration. An even more bizarre alternative was offered by J. D. Crossan at the end of the twentieth century. According to Crossan, after the crucifixion Jesus' corpse was probably laid in a shallow grave, barely covered with dirt, and subsequently eaten by wild dogs.[10] Apart from the pejorative language, it is worth noting that every element in that scenario is an unsubstantiated assumption. On reflection it is extraordinary that opponents of the resurrection should feel free to make such outlandish assumptions and feel no need to justify them.[11]

Having mentioned the absence of alternatives, in the preceding paragraph, it is instructive to take a look at the alleged mythological explanations. In the literature of the ancient Near East there are a number of myths describing the gods' coming to life again. The myth of Osiris is a useful example.[12] Osiris was a culture hero who, in antiquity, taught the Egyptians the arts of agriculture and metal working. His sister and wife was the goddess Isis, who ruled over Egypt with him. In the twenty eighth year of his reign Osiris was killed by his brother Seth (sometimes called Typhon). At a feast with seventy two fellow conspirators, Seth persuaded Osiris for a joke to allow himself to be shut up in a chest, which they then threw into the Nile. The chest floated down the river into the sea and was carried across the Mediterranean to the Syrian coast at Byblos. Isis in great grief searched for the body, found the chest at Byblos and brought it back to Buto in Egypt. (Another tradition records that in Byblos a sycamore tree grew over the place where the chest had been deposited; nevertheless Isis recovered the chest). The narrative continues telling how Seth, hunting by moonlight, found the chest

[10] Crossan,J.D.(1994), *Who Killed Jesus ? Exposing the Roots of Anti-Semitism in the Gospel /Story of the Death of Jesus.* San Francisco: Harper, ch. 6, quoted in Davis, Kendall O'Collins, op. cit. p.249.

[11] Without wishing to be too pedantic about it, Roman law permitted the bodies of executed criminals to be given to anyone who should wish to bury them. The provision is in the Digest of Justinian XLVI, 24, 1 & 3 where he states that the law was in force in the time of Augustus. Mommsen,Th.(ed.), (1872), Berlin, p.821.

[12] Hooke. S.H. (1963), *Middle Eastern Mythology,* Harmondsworth: Penguin Books, pp.67 - 69.

containing the body of Osiris, cut up the corpse into small pieces and scattered them though the land of Egypt. Once more Isis renewed her search and recovered all the pieces of her dead

husband's body, except the reproductive organ which had been eaten by the fish at Oxyrynchus. She put the limbs together, and with the assistance of her sister, the goddess Nepthys, she performed magic ceremonies over the body and restored it to life.

The differences in detail, and the overall tone, in comparison with the New Testament account of the resurrection of Jesus are clear. As with all myths, the characters are not historical personages but legendary figures. There is no precise point in time when the incidents are alleged to have taken place. In fact Osiris is the personification of vegetation fertility, which in Egypt was controlled by the Nile. His death and return to life is a personification of the death of plants in winter and their re-generation in spring. The nature cycle of the growth of vegetation in the spring has been the inspiration of a number of myths. The other perennial factor was the rivalry between upper and lower Egypt reflected in the struggle between Osiris and his brother Seth. In the course of the narrative there is no suggestion that the events concerned recognisable individuals, who were known locally, nor that the drama was witnessed by living contemporaries who wrote the accounts for posterity . In short , the attempt to relegate the resurrection of Jesus to the genre of myth is totally gratuitous.

SECTION 2 : THE AUTHORITY OF THE BIBLE.

Having dealt at length with the reliability of the New Testament accounts of the conception and resurrection of Jesus, the time has come to consider a deeper quality of the biblical writings namely the fact that they are inspired. This status is accorded to the bible by all Christian Churches and it means that the books were written under the special influence of God. That plain statement is deceptively simple, because the process is very subtle since it must respect the intelligence and freedom of the human author. There have been many theories to explain the interaction of the divine influence and the human writer.[13] It is important to recall the relationship between revelation and inspiration. The former category is more restricted, and the inspired books have a larger remit than simply recording the saving acts of God, and the information about God's nature and our relationship with him. The amplitude of inspiration is expressed succinctly in II Timothy 3:16, 17 :- " All Scripture is inspired by God and profitable for teaching, for reproof, for correction , and for training in righteousness, that the man of God may be equipped for every good work." In other words, inspiration is not confined to recording God's revelation, but its primary purpose is to fortify the morale of the community of believers.   The application of that text was the centre piece of the theory elaborated by two Dominicans Synave and Benoit.[14] The background to their theory was that God was the principal cause in the operation and the human writer was his instrument. Also they distinguished within the intellectual operations of a human being what they called the speculative intellect and the practical intellect. That division of operations has not been accepted universally, yet it is more relevant than many would concede. A tragic

---

[13] An excellent survey of the question is to be found in Burtchaell,J.T. (1969), *Catholic   Theories of Biblical Inspiration since 1810,* Cambridge: Cambridge University Press.

[14] Synave,P. & Benoit,P, (1947) *La Prophétie,* Paris: Désclée (Éditions du Cerf), appendix II, pp. 269 - 376.

example may help to illustrate the point. At the start of World ar II a Cambridge lecturer,

serving in the R.A.F. as an air-gunner, shot down a British plane. It serves to illustrate the theory which I have mentioned. Utilising this distinction Synave and Benoit stated that the business of inspiration of the scriptures concerns the practical intellect, (whereas revelation is more in the sphere of the speculative intellect). It also accounts for the inspiration of the narratives of events which the writer had seen for himself, which shows clearly that revelation is something quite distinct. I have in mind many incidents in the Acts of the Apostles which St.Luke saw with his own eyes. At a later stage in his life , when writing the Acts he would have said to himself something like, "What incidents shall I select to compose a narrative which will give spiritual comfort to the nascent communities."

Possibly the most difficult aspect of divine inspiration is to envisage how it leaves intact the free will of the human author. An illustration is furnished by an incident in the career of a musician.The famous soprano Janet Baker gave an interview on the radio.[15] She described the experience of singing a complicated quartet with other singers under the conductor Karl Richter. He was so skilful that the singers became oblivious of his presence. Far from being absent, his skill was so great that he drew from them exactly what effects he intended, using their talents to the best of their abilities, but without their being aware of anything like compulsion. That was the manner of a musical genius directing singers who were anything but passive performers of their art, and I think that it affords something of a valid insight into the inspiration of the biblical writers.

The famous biblical scholar M.J. Lagrange introduced an important corollary to the notion of inspiration at the end of the nineteenth century. He pointed out that inspiration applies not only to the author's choice of words but equally to the choice of literary form: was it to be poetry or history.[16] That famous distinction solved many problems which had troubled the literalists of previous generations. It means that inspiration did not convert myth into history , or poetry into a code for moral conduct. This insight provided the solution for the problems like that of Genesis and its chronology, over which the previous generation of believers had agonised.

In the previous paragraphs the concept of revelation has been mentioned several times. The time has come to explain it . It can be described quite simply as God's self disclosure to human beings. It is a broad concept and includes his communicating to prophets and others information about his own nature and his plans for the human race. It also includes his activities by which he shows his intentions towards his creatures. A well known example of this is the Exodus from Egypt by which God indicated his good will towards the Israelites, and his power to protect them. The bible is the record of God's revelation, but it is not the only vehicle for transmitting the information about God and his saving activities. The other vehicle for passing on the knowledge is technically called Tradition, which is basically the verbal method as opposed to the written form. In the course of history the bible has received a great deal of attention because the manuscripts on which it has been written are a tangible

---

[15] B.B.C, Radio 3, on 27th April 2006.

[16] cf. Burtchaell,J. op.cit.p. 140 ff.

possession of the Church, whose copying and commentaries have occupied the efforts of countless scholars.

However we should not allow our enthusiasm for the written bible to overshadow the importance of the oral transmission of doctrine. For the major part of that history and for most of the people, teaching and all communication was by word of mouth, and people of that epoch seem to have had prodigiously accurate memories. The bearing of these considerations upon the life of Jesus will become clear on a few moments reflection. The whole of the New Testament can be read in the course of one day, and the gospels in just a few hours. That being the case, it is impossible that they should contain everything which Jesus said. It is probable that only a small proportion of all that he said, and what was perceived by his contemporaries, came to be written down in the New Testament. It is equally probable that they recorded the most significant events and sayings, but that should not lessen our respect for the unwritten traditions.

Having originated as oral tradition much of its content came to be written by the scholars of the infant Church. The period of patristic writing was an epoch of intense intellectual creativity, as the early Christians debated their spiritual heritage, defended it against attacks from the pagans, and from heretics from within their own ranks. All of this led to a greater sophistication in understanding and presentation of the simple message of Jesus. This gives rise to the question, were they innovating, and inventing ideas which Jesus would never have dreamed of ? This leads to the important consideration of the evolution of doctrine, more usually known by the name of development, thanks to the title of its classical formulation by John Henry Newman.[17] His basic insight was that the only sign of life is growth, and that the growth in sophistication of Christian doctrine took place thanks to its intermingling with other cultures. The most creative cultural influence was that of Greek philosophy. Other factors too which enriched the understanding of the Christian message were the theological debates among Christians, as well as their polemical disputes with opponents, all of which provoked the believers to delve more deeply into what was entailed in the simple gospel message. Newman also formulated a number of criteria with which to distinguish authentic developments from erroneous deviations. The resultant evolution of doctrine could be likened to the growth of a human being whose authentic self identity is always preserved through the process of developing from infancy to maturity and into old age. Armed with this concept one can understand how Christian theologians have confidently embraced new intellectual opportunities , such as the re-discovery of Greek philosophy in the middle ages,. In the twentieth century the advances of psychology have elucidated our understanding of the human psychology of Jesus.

SECTION 3 : JESUS IS ACCEPTED AS THE MESSIAH.

Having discussed the reliability of the bible, and the notions of inspiration and revelation, the time has come to return to the mission of Jesus and the message that he taught. At the risk of some oversimplification it can be divided into two main categories, namely his own status as Messiah, and secondly the concept and programme of the Kingdom of Heaven.

---

[17] John Henry Newman, J.H. (2nd. ed.1878) *An Essay on the Development of Christian Doctrine,* London: Longmans Green & Co.,

To Christians the notion of Jesus as the Messiah is thoroughly familiar, and in English

speaking countries this may owe something to the popularity of Handel's oratorio of that name. However in the history of Israel the concept was by no means so clear. A number of strands can be seen in the Old Testament, whose ultimate harmonisation became apparent only after the mission and resurrection of Jesus. The word itself comes from the Hebrew verb to anoint, and that was the high point of the inauguration of the kings and priests. Before the monarchy was established in Israel there were various promises in the patriarchal period about a future leader who would safeguard Israel and its religion. After the time of king David this leader was depicted by the prophets as an ideal king, a descendant of, and the personification of a new David who would be faithful to God and guide the people in their fidelity to Yahweh. In the period of the Exile and the restoration to their homeland other elements entered the Messianic picture. They looked ahead to a moral re-generation of the nation, prefigured in some sense by the political restoration of the sixth century. A new covenant was promised, and a future kingdom was foreseen where the will of God would be sovereign. This notion of a future kingdom was taken up in the late non-canonical literature and given a decidedly political slant. This explains why Jesus was so circumspect in disclosing his Messianic identity, lest it should give rise to a secular political movement which would be at variance with the spiritual aims of his teaching. After the miracle of the multiplication of the loaves and fishes, St. John records : - "Perceiving then that they were about to come and take him by force to make him king, Jesus withdrew again to the hills by himself." (John 6:15).

It is a fact, worthy of serious reflection, that Jesus never announced that he was the Messiah; he allowed his companions to discern it. The synoptic gospels have numerous incidents where for example the grateful recipients of miraculous cures, acclaim him as the Son of David, or the saviour of Israel, but he always tried to enjoin silence upon them. For the apostles, as his constant companions the realisation must have come quite early in the public life. It is recorded in a simple form in Mark 8: 27 - 30 "On the way he asked his disciples: ' Who do men say that I am ?'. And they told him 'John the Baptist, and others say Elijah, and others one of the prophets.' And he asked them , ' But who do you say that I am ?' Peter answered 'You are the Christ.' And he charged them to tell no one about him." The longer version in Matthew 16:16 displays more theological sophistication. "You are the Christ, the Son of the living God." This version alludes to one strand of Old Testament messianism, namely that the Messiah will be a descendant of King David which in its turn contains the belief that the Kings of Juda were in some sense the adopted sons of God. (cf. Psalms 2:7, and 110: 3, the latter being well known because it occurs in Sunday Vespers, immortalised by Vivaldi's "Dixit Dominus"). Matthew's account of the recognition is one of those enigmatic passages of the gospels , whose full meaning would not have been understood at the time, but which later on furnished the infant Church with the incredible conviction that the Messiah was also divine; and that concept I will elaborate in Chapter Six. The only exception to Jesus's reluctance to announce himself as the Messiah is the dialogue with the Samaritan woman in John 4:25, " The woman said to him 'I know that the Messiah is coming (he who is called Christ); when he comes, he will show us all things.' Jesus said to her 'I who speak to you am he." Although it is an apparent exception, one may surmise a considerable measure of later theological reflection had gone into the writing of that dialogue, as is the case with much of the fourth gospel.

Towards the end of his public life Jesus accepted the designation as Messiah in highly significant situations. At his entry into Jerusalem on Palm Sunday he accepted the acclam -

ation of the crowds shouting " Hosanna to the Son of David" (Matthew 21:9). After his arrest, and when there was no possibility of his followers starting a purely political uprising, he no longer needed reticence. When he was on trial before the High Priest his explicit acknowledgement is recorded :- "And the high priest said to him 'I adjure you by the living God, to tell us if you are the Christ, the Son of God'. Jesus said to him, 'You have said so. But I tell you hereafter you will see the Son of Man seated at the right hand of power, and coming on the clouds of heaven." This too (an allusion to Daniel 7:13) was another saying which would furnish material for the early Church to understand that he was divine as well as being the Messiah. After the resurrection the disciples began to understand that the mission of the Messiah was to be united with that of the Suffering Servant of Isaiah, ("Was it not necessary that the Messiah should suffer these things and enter into his glory?" Luke 24:26).

Jesus's role as Messiah was both as teacher and as liberator of the people. The role a liberator from sin and evil, is one which I will deal with in a Chapter Six. His role as teacher was to bring to perfection the revelation of the true God to his chosen people which had commenced with Abraham approximately two thousand years earlier. The unifying theme which Jesus employed for this purpose was to present to his hearers the concept of the Kingdom of Heaven, which was not a theoretical idea but a practical reality. At the risk of some over - simplification it can be described as a network of relationships between God and men, and among human beings themselves. The relationships are all based on love (as opposed to hostility and exploitation), reconciliation, equality of persons and mutual respect. The kingdom is open to all races and both sexes on a basis of equality. This network of relationships was destined to be institutionalised as a community, so that it would have stability. That community is the Church. Having summarised the Kingdom in just a few plain sentences above, I feel it is imperative to say no more, but to urge my readers to read the four gospels for themselves. The message of Jesus must speak for itself. At this point any further attempt on my part to elaborate those high moral ideals would only impoverish them.

Over the centuries Christian scholars have reflected carefully on message of the New Testament and for the sake of clarity, largely in the process of teaching, they have systematised it into categories such as sacraments , virtues and so on. This is a useful process provided that the plain text of the gospels and epistles is not relegated to second place. It is to that systematisation that I will turn in the next few chapters.

CHAPTER FIVE : THE CHURCH

SECTION 1 : THE CORE REALITY

At various times in the previous chapters I have referred to the Church as the vehicle for transmitting the Scriptures and Tradition so as to hand on the message of Jesus to future generations, and to present the invitation to faith in Jesus to potential believers. The time has come to explain more fully the nature and function of this community.

As with much else in Christianity, the origin of the Church itself was modelled on Judaism. The act of inauguration was the initiation of the New Covenant by Jesus at the Last Supper, which was modelled on the establishment of the Old Covenant through Moses on Mount Sinai about a thousand years earlier. A comparison of the two narratives makes this perfectly clear. The establishment of the Mosaic Covenant is recorded in Exodus 24: 3 - 8 :- " Moses came and told the people all the words of the Lord and all the ordinances; and all the people answered with one voice, and said 'All the words which the Lord has spoken we will do.' And Moses wrote all the words of the Lord. And he rose early in the morning, and built an altar at the foot of the mountain, and twelve pillars, according to the twelve tribes of Israel. And he sent young men of the people of Israel, who offered burnt offerings and sacrificed peace offerings of oxen to the Lord. And Moses took half of the blood and put it in basins, and half of the blood he threw against the altar. Then he took the book of the Covenant, and read it in the hearing of the people; and they said, ' All that the Lord has spoken, we will do , and we will be obedient.' And Moses took the blood and threw it upon the people , and said, 'Behold the blood of the Covenant which the Lord has made with you in accordance with all these words."

The narrative of the Last Supper is clearly modelled on that of the Sinai Covenant, to indicate that an inauguration of equal magnitude was being enacted. The crucial event is recorded in the three synoptics and in St. Paul's First Letter to the Corinthians 11: 23 - 26, (from which I will quote, because it is the oldest account).[1] The variants between the four accounts are slight and do not affect the substance of the momentous transaction. " For I received from the Lord what I also delivered to you, that the Lord Jesus on the night when he was betrayed took bread, and when he had given thanks, he broke it and said, ' This is my body which is for you. Do this in remembrance of me'. In the same way also the cup, after supper, saying, 'This cup is the new covenant in my blood. Do this as often as you drink it in remembrance of me."

The Second Vatican Council revalidated the concept of the People of God, which had been neglected in Catholic theology in the preceding centuries. In the decree on the Church, the whole of chapter two is devoted to this theme.[2] I recommend my readers to read the whole of that decree, since the short quotations which I will print hardly do justice to the theological richness of the whole document. Chapter two begins with the words :-"At all times and among every people, God has given welcome to whosoever fears him and does what is right. It has pleased God however, to make men holy and save them not merely as individuals

---

[1] Matthew 26: 26 - 29, Mark 14: 22 - 25, Luke 22: 14 - 20.

[2] Dogmatic Constitution, *Lumen Gentium* Chapter 2, English translation by Walter, M. Abbott, (1966), *The Documents of Vatican II*, New York : Guild Press, pp. 24 - 37.

without any mutual bonds, but by making them into a single people, a people which acknowledges him in truth and serves him in holiness. He therefore chose the race of Israel as a people unto himself. With it he set up a Covenant. - - - - - - -All these things , however, were done by way of preparation and as a figure and that new and perfect covenant which was to be ratified in Christ, - - - - - - -- - - - Christ instituted this new Covenant, that is to say, the New Testament, in his blood, by calling together a people made up of Jew and Gentile, making them one , not according to the flesh but according to the Spirit. This was to be the new People of God."[3]

A little further on in the same chapter, the Council introduces the identification of the People of God with the concept of the Church:- " God has gathered together as one all those who look upon Jesus as the author of salvation and the source of unity and peace, and has established them as the Church, that for each and all she may be the visible sacrament of this saving unity."[4]   The important technical term, Church, used in that document and occurring frequently in Christian theology and worship, is the translation of the Greek word *ekklesia* . In secular usage it referred particularly to the political assembly of the city state which was summoned when the herald called out the citizens to attend the meeting. The Greek translators of the Old Testament used it as the most appropriate equivalent of similar Hebrew words for political, and more especially, religious assemblies (like the gathering at Sinai, mentioned above). By extension it also came to designate the permanent community of the people who attended those assemblies, and by derivation in Christian times, it was used ultimately of the buildings in which they held their liturgical meetings.

From its very beginnings entry into the Church was by means of baptism, given to those who had expressed faith in Jesus. Also from the start it was open to men and women on a basis of spiritual equality. An even more momentous innovation was that very early in its history the Church admitted all races and nations on an equal footing. This was a quite extraordinary innovation. In the ancient world all religions were more or less coterminous with the tribe or nation, so much so that after wars which entailed the occupation of the vanquished nation, the people had to accept the gods of the conquerors. It was intimately connected to patriotism, and the forging of national unity.

It was clear from the very beginning that this assembly of Christ's followers would be a visible community. However they were aware that the visible community was the manifestation of more profound reality, namely the invisible bond of grace which united them spiritually with Christ and with one another. I will have more to say about the nature and workings of grace in a later chapter. For the moment let me describe it briefly as a God - given gift comprising faith, hope and charity, which enables us to understand God, our fellow humans, and the whole world in an entirely new perspective. We are enabled thereby to love God and our neighbours realistically, and have confidence to chart our lives on a course of creative benevolence to the whole of creation. It raises man to a totally new programme for living which is the remedy to the unregenerate pattern of selfishness, competition, aggression, violence, exploitation and deceit which has characterised so much of human history. In order

---

[3] *Lumen Gentium,* section 9, ed. Abbott, p. 25.

[4] *Lumen Gentium,* section 9, ed. Abbott, p . 26.

to do justice to this intimate, invisible bond with Christ the writers of the New Testament have devised various images. The two most vivid are that of the vine and the branches (St. John's gospel, chapter 15) and that of the head and the body which occurs frequently in the letters of St. Paul. The latter image has come to occupy the most prominent position in Christian thinking, probably because it does justice to the unique position of Christ as the head of the body. Later theology also formulated the expression, used in the creeds, of the "communion of saints', to emphasise the sharing of spiritual strength between the members of the Church. St. Paul had spelt it out clearly in I Corinthians 12: 14 - 26, stating from the comparison with a human body, that weaker members of the Church are fortified by the strength of the heroes, saints, and martyrs.

The functions of this community can be reduced in practice to one comprehensive operation, namely to act as the instrument and sacrament for spreading the Kingdom of Heaven. This requires some explanation. As I said in the previous chapter the Kingdom preached by Jesus was the establishment of a network of inter- personal relationships enabling men and women to live and work in collaboration rather than in mutual exploitation. Ideals of that kind require some kind of institutionalisation if the objectives are to take root in daily life and shape the course of events. In this context the universal Church and each local community can be described as a community of charity, worship, witness, and apostolate.

Having said a few words about the nature of the Church and its tasks, it is important to be clear about inspiration which takes the initiative and guides the whole operation. It is the Holy Spirit. But this simple fact is frequently overlooked in a Church which has a powerfully organised hierarchy. An overall view of the New Testament makes it clear that far more is said about the Holy Spirit and his guidance of the Church, than about the human beings who received authority to serve that community. In fact the initiative of the Holy Spirit begins with the life and mission of Jesus himself even before he commends his followers to the leadership of that same Spirit.

It is perhaps superfluous to recall that the conception of Jesus was by the power of the Holy Spirit (Matthew 1:18, Luke 1:35). John the Baptist predicted that Jesus would baptise by the power of the Holy Spirit (Matthew 3:11), a point which was emphasised by Jesus in his discussion with Nicodemus who came to him by night (John 3:5). When Jesus accepted baptism at the hands of John, his Messianic mission commenced with the spectacular theophany of the appearance of the Holy Spirit as a dove (Matthew 3:16). After that Jesus was driven into the wilderness by the power of the Holy Spirit (Matthew 4:1, Luke 4:1). From there he returned to Galilee in the power of the Spirit (Luke 4:14). There he announced his mission in the synagogue at Nazareth employing the words Isaiah used of the vocation of the Messiah who had been anointed by the Holy Spirit (Luke 4:18 quoting Isaiah 61 : 1- 2). In his miracles it is by the power of the Holy Spirit that Jesus cast out demons (Matthew 12:18), and he foretold that when his disciples would be on trial for the faith, the Holy Spirit would guide them in speaking their defence (Matthew 10:20).

At his final meeting with the apostles, just before the Ascension, Jesus instructs them to wait in Jerusalem until they should receive the gift of the Holy Spirit (Acts 1: 5-6). Only after that were they to go out and evangelise (Acts 1: 2 - 8). After his departure to heaven they duly returned to Jerusalem and on the feast of Pentecost they received the gift of the Holy Spirit in the well known spectacular demonstration of parted tongues of fire which appeared over each

of them (Acts 2: 1- 4). The date was important because in the Jewish religious calendar Pentecost commemorated the day on which Moses had promulgated the covenant on Mount Sinai. The symbolic message could not be clearer. The former written covenant was being replaced by an unwritten one. Henceforth the guidance would not be from written rules but from the untrammelled Spirit of God whose initiatives could not be foreseen, and whose power could not be contained or limited by man-made written regulations, or categories of thought. The first manifestation of the new source of power was the transformation of the apostles from terrified deserters to totally confident preachers of Jesus and his message.

As the mission of the infant Church progressed each crucial step is seen to have been guided by the initiative of the Holy Spirit. Peter's bestowal of baptism on the first pagan, the centurion Cornelius, was in response to a vision, and the specific instruction of the Holy Spirit (Acts 10:19). As Peter was preaching to the household of Cornelius the Holy Spirit came upon all of them (Acts 10:44), and this convinced the doubters among Peter's companions that it was the will of God that pagans should enter the Church as well as Jews.

After twenty centuries of Christianity, it is difficult for us to appreciate just how momentous was the decision to admit the gentiles into the true Church on a basis of equality with the Jews. The Apostles and their immediate community seem to have appreciated just what was at stake, and summoned a council in Jerusalem to discuss the question and make a collective decision which would reflect the seriousness of what was at stake. The principle of gentile equality was agreed, and their awareness of being guided by the Holy Spirit could not have been made clearer. Their final decision stated :- " For it has seemed good to the Holy Spirit and to us, to lay upon you no greater burden than these necessary things." (Acts 15:19).

After the Council of Jerusalem, St. Paul's missionary journeys went further afield. In the second journey the initiative of the Holy Spirit is remarkable. When St. Paul and his companions were in what is now north western Turkey, they intended to proceed into the province of Asia, but the Holy Spirit prevented them (Acts 16:6). Their next plan was to go into Bithynia (Acts 16:7), but once again they were forbidden by the Holy Spirit. Eventually after a vision to St. Paul, the party realised that God wanted them to cross the sea to Macedonia, which they did. Thus did St. Paul make the momentous step of bringing Christianity to Europe, with consequences for the future which he could not possibly have foreseen.

In contrast to this massive amount of guidance by the Holy Sprit the gospels contain only two references to the authority which would be bestowed on the human leaders of the Church, namely the grant of authority to St. Peter (Matthew 16:18) and to the apostles generally (Matthew 18:18). There would always be potential for tension between the visible and invisible guidance of the Church, and St. Paul warned human office holders of the danger of quenching the Spirit (I Thesssalonians 5:19).

SECTION 2 : STRUCTURED ORGANISATION .

The history of idealistic movements makes it clear that their enthusiasm must be canalised by some minimum of institutionalisation or the idealism will evaporate. The peace movement in

Northern Ireland demonstrated this principle in one disappointing initiative of the 1970's.

After particularly brutal bombing two perfectly ordinary women summoned up their courage and in the face of the gunmen they said "We've had enough". Their sentiments were echoed by countless other ordinary citizens who had been horrified by the long tale of indiscriminate violence. With great courage they inspired hundreds of people to take to the streets and protest in the name of peace. The movement snowballed, it caught the imagination of people in other countries, and the two women were eventually awarded the Nobel Prize for Peace. However one experienced observer of the Ulster scene remarked to me when the momentum seemed to be unstoppable, that unless they organised it with some proper structure it would all fizzle out. That is exactly what happened. Quarrels broke out within the inner circle, there were accusations of the misappropriation of funds, personality differences got out of hand, and the whole movement dissolved into ineffectuality.

Civil society, the army, education and the arts all require appropriate structures if the energies of their participants are to be canalised effectively. Many people have a reluctance about this process since it would seem to crush spontaneity and creativity. One can sympathise with this anxiety, but the real problem is not the existence of a structured framework, but the imposition of a structure which is alien to the movement, such as when the army takes over the civil government of a nation, for example.

Religion is no exception to these rules, and the infant Church manifested a remarkably sustaining and sensitive organisation which fostered the spiritual progress of Christianity. A convenient starting point to study this structure is the organisation which is alluded to in the Letters of St. Ignatius of Antioch, whose composition can be assigned to the year 110 or shortly before it. When he was being taken to Rome as a prisoner, destined to die a martyr's death, he had the opportunity to write letters to seven communities in Asia Minor, as his ship put into port from time to time, on the voyage to Italy. He encourages the communities to remain strong in the face of persecution, and points to the sources of their spiritual strength, namely confidence in God, sound doctrine, prayer, a strong community and obedience to the Church authorities. The authorities in question are the same in each city. There is one *episkopos* assisted by a small group of *presbuteroi* and *diakonoi*. In modern times those offices have acquired the names of bishop, priest and deacon. It would be more accurate to translate the Greek terms as overseer, elders and servants. The latter category should be understood not in the sense of menial work, but like the modern designation of civil servant. In other words it was an administrative role, and by the fourth century the deacons had become the financial administrators of the dioceses.

The bishop's role was the most important since he was responsible for preaching and hence for doctrinal orthodoxy, and he also presided at the weekly eucharist, and baptisms. Those functions were entrusted to the elders only at a later stage. This pattern was almost certainly inspired by the organisation of Jewish synagogues which had an almost identical organisation. It is important to remember that this system of bishop, presbyters and deacons which eventually became universal in the whole Church, was not immediately adopted by all communities. When St. Ignatius extolled its virtues at the beginning of the second century, the important communities in Corinth and Rome for example, seem to have been governed by a committee of presbyters without the guiding hand of a bishop. [5]

In the half century before the Ignatian letters, the evidence for Church organisation is sparse but consistent. In addition to the Jewish model which was there for the Christians to copy, the roles had been prepared by Jesus, and by St. Paul. During his missionary journeys St. Paul did not leave the new converts simply to reflect on his message, but the newly baptised Christians were carefully grouped into communities. When he considered that they were sufficiently strong to survive without him he appointed presbyters (cf. Acts 14:23 , 20:17, and Philippians 1:1). The letters to Timothy and Titus describe the qualities to be sought in candidates for the roles of bishop, presbyter, or deacon (cf. I Timothy 3:2 ff, 3:8 ff, 5:17, Titus 1:7) namely mature family men who have earned the confidence of their fellow citizens on account of their integrity of character. Then, displaying remarkable confidence in the newly converted Christians, he moved on to evangelise other cities.

In the second century episcopal government flourished, and by the end of that century it was the pattern of organisation for every community for which records survive. Two important tasks required their attention, and in the settling of them their own authority was reinforced, namely the establishment of the canon of Scripture, and the vindication of orthodox doctrine against the gnostics. Their method of work seems to have evolved quite simply. They arrived at jointly agreed policies by the exchange of letters (of which many have survived) and by holding regional councils. These councils were quite frequent, and widespread by the end of the second century.

For the Old Testament the Church adopted without any misgivings the canon of the Septuagint, that is to say, the Greek translation of the Old Testament made in Alexandria in the second century B.C. by bi-lingual Jews living in that city. It also contained books written originally in Greek (like the Book of Wisdom) about which category later Jewish communities would have misgivings. From an early stage the Christians accorded to the gospels and letters of the apostles the same status as the inspired books of the Old Testament.

The second problem which the early episcopate coped with was that of Gnosticism. This was the generic term used to describe a number of sects which had sprung up among the Christians and whose members claimed "insider knowledge" . They alleged that they were the recipients of special privileged knowledge that Jesus had given only to a select few, and had been passed on to them, and not to the generality of believers. They also held that Jesus was not the unique mediator between God the Father and the human race, but that he was one among several intermediaries between the human race and the infinite God.

The general line of defence against them adopted by the orthodox Christians was that it would be inconceivable if Jesus had given them special doctrines which he did not give to the apostles and their successors. It was in the context of this dispute that the bishops' authority in safeguarding true teaching was brought to the forefront. Since both heretics and orthodox possessed the scriptures which all could read, the defence was to emphasise the tradition of true doctrine transmitted by the apostles to the men whom they had appointed as leaders of the communities which they had founded in their missionary journeys. This was the origin of

---

[5] cf. Lampe, P. (2003), *Christians at Rome in the First Two Centuries,* (Eng. trans. Michael Steinhauser), London: Continuum, pp. 397 - 408.

the concept of Apostolic Succession, namely that the bishops who could trace their appointment and consecration back to the apostles, via validly appointed predecessors, were competent to decide what was the authentic teaching of the apostles.

A remarkably explicit explanation of the apostles' provision for the transmission of their authority to the next generation of leaders is to be found in the letter of Clement of Rome to the community at Corinth. (It goes without saying that some aspects of the apostles' first generation role were not transmitted to their successors, such as being witnesses of The Resurrection). The composition of this letter may confidently be ascribed to the year 96. The event which gave rise to it was a bitter dispute within the church at Corinth, in which some of the presbyters had been expelled from office. The actual statement about the Apostles provision for the handing on of authority is so important that I will quote the relevant paragraph in full:-

" Our apostles too were given to understand by our Lord Jesus Christ that the office of bishop would give rise to intrigues. For this reason, equipped as they were with perfect foreknowledge, they appointed the men mentioned before, and afterwards laid down a rule once for all to this effect: when these men die , other approved men shall succeed to their sacred ministry. Consequently we deem it an injustice to eject from the sacred ministry the persons who were appointed either by them, or later, with the consent of the whole church, by other men in high repute and have ministered to the flock of Christ faultlessly, humbly, quietly, and unselfishly, and have moreover, over a long period of time, earned the esteem of all."[6]

Although this letter implies that the Roman community had some sense of responsibility for Church affairs far off, it does not contain anything like an explicit statement of papal supremacy. This is not surprising, granted the primitive state of the Church. Newman remarked that "St.Ignatius's failure to mention the primacy of Rome is no harder to explain than the silence of Seneca or Plutarch about Christianity itself".[7] And in a slightly different context the same author stated "It is a less difficulty that the papal supremacy was not formally acknowledged in the second century, than that there was no formal acknowledgement on the part of the Church of the doctrine of the Holy Trinity till the fourth. No doctrine is defined until it is violated."[8]

The gnostic crisis had crystallised the bishops' authority as deriving from the apostles. An extension of the same principle would give pre-eminence to the bishop of Rome, being the successor of St. Peter, whose special position had been indicated by the words of Jesus that it was upon this rock that he would build his Church (Matt. 16:18). An early indication of how the Roman community was esteemed has been supplied by Irenaeus. He was the bishop of Lyons some time after 177. Writing in the context of the gnostic disputes he stated that the true doctrine was to be found in the churches of apostolic foundation. He adds though, that it would be a lengthy process to trace the teaching of all the apostolic churches, so he

---

[6] Translation of James A. Kleist, op. cit. p. 36.

[7] Newman, J.H.(ed. of 1878), *The Development of Christian Doctrine* , London: Longmans Green & Co., p.149.

[8] Newman, J.H., op.cit. p. 151.

recommends a theological short cut. They should consult the church of Rome. He states this in the context of the apostolic churches being careful to keep a list of all their bishops going back to the founding apostle. "But it would be very long in a book of this kind, to enumerate the episcopal lists in all the churches, but by pointing out the Apostolic tradition and creed

which has been brought down to us by a succession of bishops in the greatest, most ancient and well -known church, founded by the two most glorious apostles Peter and Paul at Rome, we can confute all those who in any other way, either for self-pleasing or from vainglory or blindness or badness, hold unauthorised meetings. For with this church, because of its stronger origin (potentiorem principalitatem), all churches must agree, that is to say, the faithful of all places, because in it the apostolic tradition has always been preserved by the faithful from all places."[9] Unfortunately the original Greek has been lost, but the Latin translation is reliable, and dates from the beginning of the third century. Its meaning is perfectly clear: the community of Rome is a theological yardstick for the orthodoxy of the whole Church.

In the third century several factors came together which threw into high relief the unique status of the Bishop of Rome. First of all there was the rapid numerical increase and geographically wide diffusion of the Christian communities. Clearly a world-wide organisation of that kind would sooner or later feel the need for some sort of supra national focus of unity.

It is worth while reflecting on just how rapid was the Christian expansion and how far it had penetrated by the middle of the third century. By that time Christian communities were located all around the Mediterranean, deep into the interior of Gaul, as far away as Syria, and possibly too in Britain. The first documentary evidence for Christianity in Britain is the astounding but totally unselfconscious record of British bishops attending the first council of Arles in 314 . Among those present were the bishops of London, Lincoln, and York.

The development of the bishop of Rome's position in relation to other communities became complicated in the two or more centuries after Ireneaus. By the fifth century the normal pattern emerged after serious crises of heresy within the Church and imperial interference from outside. If the reader should feel uneasy that such a central plank of Church organisation took so long to be clarified, it is helpful to remember that it took just as long for the understanding of the precise status of Jesus to acquire similar clarity.

Up to that time three theories of episcopal government are to be seen. First of all was St. Cyprian's theory of the equality of all bishops, canvassed in the middle of the third century. Secondly there was the idea that the authority of the bishop might depend upon the political status of his city, and its corollary that the emperor had the right to intervene in Church affairs. Thirdly was the theory that the universal communion of all the dioceses (i.e. the whole Church) was secured by all bishops being in communion with one special see, that of Peter's successor. In a book of this scope it would take too long to discuss all the vicissitudes of the three theories up to the fifth century, so I will limit myself to the bare essentials, and leave the reader to look elsewhere for a fuller treatment.[10]

---

[9] Ireanaeus, *Adversus Haereses,* III,3,2. quoted in Winter, op.cit. p. 126.

[10] A well balanced account is that of the still valuable study by Jalland, T.G.,(1942),*The Church and*

St. Cyprian's theory of the equality of all bishops suffered from his relatively brief theological education. In view of the impact which his powerful personality had on the Church, it is hard to realise that he went from baptism to martyrdom (in 258) in little more than a decade, which did not leave too much time for theology. His remarkable personality dominated the Church in north Africa (as bishop of Carthage) and he appears effortlessly to have secured unity in the African episcopate in their regional councils. However his theory had simply no remedy if bishops should disagree to the point where they would act differently on important matters of principle. His rather touching naivety that bishops would always be in agreement must be put down to his lack of experience of Church affairs.[11]

One pragmatic remedy for settling differences between bishops might be to ask the civil power to intervene, particularly if that power should be a Christian emperor. Yet there is no warrant in the New Testament or the authentic tradition of the Church which gives the civil government (of whatever form) the right to adjudicate in the affairs of the Church. In spite of that, considerable damage was done to the life of the Church when the bishops of Constantinople tried to promote the prestige, power, and authority of their position, arguing that it was due to them as being the bishops of the capital of the empire. The orthodox traditionalists resented it because the see of Constantinipole had not been founded by an apostle, nor was there any precedent in the life of the early Church that the popes claimed primacy on account of Rome's having been the capital of the empire.[12]

The third position which ultimately prevailed was that of securing universal communion through the bishop of Rome. The concept of communion has overtones of administrative tidiness, but basically it expresses the relationships of harmony, concord, and charity between all Christians, epitomised in the person of their bishops, in charge of the local communities. It was not just a vague attitude of goodwill to all other Christians, but it was based on unity of belief, and mutual acceptance of valid sacraments, particularly baptism by which the individual was constituted as a member of the Church. A basic minimum of doctrinal agreement was required by the popes, and if this was not forthcoming communion could be withheld by him. In normal circumstances this was epitomised by the exchange of letters of communion between the principal apostolic dioceses when a new bishops were elected. In abnormal circumstances, when orthodox belief had to be defined the popes would give or refuse assent to general councils. If individual bishops had been the victims of injustice the pope used to act as a court of appeal.

The securing of this simple and efficient form of Church order was largely due, not to any one pope, but to St. Ambrose, the bishop of Milan from 374 to 397. He did not formulate an explicit theology of the papacy, but he secured the foundations thereof, by establishing that

---

The Papacy, London: S.P.C.K. A briefer treatment of the field is to be found in the present author's *St. Peter and the Popes,* London: Darton Longman & Todd, 1960.

[11] Chapman, H. J. (1928), *Studies in the Early Papacy,* London: Sheed & Ward, p.44.

[12] cf. Hastings, Adrian. 'The Papacy and Rome's Civil Greatness', in *The Downside Review,* 1957, p.366.

the Church was a self governing organisation independent of the emperor's political authority. His policy has been epitomised in one famous sentence : "The Emperor is within the Church not above it".[13] His policy was successful, at least in the West, which meant that left to its own devices, and free from imperial interference, the Church settled its internal

differences by its own methods. The position of the pope as ultimate arbiter of episcopal disputes or doctrinal aberrations was secure.

The benefits to the Church of this arrangement can be seen at their best in Pope Leo the Great's dealings with the Christological disputes which generated the definition of the Council of Chalcedon. Briefly what happened was this [14] . A well respected monk of Constantinople, Eutyches, was accused of teaching a heretical theory about the human nature of Christ. This sparked off a bitter dispute in the East, whose ramifications went well beyond the domain of theology. The emperor Theodosius II, without reference to the pope, summoned a council at Ephesus in 449. It was a disaster, ending in scenes of violence as soldiers intervened to restore order. Several bishops who had been ill treated appealed to Pope Leo. The Pope refused to accept the decisions of the council, and after the death of the emperor another council was called which conducted its business properly. At the conclusion of that council, at Chalcedon in 451, the assembled bishops wrote to the Pope to ask his approval of the decisions.

The disputes and eventual settlement of the affairs of the two closely linked councils demonstrate clearly the acceptance of papal authority in the Eastern part of the Church , as well as the West. When normal ties of communion had broken down, and doctrinal orthodoxy was under threat, the pope was recognised as having competence to act as court of appeal for the wronged bishops, and his assent was required for the council to have the special status of a General or Ecumenical Council.

The status of General or Ecumenical Council was and still is an important element in the preservation of true doctrine in the universal Church. As I indicated above, the origin of local councils in the second century was a spontaneous development among the bishops, in ascertaining what one could call the collective consensus of the Church on disputed questions, like the Gnostic crisis. From that simple origin, the development of larger councils was was consistent with factors such as the numerical expansion of the Church, the cessation of persecution, and the increasing seriousness of the heresies. It is important to bear in mind that they are just one expression of the Church's competence to make binding decisions on matters of doctrine. This competence was exercised in other ways in different circumstances. For example from early in the third century until the late fourth century there was a widespread debate as to whether baptism, administered by Christians who had lapsed into heresy, was valid or not. The debates on that question lasted for almost two centuries and it was agreed eventually that heretical baptism was valid. The difference between the long drawn out disputes over baptism and the quick solution of general councils for the christological battles, was because the latter aroused great bitterness, there was interference by the emperors, and the unity of the church was threatened. In the baptismal dispute these threats were absent. The

[13] Ambrose, *Sermon against Auxentius* section 36, in Migne, *Patrologia Latina* vol. 16 col.1018.

[14] A fuller account of the matter can be found in Winter, op.cit. pp. 213 - 223.

parties were content to debate the issue within the normal bonds of communion. In this perspective General Councils can be regarded as emergency measures adopted to cope with fast moving crises.

Both methods are expressions of the Church's doctrinal competence, under the guidance of the Holy Spirit, and the decisions have always been regarded as irreversible, whether arrived

at by gradual consensus, or by swift conciliar debate in an emergency. The irreformability of the decisions implies that they were free from error. This does not mean that they were totally comprehensive definitions about mysterious aspects of the infinite God, but it does mean that they had blocked off deviant paths which would lead to error. Later in the history of the Church this degree of surety would receive the name of infallibility. Newman maintained that some form of infallible teaching authority was to be expected in connection with a revelation which disclosed the inner mysteries of God, and whose understanding would develop over the centuries. To use his own words "If the Christian doctrine as originally taught, admits of true and important developments, as was argued in the foregoing Section, this is a strong antecedent argument in favour of a provision in the Dispensation for putting a seal of authority upon those developments."[15]

SECTION 3 : LONG TERM MALAISE IN CHURCH AUTHORITY

Despite the clarification of ideas at Chalcedon on Church authority and the pope's position of ultimate arbiter, the Christian emperors at Constantinople continued to interfere in the affairs of the Church. Eventually the Eastern part of the Church became effectively under the control of the emperors who appointed the bishops of the principal sees. This pernicious practice was so enracinated that it continued after the conquest of the Eastern empire by the Muslims in the fifteenth century, and the Muslim rulers took over the strongly entrenched custom of appointing the bishops of Constantinople. The same principle applied in all nations where the Eastern Orthodox Church was the national Church. In Russia the same custom persisted and when the rule of the Tsars had been abolished in the revolution of 1917, the appointment of Russian patriarchs was done by the communist government. Needless to say that practice undermined still further the likelihood of re-building unity between the Eastern and Western branches of Christendom.

Sadly the two halves of the Church drew apart in the middle ages owing to considerable cultural differences, but the real damage to Church unity was done by the crusades. The West European military campaigns in Palestine damaged the Orthodox Church, by such insensitive measures as removing the Greek speaking bishops and replacing them by Latins. Worst of all was the fourth Crusade which attacked and sacked Constantinople on the way to Palestine. The Crusaders occupied the city and most of its western territories for close on a century.

The Western Church had similar problems. In the middle ages the popes resisted the incursions of the Holy Roman Empire (approximately coterminous with modern Germany and Austria), by using the emperors' methods. The Papal States became thoroughly secular in character with armies, bureaucracy, and the rest. The popes successfully resisted the

---

[15] Newman, J.H.,(1879) *An essay on the Development of Christian Doctrine,* London: Longmans Green & Co, Chapter 2, section 2, especially p.79.

emperors, and maintained the independence of the Church but at a terrible price. The internal organisation of the Church , with a strongly centralised bureaucracy was the mirror image of its great rival, the empire, and worked by the same methods of compulsion, even using the death penalty for heretics.

The aggrandisement of the pope's power within the Church reached its apogee in 1870 at the

First Vatican Council. In the decree *Pastor Aeternus* the council defined the juridical supremacy of the papal office within the Church and also the papal infallibility. [16] The latter power was defined with carefully thought - out checks and balances attaching to it, but the former (the pope's supremacy) received no such limitations. By the 20th century it had extended its scope so much that it stifled the role of bishops and laity in the Church.

In Chapter Two I pointed out that dysfunctional aspects of ecclesiastical administration acted as a deterrent to people of good will who might wish to join the Catholic Church, since such practices obscured the the goodness of the gospel message and the person of Jesus. Having just discussed the normal structure of the institutional side of the Church's life, the time has come to return to its abuses in order to clarify what should be normal in the life of the Church, and what must be remedied if it is to pursue its mission properly, and present itself as credible to potential converts.

The newly enhanced concept of papal supremacy showed itself quite soon after the First Vatican Council, when Canon Law was codified in 1919. What is theologically significant was that it was promulgated on the authority of the pope alone. In the previous history of the Church large bodies of legislation had been issued on the authority of general councils. Individual regulations had been promulgated by particular popes, but never before had the totality of Church law been promulgated by the pope on his own.

The centralising tendency did not stop merely with the promulgation of the Code of Canon Law in 1919. Within that Code, for the first time in the history of the Church, the pope was accorded the right to appoint practically all the bishops in the Catholic Church. It is difficult to overestimate the significance of that innovation. Theoretically it is done in the name of the pope, but as there are approximately 3000 bishops in the Church, he cannot be personally responsible for the choices. It is difficult to think of any activity in the Church today which is further removed from our ancient traditions. In the middle of the 19th century the Catholic Church had 646 ordinary bishops in the whole world. Of those, 555 were nominated by various forms of secular authority, lay patronage, noble families or heads of state. A further 67 were elected by cathedral chapters of canons, and a mere 24 were nominated directly by the pope. [17] The details of the historical shift of power are too well known to need repeating here. It was a combination of the French Revolution and the Italian Risorgimento. The secularist governments of those nations (and others which followed the same path) did not wish any longer to nominate bishops, and handed the responsibility to the pope just about the time that Vatican I had defined his universal jurisdiction in extremely centralising terms.

---

[16] Denziger, 3053 to 3074.

[17] These numbers were researched originally by Rev. G. Sweeney, and published in Hastings, Adrian (ed.) (1977) *Bishops and Writers*, Hertfordshire, p. 207.

The relationship between the bishops and the papacy is an example of an imbalance of power. The Second Vatican Council clarified the theological status of the episcopate. Bishops are the successors of the apostles from whom they derive their authority. They are not deputies of the pope nor do they derive jurisdiction from him as if they were his delegates. By contrast all members of the Roman Curia function as delegates of the pope from whom they derive

whatever jurisdiction they might enjoy. The world-wide episcopate has a collective responsibility for the whole Church, in union with the pope. This status has been described as collegiality.[18] The notion of collegiality has not been very firmly enshrined in the 1983 Code of Canon Law, but the late Bishop Christopher Butler maintained that the post-conciliar popes now have a moral obligation to deal with bishops according to the principles of collegiality as laid down by Vatican II.

In the post-conciliar period those insights have not been matched by the establishment of structures which could make them effective in practice. A number of episcopal synods have been held, but none of them has fulfilled the conditions for collegiality. The bishops were not exercising real responsibility. The agendas had been prepared by the Vatican, and Curial nominees were so numerous that they were able to control the outcome. If individual bishops expressed opinions outside the programme their views were simply ignored, as was the case in the Roman Synod of October 2005 when some bishops made a serious plea for the ordination to the priesthood of mature married men. The suggestion was simply brushed aside by the presiding Cardinal.[19]

The power of the Roman curia was also the main cause for the birth control debacle of the 1960's, but I will leave the details of that dispute to the section on marriage, in Chapter Seven on the Sacraments.

This limitation of episcopal responsibility is serious from the theological point of view, and it is equally disquieting from a purely practical standpoint. Quite simply it means that the Vatican is appointing to the episcopate men whom they do not trust; hence the tight control on their activities. Alternatively it could mean that the personnel of the Roman Curia so much enjoy the exercise of power that they have been taking over gradually the rightful powers which bishops ought to be exercising. Either of those two possibilities is extremely serious for the well being of the Church, and constitutes yet one more element of what I have been describing at length in this chapter, namely that there are elements in the way in which the Church functions which constitute a deterrent to an outsider looking for belief.

SECTION 4 : RENEWAL AND REFORM IN THE MODERN PERIOD

In this and in previous chapters, I have indicated that there are serious shortcomings in the present administrative structures of the Church in relation to eliciting and sustaining faith. This malfunction has arisen mostly on account of the retention of institutions which might

---

[18] Vatican II, Constitution on the Church, *Lumen Gentium,* sections 19 - 23, Eng. trans. Abbott, pp 38 - 45.

[19] Vatican web site, www.vatican.va Oct.29, 2005, Press Report number 31.

once have been useful, but which in the modern world have become obstacles to the apostolate. The time has now come to study how we should proceed from the present inadequate organisation to one that is purposefully orientated to its pastoral objectives.

In this section I am deeply indebted to Yves Congar's book on Church reform, which was one of the seminal theological studies of the twentieth century.[20] In the course of its history the

Church has undergone reforms of three basic kinds, namely reforms of doctrine, morals and structures. Doctrinal reform was the principal issue at the Council of Nicaea in 325 when orthodox doctrine about the divinity of Jesus had to be clarified in the context of Arianism. Moral reform was most effectively carried out by the saints, such as St. Francis calling back the wealthy and politicised mediaeval Church to the ideals of the New Testament. Structural reform can be seen at various levels, such as monasticism. St. Benedict was not the originator of the monastic movement in the Church but he devised a way of life embodied in his rule which has proved remarkably durable and adaptable in fostering dynamic spiritual communities. In the sixteenth century the Council of Trent achieved various reform measures in the structures of the Church whose value is sometimes overlooked. For instance, that council created the Congregation then known as Propaganda Fidei (for the propagation of the faith). It co-ordinated the whole international missionary movement, and did it smoothly. This was a remarkable achievement, when one considers the potential conflict of interests in the national rivalry between different colonial powers, competition between religious orders, and the possibility of friction between secular and regular clergy. It is an example of structural reform at its best.

Congar pointed out that whatever the nature of the reform, four conditions had to be fulfilled if it was to be successful, in other words an authentic renewal of the Church's spiritual energies, rather than a superficial modernisation. These four conditions are that it must be motivated by apostolic zeal and charity, it must entail a return to the sources, it must preserve the unity of the Church, and its advocates must observe *patientia*. I have retained the Latin form of that word because the English translation as 'patience' does not do justice to its meaning. Its authentic sense includes not only a willingness to endure the passage of time, but also to endure suffering and reversals and not be deterred from pursuing one's objective. In Christian antiquity it was the martyrs who displayed the true patientia because they endured any amount of suffering, long-term imprisonment or violent torture without being turned away from their loyalty to Christ. It was also displayed by the orthodox party after the Council of Nicea. The council had decided upon the true formulation of the doctrine of the divinity of Jesus, but within a few years the whole Roman world descended into theological chaos because the successors of Constantine favoured the Arian party and removed the orthodox bishops from office. Late in the fourth century there was scarcely a single orthodox bishop left in any important diocese. Long term tenacity was displayed by true believers, who ultimately triumphed.

The condition of charity and apostolic zeal can best be appreciated in contrast to some less well thought out reforms. For example in the eighteenth century the Austrian Emperor Joseph II carried out a certain number of reforming measures on the Church in his dominions. He was

---

[20] Congar,Y.M.J. (1950) *Vraie et Fausse Réforme dans l'Église,* Paris : Éditions du Cerf.

78

chiefly concerned with administrative tidiness and the rationalisation of the Church's considerable wealth. It is not the kind of updating that the Church needs for the transfor - mation of its spiritual life. The Franciscan movement embodied this characteristic perfectly.

The return to the sources is in a way the most basic of the four conditions. The vision of the Church as presented in Vatican II is a good example of this. Thanks to nearly a century of renewed biblical and theological study, the consensus among theologians about the Church on

the eve of the Council derived from the New Testament and the patristic understanding of it. Namely it was an invisible mysterious entity of the union of baptised believers with Christ (the Mystical Body) which showed itself in the visible world as a community, which could be described as the People of God forged by the New Covenant, on a parallel with the People of the Old Covenant. Any organisational structures like the episcopate had to be regarded as of secondary importance in relation to the fundamental community. The significance of those insights can be appreciated by contrasting that vision with what was implied in the reform of Canon Law in 1918. The codification of the law book was merely an operation of administrative tidying up. It was not a return to the sources of anything and did not renew the Church spiritually. The architects of the Code probably did not have that ambition anyway.

The preservation of unity is, in sense, the acid test as to whether the reform had been authentic or not. Any organisation can improve its performance by creaming off the talented people and leaving the others behind. A example comes to mind from another sphere of life. Schools which are ruthless in shedding less intelligent pupils may improve their examination performance, but such measures may not represent any real improvement in the quality of the teaching. Religious reform which creams off the zealots and forms a separate Church has largely evaded the overall problem of reforming the parent body.

How should we apply those four conditions to the reforms which the Catholic Church needs today if it is to transmit the faith to its own younger generation and to a secular society ?

I will now return to Congar's basic insights. He maintained that in the middle of the 20th century the Catholic Church did not need a reform of morals or doctrine, but a reform of structures to enable it to exercise a realistic apostolate to a post-Christian society. When the man-made structures of the Church become incapable of attaining their objectives it usually happens that their deformations falls into one of two categories, either the Church gone worldly or the Church gone churchy.[21] In the late middle ages the Church had become very worldly, having vast wealth and being immersed in the secular politics of the age. Cardinal Wolsey's career is a classical example, but that problem does not concern us in the modern world. The plight of the Church gone churchy is what we are suffering now. It is a situation characterised by an almost obsessional preoccupation with ecclesiastical rules as ends to be pursued in their own right, regardless of clear connection with advancing the Kingdom of God. One whole area which springs to mind is all that goes with the privileged status of the

---

[21] For those apposite epithets worldly and churchy, I am indebted to Cicely Hastings who made the English translation of Hans Küng (1961), *Konzil und Widervereinigung,* Freiburg, (English title *The Council and Reunion),* (1961), London: Sheed & Ward, p. 30.

clergy as a separate class, particularly its manifestation in details of dress. Before the Council it was more rigid, but it still lingers on even to the absurd details such as Monsignors being allowed to wear purple socks. Religious orders have had their own problems, such as the disputes as to whether Capuchins were obliged to wear beards, and whether or not they might trim them.

Apart from trivialities which are just irrelevant or disedifying, there are deeper problems of the churchiness such as the sharing of power. Despite the Second Vatican Council's

admirable theological vision of the Church, the post conciliar reforms have not rectified the imbalance of power in any satisfactory structures. There are two principal areas in need of re-organisation. At the risk of some oversimplification I would describe the two problems as the laity being oppressed by the clergy, and the bishops being oppressed by the Roman Curia. The latter scenario was explained above (pages 75 and 76) in the context of the over-centralising tendency of the Vatican. The reversal of that tendency will probably have to await the arrival of a reforming pope like John XXIII. In the meantime a totally unforseen factor has entered upon the scene. The Second Vatican Council sanctioned the principle of free speech within the Church, by declaring that lay people had the right to make known to their religious superiors their views on what would benefit the life of the Church. The principle was also enshrined in the Code of Canon Law in 1983.[22] In the subsequent years it has turned into constructive criticism, where necessary it has also become active protest, and it is unstoppable. A clear example occurred in Austria in the spring of 2009. The Vatican nominated as auxiliary bishop of Linz a priest who was known to be rigidly conservative. After more than one disastrous episcopal appointment in Austria's recent history, there was widespread protest. In the diocese of Linz the 32 out of the 35 deans declared that the candidate was unacceptable. Within a few days the papal nominee resigned his appointment.[23]

The situation of the laity is the simpler and will only require a few paragraphs. It is a truism which is not always appreciated that the clergy exist for the sake of the laity and not vice versa. Far too much of ecclesiastical custom and Canon Law favour the comfort of the clergy and neglect the well-being of the laity. At present the laity have no part in the selection of the priests who are sent to take charge of the parishes. There is no insuperable theological problem in presenting a parish committee with a number of candidates and asking them to express a preference. The bishop would make the ultimate choice, and confer jurisdiction in making the appointment. (Incidentally there is no absolute obligation now for the clergy to provide for an elected representative committee for the parishioners). This principle could be extended to the election of bishops. In antiquity bishops were elected by the laity and clergy of the vacant diocese. The bishops from neighbouring dioceses in the province performed the consecration. In addition to conferring episcopal ordination on the candidate the ceremony thereby inserted him, theologically, into the apostolic succession.

The most successful way of effecting institutional reform is not by issuing more rules within the existing structures, but by changing the structures in question to make them better adapted to achieving their operational goals. In chapter Two I described the kind of basic communities which would be necessary for the satisfactory transmission of faith. If these

[22] Vatican II, *Lumen Gentium* § 32 , *Gaudium et Spes* § 62. Code of Canon Law, Canon 212, § 3.
[23] The episode was reported fully in the Vienna based journal *Kirche Intern*, February 2009.

could be established widely and acknowledged as the fundamental eucharistic communities, most of the imbalances of power would be remedied automatically. Within such small groups the exercise of anything like clerical power would be impossible. This equalisation would be fortified by the financial position of their priests. Clearly the larger numbers needed and the smallness of the groups for which they celebrated mass would not require full-time fully-paid clergy. Their eucharistic leaders would be earning their living like the rest of the human race. All practical matters could be arranged by informal dialogue. They would not need to have special houses, whose upkeep entail considerable financial burdens.

SECTION 4 : ECUMENISM.

One of the most important developments in the life and self understanding of the Church in the twentieth century was the birth of the ecumenical movement. It might almost be described as an example of the beer glass. Is it half full or half empty? Up to the Second World War the pessimistic view prevailed, and one has the impression that many Christians preferred to focus their attention on the issues which divided us, rather than attend to the points of unity. In the catechism which was in common use in England up to the time of the Second Vatican Council, the children were taught that it was sinful to take part in the prayers or services of a false religion. The derogatory term " false religion" applied to every religion other than the Roman Catholic Church, namely primitive animistic religions in remote parts of Africa, fundamentalist biblical Churches, Lutherans and all other Protestants, Anglicans and the Orthodox, although the latter was recognised as having valid sacraments and belief in the same doctrinal programme as R.C.'s: the only difference being the status of papal authority. Nevertheless the Catholic s were forbidden even to recite the Lord's prayer with any other Christians. Admittedly the Catholics were not alone in living by those divisive principles.

The mere existence of so many different Christian Churches is itself a disincentive to outsiders to enquire further, and it weakens the influence which Christians might otherwise exercise in public life. Apart from the ancient and large Churches, there are so many smaller gatherings that it is quite impossible to count them all. In the tolerant societies of Europe and America there is nothing to prevent any individual picking up the New Testament and creating his or her own local Church. This is so much at variance with the explicit words of Jesus about the unity of his followers that serious minded Christians realised something had to be done to remedy it.

The Second World War provided the catalyst because its horrors shook many committed Christians out of their narrow and prejudiced attitudes. For example a priest in the German army who later became a famous theologian, namely Bernard Haring, had all his ideas shaken up when he served on the front line in the Russian campaign. When celebrating mass on the day before an offensive, he realised that half the men in front of him would be killed within a few days. At that point he decided to give holy communion to the Lutheran soldiers as well.[24] Back at home similar toleration was breaking out. The British policy of the indiscriminate bombing of civilian centres of population resulted in the destruction of countless churches. As a result of this Lutherans and Catholics started sharing the surviving buildings holding their own services at different times on Sundays, but under the same roof.

---

[24] Häring, B.(1977), *Embattled Witness: Memories of a Time of War,* London: Burns & Oates, p.5.

It is worth remembering that Haring's attitude to other Christians was influenced not only by the horrors of war, but also by examples of heroism and generosity which were bred in those tragic situations. After the battle of Stalingrad, Haring was ordered to take a party of wounded German soldiers back home. The army's situation was so serious that no transport was provided, nor rations, and they had to walk. They were dependent upon the kindness of the local population who had suffered ruthless cruelties from the invading German army. Nevertheless on one evening an elderly Russian couple gave them a meal which used up all the food which they had left in their house. On their departure Haring (who spoke Russian)

said to them: "You are so kind as to give us your last piece of bread, although we are a people of an alien nation that has brought great suffering to your country. May I ask why you do it ?" The old gentleman answered. "In times of starvation I was working in the mines, and after loosing my job I had to walk home several hundred miles. Day by day on that long journey, someone would share his bread with me, and I made a vow to God that I would never refuse hospitality to anyone in need of it." Haring observed, "This was the mark of the Orthodox believer."[25] In such circumstances was the spirit of ecumenism born.

In addition to these practical activities, the spiritual foundation of ecumenism had been prepared some time earlier by a French priest Paul Coutourier. He urged that Christians of all Churches should pray for unity, and this resulted in the world wide custom of the octave of prayer for Christian unity in January each year. He encouraged his fellow Catholics to examine how much we had in common with other Christians rather than emphasise what was different. Many traditional Catholics were quite surprised to find how many of their beliefs and spiritual practices were the same as those of other Churches. As with many other positive initiatives in Catholic practice and theology, the ecumenical movement gained the approval of the Second Vatican Council which devoted a special document to the matter, entitled *Unitatis Redintigratio,* promulgated on 21st. November 1964.

After the Council one saw the results of the ecumenical movement in a complete change of attitude among seriously committed Christians. The examples which could be cited are so numerous that I must confine myself to a small sample. When Pope John Paul II made his visit to England in 1980 he was received with full liturgical honours by the Archbishop of Canterbury in his cathedral. A more enduring partnership was that between the Anglican and Catholic bishops of Liverpool, Dick Sheppard and Derek Worlock. They worked closely on countless social problems in a difficult period of that city's history, realising that the moral principles which should govern good social policy were the same for both of them, being grounded in Christianity.

However the most important ecumenical event in the period after Vatican II was not in the Catholic Church, but the Orthodox. In the year 2006 complete reconciliation and the re-establishment of full communion was achieved between the Moscow patriarch and the Russian Church in exile. The schism occurred after the revolution of 1917 because the exiles in western Europe could not repose confidence in the Russian bishops who had been nominated by the communist (atheist) government. The reconciliation followed a few years

---

[25] Häring, B. op.cit. p.27.

after the end of communist rule in Russia, which enabled the Church there to break free of the control of the State.

The long term goals of ecumenism being realistic unity between different Christian Churches, will take a long time to achieve. In the mean time ordinary life does not stand still, and the different Christian Churches pursue their habitual practices in presenting Christianity to the societies in which they live, collaborating wherever possible with other Christians, doing their best to be faithful to the gospel, within the community life and organisational structures which I have described in this chapter.

CHAPTER SIX: JESUS THE LIBERATOR

SECTION 1: THE CONTEXT OF WIDESPREAD EVIL

The divinity of Jesus is unquestionably the central defining belief of all Christians, which marks us off from the other great world religions. At first sight it might appear to be a somewhat theoretical question destined for the intellectual exercises of philosophically minded theologians. Yet from the very first generations of Christians it was dealt with as something severely practical. That is to say, unless Jesus was divine he could not have rescued the human race from evil in all its forms and consequences. To appreciate this, I think it is important to maintain a comprehensive view of the evil which has to be overcome. It is not just a question of the individual seeking God's forgiveness for his personal sins. The prevalence of wickedness in human affairs is much more widespread than that.

Traditionally Christian theology has understood the widespread prevalence of evil in the context of original sin, which means evil in everyone going back to the very beginnings of the human race. St. Paul was the first to stress its importance and he elaborated it in relation to the totality of Christ's work of liberating all human beings from the thrall of evil. St. Paul's most thorough treatment of the matter is in the letter to the Romans (1: 18 - 23, 5:12 - 21, 8: 18 - 23). He connects the universal phenomenon of sinfulness with the well known account of the taking of the forbidden fruit by Adam and Eve as recorded in Genesis chapter three. The doctrine assumed centre stage in Christian polemics at the end of the fourth century when St. Augustine was in dispute with Pelagius. The latter had expounded a view of the moral capabilities of human nature which was so optimistic that the grace of God was not required for a good life. St. Augustine maintained that human nature on its own was not capable of that kind of goodness. We need the grace of God, because what we are called to is a supernatural vocation of intimacy with God.

During the middle ages Aquinas refined the theology of grace and original sin. He maintained that the essence of original sin is the absence of grace which ought to be there if humanity is to fulfil its authentic vocation as destined for it by God. This view of Aquinas has the advantage to the modern mind that it is not intrinsically tied up with the literalist interpretation of the account of Adam and Eve's sin in Genesis Chapter Three. For the ancients that was a mythological way of teaching that the whole human race was inescapably in a state of alienation from God.

In the context of the liberation effected by Jesus, the comprehensive repairing of all the effects of evil extends to undoing the consequences of personal sin by reconciliation with God and restitution to people whom we have injured. It also includes giving human beings enough moral strength to endure persecution and other forms of injustice without becoming crushed psychologically or morally degraded. Finally it includes a person's acquisition of enough moral strength to undertake reforms of corrupt institutions, like the slave trade, in order to free the victims of such systems so that they can lead normal lives in conditions which could be called civilised.

The adverse pressure in all the categories of inter personal evil which I have mentioned are ultimately moral choices made by the ill will of freely acting human beings. That is what I mean by comprehensive atonement, and I think that it does justice to the earliest prayer on the matter in the life of Jesus. I refer to the Benedictus which is spoken by Zachary in the gospel of St. Luke . The crucial lines are as follows (Luke 1: 71 - 75)

"that we should be saved from our enemies , and from the hand of all who hate us;
to perform the mercy promised to our fathers, and to remember his holy covenant,
the oath which he swore to our father Abraham to grant us
that we, being delivered from the had of our enemies, might serve him without fear,
in holiness and righteousness before him all the days of our life."

That programme of restoration set the pattern for the life and work of Jesus and it explains why Jesus was given the title of Liberator. It is a term which I will use in preference to other well known titles such as Redeemer or Saviour, because they have been evacuated of their full force by over exposure and have been debased in the mediocre poetry of third rate hymns and prayers. Moreover, in modern English the word Liberator is the most exact rendering of the Greek terms used in the New Testament, which are in turn translations of the basic Hebrew concept of being rescued, or delivered from evil, be it moral or physical danger, or illness.

Having indicated the technical terms which I dislike in this context, I wish to indicate one for which I have a strong predilection, namely the term Atonement, because it is so positive. As is well known it is a composite word combining three elements at - one- ment, aptly describing the restoration of unity between the human race and its Maker. It entered the English language in the sixteenth century and one cannot but admire the unknown genius who invented it.

The early Christians treated the divinity of Jesus as a practical matter because they were fully aware of just how much wickedness there was in the world, and they were equally persuaded that no human being, or indeed any creature, was powerful enough to overcome that unfathomable quantity of badness in past history and present experience. If the human beings were to be reconciled to God and to each other the agent of that gigantic enterprise would have to be endowed with power and qualities which no mere creature could ever lay claim to. In short, the success of the enterprise depended upon his being divine, and therefor endowed with unlimited powers.

SECTION 2 : THE PROCESS OF ATONEMENT

In the course of two millennia of Christian theologising, several theories have been put forward as to how the transaction was effected. For the sake of clarity I will deal with this aspect of the theology of atonement before passing on to examine how the Church came to a progressively deeper appreciation of the divinity of Jesus.

Some of the theories on the atonement have relied too heavily on concepts of sacrifice draw from primitive pagan religions, and from the oldest parts of the Old Testament, when the ancient Israelites still harboured notions about God's anger which were not yet very different from their outlook before the true God revealed himself to Abraham. For example they considered earthquakes and devastating storms as signs of God's anger, which they sought to placate by sacrifices, which were quasi compensation for their offences against God. The notion of an angry God thirsting for blood vengeance has been exaggerated in modern times, but it has acted as negative publicity for Christianity in the minds of many good people.

For a long time, Christians have been sensitive to that kind of allegation, in the quest for what one might designate as the causal process of the atonement: what actually produced the result? In the middle ages St. Anselm proposed a solution which avoided one set of difficulties, but failed to get to the root of the problem. However, his theory has been so influential that I must pause to explain it briefly. He was well aware that there could be no question of a juridical transaction between God and humans in the making of compensation to God for our evils, precisely because we are not equal to God. Transactions in the realm of justice, including infringements of rights and compensations thereof, only take place between equals, who can claim rights from one another. St.Anselm overcame this problem by saying that the sins of mankind did not injure the rights of God, but they constituted an affront to his honour. With the passage of time one can see how much that theory was influenced by the sociology and class distinctions of mediaeval society. According to St. Anselm the death of Jesus was a heroic undertaking of infinite worth because he was divine, and so the balance of honour was satisfied, and the Father could welcome back his errant creatures into peace and concord, without any fictitious whitewashing of their sins.

On sober reflection it is clear that all such theories are extrapolations from the parallel concepts of compensation for material damage or financial fraud, and they cannot be applied to God. Moreover a careful reading of the New Testament makes it clear that nowhere in its pages is the atonement presented as a compensation to appease the displeasure or anger of God. What the New Testament yields is about half a dozen differing theologies of the atonement, with no attempt to harmonise them. Sacrifice is indeed spoken of in the context of the death of Jesus, but there is no sense that it was demanded by God the Father, nor is any causal link demonstrated between his pain and our receiving the Father's benevolence. Because the practice of sacrifices in the temples of the Jews and pagans was so widespread at the time, it should not surprise us that the crucifixion should have been described as a sacrifice by the writers of the New Testament. Indeed the term was still used in the twentieth century when soldiers killed in warfare were described as having made the supreme sacrifice.

A satisfactory understanding of the "economics" of the atonement (if one may use such a term) can best be approached by looking at the different theologies of the matter as presented by the New Testament, of which there are about half a dozen. The Church has never made a dogmatic definition about the cause of the redemption, probably because the debates on the matter have never threatened the unity of the Church, and possibly because the authors of the New Testament seem to have been content to present several theologies on the matter without being anxious to harmonise them. After all they are complementary and not mutually exclusive.

I will give a list of the half dozen schemes, but it would be outside the scope of this book to explain them all in detail. The first ascribes the causality simply to the resurrection of Jesus (ICor. 15:17, Romans 4:25, and Hebrews 5: 8 & 9), next is the theory of the perfection of Jesus though suffering, thus making him the liberator (Hebrews 2: 10 & 11). In Luke the suffering of Jesus is presented as a pre-condition of the liberating work (24:26 and 24: 45 – 47). The whole of the liberation is ascribed to the Holy Spirit in Titus (3: 4 – 7). Finally the complete causality is assigned to the intercession of Jesus in Romans 8: 33 & 34, as well as Hebrews 7: 23 – 25.

Having indicated a variety of theologies of liberation in the New Testament, it is worth while mentioning that the overall tendency of the Greek Fathers was to ascribe the causal role for humanity's redemption to the plain fact of the Incarnation itself. It is as if the Incarnation had established the great bridge between the human race and the infinite God, in relation to which all intermediate mechanisms were of relatively minor significance.

Having sketched out the broad canvass, I wish to develop a little further the theology of Intercession. The gospels record about a dozen instances where Jesus forgave the sins of different individuals. His consistent attitude in the matter of reconciliation is made clear in his dialogue with Peter (Matthew 18:21), "Then Peter came up and said to him, Lord how often shall my brother sin against me and I forgive him ? As many as seven times? Jesus said to him I do not say to you seven times, but seventy times seven." Since the constant theme of the teaching of Jesus is that forgiveness follows a sincere repentance, combined with a request for reconcilliation, it is reasonable to extrapolate that principle to the much wider context of the whole human race seeking reconciliation with God.

Before pursuing that line of enquiry further, it is important to pause and attempt to harmonise the theology of reconciliation with that of sacrifice. Although there is no question in the New Testament that God the Father demanded blood sacrifice as the price of restoring humanity to his favour, the death of Jesus is frequently described as a sacrifice of some sort. If the notion of sacrifice is pared down to its essentials one can see that it is legitimate to speak of the crucifixion in this way, without implying that the Father was being vengeful or bloodthirsty. In seeking to identify the essential elements of sacrifice I confine myself to the Old Testament sacrifices. This was the background from which both Jews and Christians drew their ideas. The concept of sacrifice in other religions is too vast to cover, and much of it contains elements which are inimical to revealed monotheism. The essential elements of Israelite sacrifice have been identified by Roland de Vaux as follows:- It is the giving of a gift to God by the worshipper, it is a sign of loyalty (and all that goes with his commitment to God), its destruction signified the irrevocability of the gift, and the performance of the rite in a holy place signified its transference to the invisible world. An element of compensation for sin might or might not be present depending on the circumstances.[1] When those elements are applied to the crucifixion and resurrection of Jesus, one can see that it was an authentic sacrifice. His death was irrevocable, and the resurrection effected

[1] de Vaux. R, (1961), *Ancient Israel, Its Life and Institutions,* trans. J. McHugh, London: Darton Longman & Todd, pp 451 - 4.

not a symbolic, but a real transfer to the invisible world.

The model for the intercessory role of Jesus was Moses, who interceded for the Israelites. The incident is recorded in Exodus 32: 9 - 14. When Moses was with God on mount Sinai receiving the Decalogue, the people at the foot of the mountain had worshipped the molten calf. God threatened to destroy them for the infidelity, but Moses asked for them to be forgiven. "Moses besought the Lord his God, and said O Lord, why does thy wrath burn hot against thy people, whom thou hast brought forth out of the land of Egypt with great power and with a mighty hand? - - - - - - - - - - - - - - - - -And the Lord repented of the evil which he though to do to his people."

That model of intercession was of a limited scale, but its essentials illustrate the much vaster work of Jesus. The essentials are all there. Moses was qualified to speak on behalf of the people because he was one of them racially by flesh and blood, and at the same time he had been designated as their leader by God. In the case of Jesus, we see the basic connections with the incarnation falling into place. Jesus can intercede for the human race because he is authentically a member of it by flesh and blood. His competence to intercede on our behalf far outstrips the role of Moses. Being divine he is with the Father the creator of the universe and indirectly the ultimate cause of the whole human race. He is therefore perfectly constituted as the mediator for humanity.

Much more could be said on this subject, but having indicated the essentials of the liberation of humanity from evil, I wish to draw attention to the connection with the doctrine of the divinity of Jesus.[2] From the earliest expressions of patristic theology on the subject the conviction was present that his redeeming work could not have been possible unless he was divine in some sense, and they set themselves the task of elucidating that problem without being unfaithful to the basic doctrine of monotheism which they had accepted unalloyed from Judaism.

SECTION 3 : HOW THE DISCIPLES BECAME AWARE
              OF THE DIVINITY OF JESUS

Relatively early in the history of the Church, Christians realised that Jesus was divine from the moment of his conception. Such a gigantic intellectual achievement on their part did not come instantly. It was the result of intense intellectual activity in the first decades after the Resurrection in which the early community, guided by the Holy Spirit, wrestled with the awe inspiring problem of reconciling the divinity of Jesus with the strict monotheism which they inherited integrally from Judaism. At that time they did not yet have an adequate theological terminology for for such a profound question. What they had to unravel was basically these daunting and difficult questions: at what time in his life did Jesus become divine ? When did he realise that he was divine ? How did he relate that awareness to the one God of Jewish revelation ? And by what stages did his disciples come to appreciate (I will not say, understand) those profound

---

[2] I have dealt with the subject at more length in a modest volume which I entitled *The Atonement,* (1995) Collegeville, Minnesota: The Liturgical Press. .

realities ?

The intricate problems indicated in the previous paragraph may perhaps become clearer by comparison with a similar situation in the life of a purely human person, namely Queen Victoria.

When the young Victoria was still a child, her father the Duke of York, died. He was a younger brother of the reigning king George IV, which already set her among the possible heirs to the throne. After her father's death, she being the only child of that marriage, there was no possibility that a younger brother might be borne to take precedence over her rank . As other members of the immediate royal family died, or their wives passed the age of child-bearing, it became more and more clear, to her mother at least, that the young Victoria might well be the next sovereign. Her mother concealed the likelihood of so great a responsibility from her young daughter, in case it might worry her. The servants were not allowed to speak about it.

With the death of George IV in 1830 it was inevitable that the young Victoria would eventually be the sovereign. Although he was immediately succeeded by his brother William IV, the succession would not pass through him since all his legitimate children had died in infancy. As she was only eleven at that time her mother and her governess, Baroness Lehzen stage-managed the disclosure with some care. On 11 th March 1830 she was having a history lesson with her governess, reading a book about the history of the kings and queens of England. On that day she noticed a page, inserted in the book, which she had not seen before, containing the family tree of the immediate predecessors on the throne. The young princess remarked to her governess "I never saw that before", to which Baroness Lehzen replied "No princess, it was not thought necessary that you should". The princess studied the page a little longer and then remarked " I am nearer to the throne than I thought". Then she burst into tears. [3]

There is an instructive parallel for the subject of this chapter. There was a young girl who was the heir to the throne, but she did not know it. The fact of her being unaware of her awesome destiny did not alter the reality of her position in the slightest. Gradually her immediate entourage all shared the knowledge, as did the rest of the nation eventually, with her accession to the throne, on the death of her uncle William IV in 1837. The parallel is not exact, but it serves as some kind of illustration of the difficult problem as to how the disciples of Jesus became aware of the reality that he had come to appreciate at an earlier stage in his life. The fact that it was appreciated only gradually did not in any way minimise the reality of the stupendous truth which was there all along, and was gradually recognised.

The principal difference in the two parallel cases is that the main revelatory event in the life of Jesus was his resurrection. That stupendous event, without parallel before or since, completely transformed the disciples' perception of Jesus. After that event, they came to realise that he was divine, but we do not know precisely how long it took for that incredible idea to take shape in their minds. Once it had been appreciated and formulated in some sort of communicable

---

[3] The incident is recorded in Longford,E.(1964) *Victoria R.I.* London: Weidenfeld & Nicholson, p.32.

88

terminology, they were able to look back on the public life of Jesus, and see its whole course in a

new light. In the context of that subsequent enlightened understanding, some of them composed narratives of important events or speeches, which were subsequently incorporated into the four canonical gospels. It was in the light of the new understanding of Jesus after the Resurrection that they crafted their accounts of the life and deeds of Jesus in the time of his public ministry.

The later writings in the New Testament contain remarkably clear statements about the divinity of Jesus. Earlier writings do not have the same precision of expression. They express the truth in less sophisticated terminology, but it would be false to infer that the reality was being created over the course of time in which those texts were being written. A vast literature exists on this subject, namely the stages by which the earliest Christian community became progressively aware of what was entailed in the fantastic realisation that Jesus was divine, and how they struggled to create the vocabulary and technical terminology in which to express it. Such an achievement could not have come instantaneously. It lies outside the scope of this book to pursue that development in detail. [4] But I will discuss briefly half a dozen passages from the New Testament to illustrate the main outlines of the development.

For the sake of clarity I will start with the latest text and move backwards. The prologue of St. John's Gospel contains an explicit statement of the divinity of Jesus and his relationship to the Father in what can be seen as technical terms designed for the purpose. The Greek word *theos* (God) is used with and without the definite article. The dense passage makes most sense if we understand that "the God" means what we would would describe as "God the Father", whereas in the absence of the definite article it is to be understood as "the divine nature". With this, somewhat stilted use of words , one can translate the first verses of the gospel as follows :-
>   " In the beginning was the Word,
>   and the Word was with the God,
>   and the Word was Divine.
>   He was in the beginning
>   with the God.

The employment of "the beginning " is a clear reference to the first words of Genesis , the beginning of time, when God created the universe. Later in the chapter, at verse 14 the evangelist makes the connection with the human Jesus in these words:-
>   "And the Word became flesh
>   and dwelt among us,
>   and we have seen his glory
>   as the only one born of the Father,
>   full of grace and truth."

---

[4] Among the vast number of books on the subject I would recommend two admirable introductions, namely Moule, C.D.F.(1977),*The Origin of Christology,* Cambridge: Cambridge University Press. And, Brown, R.E.(1994) *An Introduction to New Testament Christology,* London: Geoffrey Chapman.

In those few lines the whole of the theology of the divinity of Jesus and the relationship of the divine and human in his person is contained in germ. It is so profound and so concisely expressed

that it should not surprise us that it took several hundred years for its full significance to be appreciated. But there it is. At the end of the first century the Church had an unambiguous statement about the divinity of Jesus. Although I have presented it as the clearest statement on the matter, it is by no means the only one. Nor did it come out of a vacuum. The few other passages which I will analyse briefly will make it clear that a whole theological tradition was moving consistently towards greater and greater precision on this very same matter.

The well known hymn in Philippians 2: 5 - 11 may have been an older composition which St. Paul incorporated into his letter as it stood. The divinity of Jesus is indicated by a semitic literary device which one could describe as implied equivalence, because the author lifts a significant sentence out of Deutero Isaiah. For the sake of clarity I will quote the whole hymn:-
5) Have this mind among yourselves which was in Christ Jesus,
6) who, though he was in the form of God
did not count equality with God a thing to be grasped,
7) but emptied himself, taking the form of a servant ,
being born in the likeness of men.
8) And being found in human form he humbled himself and became obedient unto death,
even death on a cross.
9) Therefore God has highly exalted him
and bestowed on him the name which is above every name
10) that at the name of Jesus every knee should bow,
in heaven and on earth and under the earth,
11) and every tongue confess that Jesus Christ is Lord, to the glory of God the Father.

Verses 10 and 11 are an obvious borrowing of the powerful monotheistic speech in Isaiah 45: 22, 23, "For I am God , and there is no other. - - - - -*To me every knee shall bow , every tongue confess* ". The resemblance is unmistakable in the Greek version of Isaiah. [5]

An equally powerful claim to divinity is recorded from the lips of Jesus in St. Mark's gospel. The setting is the trial of Jesus before the Jewish High Priest. The high priest questioned him explicitly about his status with the words (Mark 14: 61) " Are you the Christ the son of the Blessed ?" And Jesus said "I am; and you will see the Son of Man sitting at the right hand of Power and coming with the clouds of heaven." In addition to Jesus's explicit affirmation of the question asked, the Jewish equivalents for God which he employed (whose direct naming was avoided out of a sense of extreme reverence) made his meaning perfectly clear. Moreover he combines it with an identification of himself with the heavenly Messianic figure of Daniel 7:13. Lest any doubt should linger, the assembly understood it as a claim to divinity and condemned him to death for blasphemy.

---

[5] cf. Moule, C.F.D. op.cit. p.41.

Paradoxically some of the clearest affirmations of the divinity of Jesus are to be found in the

infancy narrative of Luke, using what I have described above as the method of implied equivalence. When Mary learnt that her kinswoman Elizabeth was pregnant, she set out to visit her. This is no ordinary visit, since the literary genius who composed the passage is preparing his readers for a special message. Elizabeth states that as soon as she heard Mary's greeting the child in her womb leaped for joy (Luke 1: 44). The use of the word "leap" is deliberate. Unborn children in the womb do indeed move, but they do not leap. The author is directing the attention of his readers to King David who danced before the Ark of the Covenant (II Samuel 6: 14, 16) leaping about with all his might. This was to prepare the readers (or hearers) for the punch line: "Mary remained with her about three months, and returned to her home". This is a direct reference to II Samuel 6:11, where it is recorded that the Ark of the Lord remained in the house of Obededom for about *three months*. Jewish readers (or listeners) of that era could not have failed to understand the message. [6] The Ark of the Covenant was regarded as the dwelling place of God among men. Who was dwelling in Mary ? The answer was obvious, but the author relied on the audience to make the deduction. One must remember that in largely non-literate cultures peoples' memories are much more retentive than in our own situation. Moreover for most of them the bible was the only book with which they were familiar thanks to its being read publicly in the synagogue week by week.

In the same part of Luke, (1:16) the angel tells Zachary that his son will " turn many of the sons of Israel to the Lord their God, and he will go before him in the spirit and power of Elijah". After the birth of the boy, Zachary, having recovered the power of speech, addresses the infant with the words: "And you child, will be called the prophet of the Most High; for you will go before the Lord to prepare his ways, " (This is an implicit allusion to Malachi 3:1 and 4:5, concerning the coming of God). When all of this was incorporated in the gospel of St. Luke, the listeners would be aware that John the Baptist had prepared the way before Jesus which was a clear method of indicating that Jesus was God. [7]

SECTION 4 : THE EARLY CHURCH CLARIFIES THE DOCTRINE

As so many books have been written about the scriptural basis for our belief in the divinity of Jesus, I will not pursue the matter further in this study, but I wish now to direct the reader's attention to the painful process by which the Church assimilated the profound and mysterious doctrine that Jesus was both human and divine. The immediate aftermath of the period in which the New Testament was composed represents an apparent regress from the lofty ideas of the inspired books. This fact was commented on by Newman in his study of the development of

---

[6] Some years ago, when teaching undergraduates, I used to ask them to identify the source of the four words "New lamps for old". It is surprising how many people immediately recognise Alladin and his Lamp, in a culture which has literally thousands of books at its disposal.

[7] For these reflections on the infancy narrative of Luke I am indebted to R. Laurentin, *Structure et Théologie de Luc I - II* , Paris 1964, Gabalda, passim, but especially. pp 58 and 79.

doctrine. This was the stage of apparent regression because the inspired writers of the biblical books were followed by authors who were not endowed with the gift of inspiration, and whose

descriptions of the life and work of Jesus were not as profound as those found in the pages of the New Testament. The overall attitude of the early Church was overshadowed by some writers whose attitude seems to have been "it's too good to be true". The Church steered an orthodox path between those who considered that the body of Jesus must have been no more than an appearance, and others who considered that connection with the divine was no more than great holiness in an unusually saintly human being. The Church's staunch affirmation that Jesus was both divine and human ultimately led to theological disputes of a gigantic scale which threatened the unity of the Church. The intellectual climate in which those disputes took place was that of Greek philosophy, which furnished concepts and methods of elucidation which were new to the Church whose origins had been semitic and and whose thought patterns had been strictly biblical.

In the early fourth century, Arius, a priest of the church of St.Baucalis in Alexandria put forward a theory about the nature of Jesus which was destined to split the Church In essence he taught that Jesus was a very high grade creature. This theory avoided the intellectual difficulty of reconciling the divinity of Jesus with traditional monotheism, but it failed to do justice to the traditional doctrine, derived from the New Testament, that Jesus was divine. In 318 Alexander, the bishop of Alexandria, summoned a council of the bishops of Egypt to settle the matter. At this council Arius was condemned as was his theory, but a positive doctrinal statement had not yet been formulated. Arius did not accept the decision of the council, and sought allies in the Greek speaking world. In fact he found considerable support and the dispute became more widespread. All parties took the matter seriously, as they realised that it was not just an intellectual debate between scholars, but the bedrock of Christianity, namely the reality of the liberating work of Jesus was at stake. As I have pointed out earlier in this book, Christians realised that Jesus could not have liberated the whole human race from evil unless he was divine. The disputes became so bitter that the unity of the Church was under threat. At that point the emperor Constantine intervened, realising that a divided Church could undermine the unity of the empire. He took the established conciliar principle one stage further and summoned a universal council. In other words the bishops of the whole universal Church were invited. In the event not all of them came. Only a handful came from the western half of the empire. Probably a number of about 250 assembled in 325 at Nicaea, a town in the north west of modern Turkey, close to Constantinople.

The bishops at the council re-affirmed the condemnation of Arius and his theory. To prevent a further recrudescence of the error they drew up the famous Nicaean creed, which with additions by the second ecumenical council at Constantinople (381) is recited in the Sunday liturgies of all the main Christian Churches to this day. To put an end to all uncertainty the bishops agreed upon the technical term *homoousios*, meaning of one substance. In other words the Father and the Son were of the same divine nature and therefore equal. Underlying this phraseology was the understanding of the distinction between nature and person. The Father and Son were two distinct persons, but they shared the same one divine nature. There was some reluctance at the council about incorporating the word *homoousios* into a profession of faith, since it did not occur in the Scriptures. However the council had to cope with a problem which had not occurred during the time when the New Testament books were being written, and it was considered reasonable to

employ a non-scriptural term to a problem which had occurred after the New Testament had been written.

The impressive gathering of bishops, and the brilliantly thought out credal formula should have settled the matter once and for all. However the affairs of the Church do not always follow the path of reasonableness and good sense, and the aftermath of Nicaea is one of the worst examples of calamity. The emperor Constantine continued his involvement exiling Arius to Illyria, but then recalled him in 328. After Constantine's death his son Constantius openly espoused the Arian cause, and removed orthodox bishops from their dioceses, until all the principal cities of the empire had Arian bishops. During this period of continuous crisis the champion of Nicene orthodoxy was Athanasius, who had been elected as bishop of Alexandria in 328, but who was destined to spend more time in exile and in hiding than in peaceful occupation of his bishopric. Despite the difficulties and hazards of constantly moving to evade arrest he devoted his energies to writing endless letters and treatises against the Arians, and upholding the decision of Nicaea. After the death of Constantius in 361 the exiled bishops were recalled by the new emperor Julian. Athanasius was able to return to Alexandria, was re-instated as bishop, and died peacefully in 373. Arianism did not die out so quickly, but the major crisis was over, and it lies outside the scope of this book to pursue in detail the final demise of the heresy.

A significant milestone in that complicated process was the Second Ecumenical Council held at Constantinople in the 381. It had been summoned by the emperor Theodosius to bring order into the affairs of the Church. One hundred and fifty bishops attended, and it has always been ranked as the second of the Church's General Councils. The creed of Nicaea was re-affirmed, and a minor heresy that of the Macedonians was condemned, because they denied the divinity of the Holy Spirit. That heresy was not as serious as Arianism, and its resolution was less complicated because the principles worked out in relation to the divinity of the Son, were applied quite simply to the Holy Spirit. In other words, the distinction between nature and person was applied once again, affirming the divinity of the person of the Holy Spirit, who shared the one divine nature with the Father and the Son. In a sense it was an easier elucidation than the status of the Son, because the incarnation entailed further intellectual problems whose understanding would convulse the Church in the next century. The divinity of the Holy Spirit is proclaimed in the extended version of the Nicaean Creed which has been associated with that Council, but whose origin in perhaps more complicated.

Once the divinity of the Son had been guaranteed at Nicaea, it was inevitable that Christian thinkers would address themselves to elucidating the relationship between the divine and human elements in Jesus. Before examining this second stage of theological elaboration, it is important not to loose sight of the mysterious character of the deity and the incarnation. The theologians of that period were well aware that they were attempting to understand a limited amount about the God who is infinite. They never claimed to aim for comprehensive understanding of his nature, and the general councils which safeguarded true doctrine against heresy never envisaged that they could explain the divinity in full. Their decisions should be regarded as negative defences closing off paths which would led to distortions or falsehood if pursued any further.

The first major theory which I will consider is that which is called Nestorianism, though it is uncertain whether the putative author of the theory really taught it in the terms in which it was later condemned.[8] Nestorius was the bishop of Constantinople, and in his preaching against various heretical groups in the city he publicised a theory about the incarnation which was claimed to be erroneous. The dispute became bitter. The emperor became alarmed, and intervened (which usually made matters worse). He summoned a council to meet at Ephesus on the feast of Pentecost, June 7th , 431. The proceedings were chaotic and disedifying, but the Roman legates managed to introduce a measure of order into the scene. Eventually the theory of Nestorius was condemned as heretical and he was deposed.[9]

His theory had the advantage of simplicity, and at the rational level it is not a theoretically impossible position. Basically the idea was that Jesus who walked the roads of Palestine was a human person closely united to a divine person. At the risk of much over simplification one can say that there were four elements in him, a human nature and person, together with a divine nature and person, closely linked in moral harmony. Such an explanation contains no intrinsic contradictions, but the early Church realised that it did not do justice to the New Testament picture of Jesus. In the words and actions of Jesus there was always just one person who spoke claiming responsibility for both human and divine activities, such as "I and the Father are one", or "I thirst". Examples like these could be multiplied at length, because the gospels are constant in presenting Jesus as one person.

Although an erroneous theory had been rejected at Ephesus, the Christian thinkers had not worked out a positive account of the divine and human elements in Jesus. Twenty years of theological reflection ensued during which the matter was debated. Once again debates turned into disputes, personal rivalries entered into what should have been a dispassionate quest for truth, and various parties accused their opponents of heresy.

Bitter controversy was sparked off by the teaching of Eutyches who was the superior of a monastery in Constantinople. In order to compensate for the excessive divisions introduced into Christ by the dualism of Nestorianism, Eutyches stressed the close unity of the human and the divine, saying that the human nature of Jesus was absorbed into the divine nature like a rain drop into the ocean. In effect he was over - reacting against the two nature two person picture in Nestorianism by presenting a theory which was in effect one person and one nature in Jesus. This theory was disputed by various bishops and scholars in the Eastern part of the Church. From the start Flavian, the peace loving bishop of Constantinople, had tried to keep out of the disputes.

---

[8]   A useful introduction to the question as to whether Nestorius really held the theory which was condemned as Nestorianism, can be found in Grillmeier,A.(1965), *Christ in Christian Tradition* , trans. J. S. Bowden, London: Mowbrays, pp.496 - 505.

[9] Denziger - Schönmetzer, *Enchiridion Symboloroum,* number 264.

However he could not evade involvement after Eusebius of Doryleum formally accused Eutyches of heresy, in the course of a local synod in Constantinople in 448. Reluctantly Flavian commanded Eutyches to appear before the synod to answer for his orthodoxy. After much

evasiveness, he was obliged to state the core of his theory, namely that there was only one nature in the incarnate Christ. The synod judged that this was heretical, he was condemned and removed from his position of authority in the monastery.

Eutyches did not accept the decision of the synod, and sought support from many quarters. All the latent theological and political rivalries in the East were once again stirred up. The emperor intervened and summoned a council to meet at Ephesus in 449. It proved to be disaster, in which truth was lost sight of. Violence prevailed, and Flavian was arrested with such brutality that he died a few days afterwards. Pope Leo the Great refused to accept its decisions. Thanks to Leo's determination a regular council was held at Chalcedon in 451 which agreed the famous definition the two natures and one person of Jesus Christ. This definition which has been so important for all subsequent understanding of christology deserves to have its centre- piece quoted verbatim :-

" Following, then, the holy Fathers , we all with one voice teach that it should be confessed that our Lord Jesus Christ is - - - - - One and the same Christ, Son, Lord, Only begotten, made known in two natures (which exist) without confusion, without change, without division, without separation; the difference of the natures having been in no wise taken away by reason of the union, but rather the properties of each being preserved, and (both) concurring into one Person and one *hypostasis* - not parted or divided into two persons, but one and the same Son and Only begotten, the divine Logos, the Lord Jesus Christ; even as the prophets from of old (have spoken) concerning him , and as the Lord Jesus Christ himself has taught us, and as the Symbol of the Fathers has delivered to us."[10]

This magnificent definition represents what Newman would call a development on the New Testament picture of Jesus on account of the rational precision of its terminology. Like the creed of Nicaea it introduces technical terms from Greek philosophy precisely because that philosophical culture had given rise to intellectual difficulties unknown to the writers of the New Testament. The decision at Chalcedon had clarified the position of Jesus, it had closed off a source of serious error, but it had not closed future intellectual enquiry. Just as the fifth century Christians had gained a deeper insight into the life of the Liberator thanks to the intellectual achievements of their culture, the same process was destined to repeat itself again in the history of the Church.

 Expressing the Council's pronouncement in the simplest terms, and with some degree of over - simplification, it can be said that Jesus is presented to us as having a normal human nature like the rest of the human race. It confirms the meagre information about his childhood which is contained in the gospels. In Luke chapter 2 verse 40 we read "And the child grew and became strong filled with wisdom and the favour of God was with him". Next comes the narrative of

---

[10] Original Greek text in Denziger - Schönmetzer, op. cit. numbers 301, 302, and English translation in Grillmeier, A. op. cit. p.481.

the loss and finding of the child Jesus aged twelve:- "And Jesus increased in wisdom and in stature, and in favour with God and man." Without entering into detailed exegesis of those verses, I think it is reasonable to deduce from them that the child Jesus grew up normally, with his emotions and intellectual development proceeding like that of other children.

SECTION 5 : REFINEMENTS IN THE MODERN PERIOD

In the area of his intellectual progress there has been a notable development of understanding, thanks to the advances of modern psychology over the limitations of the mediaeval understanding of the human psyche. In antiquity Christian thinking about the intellectual perfection of the human soul of Jesus was strongly influenced by the outlook of Greek philosophy. For them knowledge was good and ignorance was a defect.[11] Following from this standpoint, and bearing in mind that Christ was perfect, Christian thinkers made extravagant claims for the extent of his human knowledge. In the middle ages the same Greek inspired influence was at work, and St. Thomas Aquinas literally crams into the human intellect of Jesus an unbelievable amount of knowledge.[12] In the light of modern psychology we can see that an unlimited quantity of facts stored in the brain is not necessarily a human perfection.

Karl Rahner has indicated the general outlines of a more satisfactory understanding of the development of the human intellect of Jesus. The starting point is the clear evidence in the New Testament that Jesus experienced the human emotions of sorrow, weeping, fear, and a sense of desolation. He exercised true freedom and made moral choices, the most virtuous of which was the decision in Gethsemane to go forward to a martyr's death. For the real exercise of freedom a measure of "not-knowing" is necessary. Rahner calls it nescience, to distinguish it from ignorance, which might have pejorative overtones. In the more general context of his whole life , Jesus's human self consciousness would have developed, over time, like ours, in which the individual gradually moves from ignorance to greater knowledge of reality via the ordinary experiences of everyday life. This process is not an imperfection but a manifestation of normality. In view of these considerations Rahner stated (and I simplify his long sentence) that Jesus "should not be regarded as a walking encyclopaedia".[13] In other words, his human knowledge developed like that of any other human being, and remained to some extent within the limits of his historical culture.

In bringing this chapter to a close, I do not wish to leave the reader with a picture of Jesus which might seem to be too much dissected by the requirements of philosophical investigation. A healthy antidote to such a slant is to recall the picture of Jesus in the popular mediaeval culture. I

[11] Rahner, K.(1966), *Theological Investigations,* trans. K. Smith, London: Darton,Longman, and Todd, Vol. 5, p.201.

[12] The details can be read in the *Summa Theologica.* Part 3, questions 9 - 11.

[13] Rahner, K. op.cit. p. 214. Readers wishing to pursue a fuller study of this matter are recommended to read in that volume, the whole of chapter 9, entitled " Dogmatic Reflections on the Knowledge and Self Consciousness of Christ ".

can only speak for the English scene, but I earnestly recommend my readers to reflect on the beauty of the mediaeval Christmas carols and the mystery plays. In the context of their charming simplicity and beauty they convey an understanding of Jesus which is hard to improve upon. They are the expressions of a genuinely popular culture in which there is a profound grasp of the

theology of the incarnation. These insights are presented to the imagination of the audience by imagery which must be described as brilliant. Some years ago, the Coventry Cycle of plays was produced in London. The role of God the Father was played by a large man with a shaved head who spoke with a strong Geordie accent, and who was raised or lowered between heaven and earth on a machine like a fork-lift truck. It is difficult to convey in writing the impact of that performance, but in the theatre the effect was one of complete and perfect reverence. That, I think, is a fitting commentary on how our mediaeval ancestors appreciated the reality and sublimity of the incarnation.

CHAPTER SEVEN : GRACE AND THE SACRAMENTS

SECTION 1 : GRACE

The reality which Christians describe as grace can only be understood properly in relation to human badness for which it is the remedy. In Chapter One I dwelt at length on the extent and gravity of evil in the world. It may be helpful at this stage to recall just how widespread and deeply rooted it is in human nature and experience. Sadly it is difficult to know where to start since there is so much material to draw upon. People who are old enough to have clear memories of the twentieth century are the best witnesses to my contention. The two European wars of that century, which with their attendant evils, spilled over into the rest of the world are too enormous to be ignored.

In addition to the wars, the same century also witnessed the cruellest revolutions, namely in Russia and China. The latter nation representing another highly sophisticated culture backed up by centuries of refined intellectual and artistic development. Those two revolutions produced almost as many violent deaths as the two European wars.[1]

Fundamentally the Christian evaluation of evil is not one of pessimism, but an extremely positive attitude since the liberating work of Jesus, described in the previous chapter, has provided the remedy for that propensity to badness. The remedy in question is a divine gift available to all human beings, which is the interior spiritual transformation of the individual enabling him to live a normally virtuous life instead of being trapped in the behaviour of greed, violence, and lies. This transforming gift has been given the technical name Grace, to stress that is is a gift, which is beyond the capabilities of human nature, of which history has all too much evidence.

Functionally the presence and operation of grace in the human soul, can best be viewed as the combination of faith, hope, and charity. This means that the redeemed individual is now enabled to view the world in a totally different light (faith), he has the confidence to pursue a higher standard of behaviour for himself and the rest of society (hope), and he has the motive to act with love instead of selfishness (charity). This latter is extremely important because one way or another he will have to bestow generous love upon people who are not really very attractive or loveable from the purely human standpoint. In case the claim about looking at the world in a different light should seem unrealistic, let me quote an example. A few years ago a friend of mine was taking an acquaintance on an informal guided tour of Cambridge. They stopped for lunch and in the afternoon she asked him if he would like to see some more. To that he replied that he saw no point at looking more old buildings, they all looked the same to him, and he settled down to watch television for the whole of the afternoon. The young man in question was not unintelligent. He had recently completed his university studies (not at Cambridge), but he was incapable of perceiving that he was being shown some of the most beautiful and historically significant buildings in England. There was some deficit in his personality which made him unable to perceive a particular kind of beauty. That example

---

[1] For the Russian revolution an admirable account is that of Orlando Figes, *A People's Tragedy,* London: Pimlico, 1996. The Chinese Revolution is best approached through the biography: *Mao, The Unknown Story,* by Jung Chang and Jon Halliday, London: Vintage, 2005.

illustrates how two people can look at the same thing with widely different levels of perception.

The Christians who are endowed with faith are capable of seeing human beings and society in general in a totally different perspective from that of the non-believer. For them human society is full of capabilities for heroic goodness, provided that the impulse comes from grace. I do not imply that all non - believers are leading immoral lives. My contention is that the transformation of the human race to something better than the pattern of the twentieth century (for example), requires something more powerful than the resources of common decency. Just how fragile is the pattern of ordinary decency can be seen once more by reflecting on the Second World War. How many ordinary men found themselves joining the armed forces through conscription or social pressure which they could not resist. Once in the ranks, of the air force, for instance, they might then volunteer or be selected for air crew. By incremental stages those same decent men would find themselves taking part in the night bombing of Germany, creating fire storms in which countless women and children were killed. In one air raid on Hamburg in July 1943 a fire storm was created which killed more than 40,000 people in one night. Yet how many men refused to take part in such indiscriminate barbarity? There are no records of any refusals.

Moving from the functional manifestations of grace, one must try to penetrate the reality more deeply and try to understand something of its mysterious inner essence. Among the various descriptions offered by the New Testament, several stand out with particular clarity. The first of them which I will consider is St. John's description of grace as a form of life. The believer commits himself to Christ in faith , and the reward is life: not just biological life which we all have, but something richer. Quoting the words of Jesus he states " I have come that they may have life and have it abundantly"(John 10:10). What is special about this life is that it is eternal, and this supra mundane quality is present here and now. This sharing of life with God is illustrated in the parable of the vine and the branches. " I am the vine, you are the branches. He who abides in me and I in him, he it is that bears much fruit, for apart from me you can do nothing."(John 15:5). It is this sharing of life, initially with Jesus which enables the believer to have relationships of intimacy with the Father, with Jesus, and with the Holy Spirit. About these relationships I will have more to say in the chapter on Prayer.

St.Paul' favourite image of the life of grace is that of a human body. The underlying reality of a shared life is implied throughout, but St. Paul focusses his attention on the person of Christ whom he likens to the head of the body, on account of its superior position, and the believers are like the limbs. This model of the life of grace has the advantage that it conveys quite simply the factor of solidarity which means that the Christians benefit one another, automatically one might say, just as the various organs of the body cannot enjoy health or weakness independently, but all thrive or suffer together. The words of St. Paul cannot be improved upon, and I advise readers to turn to the first Letter to the Corinthians and read carefully chapter 12, verses 12 to 27.

When St. Peter speaks of grace, he makes perhaps the boldest claim of all, reassuring his readers that they share in the divine nature. His own words are :- "His divine power has granted to us all things that pertain to life and godliness, through the knowledge of him who called us to his own glory and excellence, by which he has granted to us his precious and very great promises, that through these you may escape the corruption that is in the world

because of passion, and become partakers of the divine nature."(II Peter 1: 3-4).

A few paragraphs above I pointed out that this inner transformation of the individual is called grace to emphasise that it is a gift from God which we cannot produce by our own efforts. Nothing similar to education or athletic training can generate it in the soul. This raises the question as to how exactly do we receive it ? In addition to the unforeseeable initiatives of God's generosity, there are basically two ways in which it comes to us, prayer and the sacraments. I will discuss the process of praying for grace, and other divine favours in Chapter Nine on Prayer. In this present chapter I will describe the role of the sacraments.

SECTION 2: THE SACRAMENTS AS CHANNELS OF GRACE

In the simplest terms one can say that sacraments are causes of grace which coming from God are more powerful in conveying grace to believers, than are their own prayers. And this is totally consistent with the theology of grace. There are two levels at which we can consider the sacraments, simple and profound, and they are complementary perspectives. First of all at the more descriptive level we can consider the sacraments as religious ceremonies which are signs or symbols of invisible grace. The symbolism in each case denotes something of the spiritual transaction which is taking place such as baptism signifying a washing away of moral stains and evil. These are not simply edifying gestures. Since the earliest times the Church has taught that they are effective, namely that they produce what they signify. Later theology would describe them as causes of the spiritual effects which they symbolise. A useful example is sex, which when it takes place between two people who love each other is a sign of that love, and at the same time it is a powerful energiser to increase that mutual love. Admittedly the parallel is not exact, but it serves to illustrate how a visible activity can both symbolise and produce an increase in something which is basically invisible, namely love.

The causality of the sacraments, as it was described in the middle ages, was disputed by the first generation of Protestants because it seemed to them that it was incompatible with the gratuitous character of grace. To them it seemed more like magic: words and signs were enacted, and divine grace followed. There is one simple explanation which avoids any such misunderstanding and also absolves the system of being too reliant upon mediaeval metaphysics, namely that the sacraments should be understood as instances of covenanted grace. In other words the predictability of the outcome is due to the fact that God has covenanted or promised his gifts to the recipients of these sacred transactions, in spite of the limitations of the recipient or the spiritual lethargy of the officiating priests. What the Catholics call the efficacy of the sacraments is entirely due to the reliability of God's promises.

All the sacraments were instituted by Jesus, as I will show later in this chapter when dealing with them individually. The clearest narratives of their institution are to be found in the cases of baptism and the eucharist.

In the fourth century the Church had to deal with a dispute which was intimately connected with the very heart of the sacraments. If they were of divine institution and conveyed divine gifts to the soul in a manner which human endeavour could not do, could the human beings impede their effectiveness? This can be viewed in two ways, namely the barriers constituted by the recipient or the officiating minister. The first instance can be answered easily. If the

recipient is not properly disposed to accept the divine gift of grace, and is lacking in basic good will, then the ceremony is meaningless and ineffective. Anything else would be simple superstition or magic.

On the other hand , if the minister of the sacrament is less than virtuous the situation is more complicated. The Donatists (which is the name of the party who caused this dispute) taught that a spiritually unworthy minister could not confer a sacrament effectively. This gave rise to the obvious question, well, just who is really worthy to bestow for example, spiritual regeneration in baptism? The same applies to all the other sacraments too. Strictly speaking no human being is spiritually good enough to pass on these gifts of God. It is consistent with the theology of grace to maintain that the officiating minister, although he is not leading a life of heroic sanctity, cannot impede or invalidate the gifts of God transmitted in the sacraments. To put it in simple terms: the officiating minister does not create the water, he merely turns on the tap. In more elegant terms, the Church clarified the position maintaining that the sacraments were efficacious in themselves regardless of the lack of virtue in the minister bestowing them. The same does not hold for his sermons or spiritual guidance, both of which are directly linked to his own life style and the moral goodness which it embodies.

Although the Church's stand against the Donatists was perfectly correct, it has had one unfortunate consequence. When the Church's collective spiritual life has been in periods of low ebb, unworthy priests have been allowed to remain in office, when they ought to have been dismissed largely on account of the unspoken assumption that the sacraments which they bestow are valid.

The second and more profound way of studying the sacraments is to link them closely to the incarnation of Christ. This perspective has been embraced by the Second Vatican Council. If we take as our starting point the principle that a sacrament is an active agent as well as a visible, palpable symbol of invisible spiritual power, then it is quite natural to regard the incarnate Christ as the basic sacrament, in the widest sense of that term. [2]

The Church as a community, proclaiming and activating the Kingdom of God throughout the world also has this twofold character. Namely it is a visible functioning society, within which the invisible graces of God are communicated to the human race. Before one focusses attention on to the particular channels of of grace and the variety of ways in which divine gifts are bestowed on individuals in the context of the Church, it is profitable to perceive the Church as a whole as having that basic sacramental character, as was stated clearly in the decree on the Church in Vatican II. [3]

In this wider context of linking the sacraments both which Christ and with the Church it is possible to speak of the causality of the sacraments in a more comprehensive and less

---

[2] Without employing the actual word 'sacrament' the Second Vatican Council speaks of Christ in this way, cf. *Lumen Gentium*, section 7, ed. Abbott p. 20.

[3] Vatican II, *Lumen Gentium*, section1. ed. Abbott, p. 15.

mechanistic manner. This is precisely what Karl Rahner did half a century ago. At the risk of some measure of over simplification, Rahner indicated that when the Church focusses itself at

a high degree of self actualisation conferring grace to the individual, there we have a sacrament. As the concepts are profound and deserve to be evaluated with exactitude, I would recommend the reader to study Rahner's own words in *The Church and the Sacraments*.[4]

SECTION 3: THE INDIVIDUAL SACRAMENTS

Baptism and Confirmation

I am treating these two sacraments together, because in antiquity they were bestowed in the same liturgy, which was the long admission ceremony for converts to Christianity. At a later stage in history confirmation was detached and administered at a separate ceremony some years later. The separation of the two became established when infant baptism became the commonest form for the reception of that sacrament.

The symbolism of baptism is transparently simple, namely being immersed in water as a sign of washing, and in this case the washing away of moral guilt and not just physical dirt. In the time of Jesus the Jews employed a similar ceremony for the admission of neophytes, and its use by St. John the Baptist is too well known to require comment. The symbolism is very profound and is occurs in non - Christian religions too. It seems to be deeply embedded in human nature, possibly at a subconscious level, as the following example will show. Towards the end of the Second World War a group of Hungarian Jews, who had been interned in Belsen concentration camp, were being moved westwards to another camp at Magdeburg. However they never reached that destination. On 13 th April 1945 the advance of the American troops was so swift that the 743 rd tank battalion stopped the train. The SS guards fled swiftly. The American soldiers freed the prisoners from the train and sent for food. The liberated prisoners, experiencing the joy of freedom, wandered about quite near the train which had been stopped in open country. Presently some of them came upon a stream and an unexpected sequel followed. I will quote the exact words of one of the survivors:- "While we were waiting, we found a stream and washed ourselves as best we could in the ice cold water. I realised many years later, as we reconstructed the events of the day of our liberation that this was more than the abortive attempt to clean ourselves of the grime of the journey, but a symbolic gesture: an eradication of the evil of the past months, and attempt to wash away Bergen-Belsen, Wiener Neustadt, Strasshof, the ghetto in Szeged, the ghetto in Mako. To purify ourselves of the sins of others."[5] That moving testimony speaks for itself and requires no further comment.

The characteristics of baptism can best be studied in relation to adult baptism which was the normal form of its bestowal in the early Church. What was required of the newcomer was total conversion. He or she had make a public declaration of faith in the three persons of the Trinity, as indicated in the foundational proclamation by Jesus just before the Ascension

---

[4] Rahner, K.(1963), *The Church and the Sacraments,* London: Burns & Oates, Freiburg: Herder, p.22.

[5] Lantos, P. (2005), *Parallel Lines,* London: Arcadia Books, p. 136.

102

(Matthew 28:18). That command associated with the injunction to make disciples of all nations, indicated that the sacrament and entry to the Church was open to all nations and races

on the basis of equality. That innovation was so startling that the first generation required some time to appreciate its implications, as I pointed out in Chapter Five on the Church.

The newcomer also had to profess a complete break with any sins in the past life. (Baptism was then the normal sacrament for forgiveness. Admittedly the sacrament of penance existed, but most practising Christians would go through life without availing of it, as I will show later in this chapter). The ceremony was performed by total immersion. It was recognised as the point of entry into the community of the visible Church and the invisible union of the mystical body of Christ. It was never repeated, as its effects were recognised as being permanent. Although the solemn liturgy of adult baptism was performed by a bishop, it was recognised that lay people were competent to bestow it validly. This would most naturally have been done by parents if an infant was in danger of death. The validity of infant baptism was not disputed in antiquity, and it became the norm after several centuries. This has caused disquiet to some Christians because the infant cannot make an act of faith. However it is bestowed on infants only on the understanding that they will make a personal act of faith when they are old enough to do so. Admittedly it is a problem, but it may help to set it in a wider context of the total development of an infant. Centuries ago a baby's mind was described as a *tabula rasa* (colloquially, a clean slate). Modern science, particularly biology and psychology have shown that a child's body and psyche are anything but empty. At birth, and even earlier, the baby's patrimony of DNA ensures that vast areas of his future intelligence, health, temperamental inclinations and subconscious predispositions are already firmly established. In his or her first years far reaching decisions are made on the child's behalf by parents on matters ranging from immunisations, to the choice of diet, a whole raft of decisions about upbringing, and the selection of a school. It is not totally alien to a child's progress through life that an important religious decision, i.e. entry to the Church should also be made by the parents. Nationality is assured by a much more automatic process!

Confirmation can best be studied in the context of the fully developed liturgy of the early Church as described, for instance, in the third century Apostolic Tradition of Hippolytus of Rome.[6] The initiation of newcomers to the Church was conducted during the night of Holy Saturday, when the community celebrated a long liturgy of the Resurrection. Their final instruction was conveyed in the series of bible readings, such as have been preserved to the present day in the liturgy of the Holy Saturday. In the Apostolic Tradition it is stated that the actual baptism started literally at the time when the cock crows. The neophytes were given baptism by total immersion.

After the baptism they were instructed to dry themselves, put on their clothes and come before the bishop again. The bishop laid his hands on their heads, prayed over them and anointed them on the head with the oil of thanksgiving. By the fourth century this latter prayer and the anointing had become a separate ceremony performed only by the bishop. It seems clear that a vast increase in numbers had made this inevitable. The eucharist too had undergone a similar modification and it was celebrated by presbyters in churches other than

[6] An accessible edition of the text is that of Geoffrey Cumming, (1976), *Hippolytus : A Text for Students*, Nottingham: Grove Books, 1976, pp. 18 -21.

the bishop's church. Similarly the presbyters increasingly became the ministers of baptism, and the final part of the initiation (later called Confirmation) was administered at a later date

the bishop. How much later it was given has varied considerably over the centuries. Like baptism it was bestowed once only, and came to be regarded as a deliberate reaffirmation of the Christian commitment by those who had been baptised in infancy. It is understood as the final strengthening of the mature Christian by the Holy Spirit for all the responsibilities of Christian life, including martyrdom. When the mediaeval theologians set out to agree upon the exact number of the sacraments, Confirmation was regarded as a separate sacrament bringing the total up to seven.

Penance

Although this sacrament is clearly understood to be a reconciliation with God, I am retaining the ancient name, precisely because of its antiquity. Whereas the theology of this sacrament has been agreed in an uncomplicated fashion since the earliest times, the practice of its administration has varied more than that of any other sacrament. The Fathers took the words of the risen Jesus at their face value: "If you forgive the sins of any, they are forgiven; if you retain the sins of any they are retained."(John 20:22). They also understood the process in he light of the power of binding and loosing, the granting of which is recorded in Matthew 18:18. That phrase was a legal technical description from Jewish practice, namely the imposition of an obligation or the declaration that the individual was free of the injunction.

The earliest historical accounts make it clear that it was administered once in a life-time and only for exceptionally serious sins, such as adultery, murder, or apostasy. The bishop was the minister and it was enacted publicly. At the beginning of Lent the sinners confessed (privately) to the bishop, they joined the group of penitents, undertook to perform a penance as directed by the bishop, and stood in a separate place during Mass. After the homily they were courteously dismissed with a blessing. The penances consisted of relinquishing various forms of bodily pleasures, such as giving up luxurious food, comfortable beds, fashionable clothing, and so on. The duration varied with the gravity of the sin and was determined by the bishop. Reconciliation took place on the Thursday of Holy Week. In Rome the penitents lay on the floor of the church while the archdeacon formally requested the bishop to absolve them. After that they were given Holy Communion at the solemn eucharist of that evening. Usually the period of penance lasted several years. Some rigorists insisted upon reconciliation only at the time of death. This severity was due to the fact that in antiquity, baptism was agreed to be the normal sacrament for the renunciation of evil, and reconciliation with God. The rigorists argued that the offer of frequent penance would encourage laxity in morals. Other rigorists disputed the Church's competence to forgive certain very serious sins, such as apostasy. The Roman community showed itself consistently moderate, bestowing absolution on all categories of sin, and not deferring it to the death bed. However for several centuries the once-only rule was maintained, and the average good Christian would go through his whole life without receiving this sacrament.

With the collapse of the Roman Empire in the West, a whole series of historical causes changed the form in which this sacrament was celebrated. Alongside the public penance another custom arose, namely that of administering it in private. The most significant modification in that arrangement was that after confession, the penitent accepted a penance, and was given absolution straight away, before the completion of the penance to which he had agreed.

The Fourth Lateran Council of 1215 wishing to legislate against spiritual slackness decreed that all Christians above the age of reason should receive the sacraments of penance and the eucharist once a year at about Easter time. Not surprisingly this minimum provision eventually became the norm and the reception of the two sacraments, later known as Easter Duties, became the established custom. The Council's decision also had the unfortunate effect of seeming to imply that confession was the normal preparation for the reception of the Eucharist, although moral theologians have always insisted that the only barrier to receiving holy communion is conscious mortal sin.

The next significant legislation about this sacrament came about unintentionally in the early twentieth century when Pope Pius X decreed that Holy Communion should be received frequently, and by children at an early age. Hitherto the first reception of that sacrament had been when young people were in the teens, but the Pope's instruction then brought it down to six or seven. The move was not thought out thoroughly, and since penance had come to be regarded as the normal preparation for the eucharist, that sacrament too was given to children usually about the age of six as it was considered a suitable way to prepare for the First Communion. The unforeseen results of that enlightened decision about the eucharist was that young children were encouraged to take up the practice of frequent confession. Since they were psychologically incapable of grave sin it has the effect of trivialising that sacrament. For many people it became a mechanical ritual devoid of real meaning. After the Second Vatican Council catechists tried to introduce the practice of giving young children their first communion without prior confession, and deferring the latter sacrament until some years later. The initiative was admirable, but received active discouragement during the pontificate of John Paul II, and it came to nothing.

Although I have spoken critically of the misuse of this sacrament, let me make it clear to my readers that when it is availed of in a responsible manner it is a remarkably effective spiritual remedy. The complete secrecy of the transaction is reassuring as is the possibility of confessing to a priest who is unknown to the penitent. Some people definitely prefer anonymity. The fact that the penitent makes an act of self accusation removes all self deception from the process. Psychologically the act of self accusation is extremely important especially if the fault has been really serious, as the following example will show. In the second half of the 20th century there was a well publicised air crash in South America. A football team returning home between Chile and Argentina crashed high in the Andes mountains. Surprisingly about half the passengers survived with minor injuries. They calculated that their best hope of being rescued was to remain near the wreckage of the plane, since it would be clearly visible to rescue planes which might be searching for survivors. Rescue was long in coming. All the food was soon used up, and the most tragic part of the drama then took place. The survivors began to each flesh from the bodies of their dead companions. After yet more days two of the most able bodied among the survivors decided to walk down the mountains to seek help. After a very difficult journey they came to a village and the first person whom them met was a priest. The first thing that the survivors did was to confess to him (evidently without any secrecy) that they had committed the sin of cannibalism. Only then did they experience inner peace.

Normally secrecy is always present. There is no possibility of unhealthy public humiliation, as appears to be the case in some Christian fringe Churches. It is the ideal situation for very sincere repentance, without any display of public hysteria or hyped-up emotionalism. One

hopes that with the passage of time the Church authorities will see that it is unsuitable for six year old children. If not they will simply abandon it later on in life because it has been presented to them when they are too young to grasp its relevance and importance.

The Eucharist

The Eucharist is the centre and indispensable source of spiritual strength for the life of the Church, as was stated clearly by Pope Benedict XVI.[7] From the days of the apostles it was celebrated every Sunday in commemoration of the Last Supper, in response to the explicit command of Jesus, "Do this in remembrance of me" (Luke 22:19 & I Cor. 11: 24, 25), by which he entrusted to the Church the performance of this fundamental ritual.

Quite soon the simple supper, which encompassed the words of Jesus over the loaf and the cup of wine, was augmented by bible readings and prayers, inspired by the synagogue liturgy. The pristine beauty of this simple eucharist was fully developed by the beginning of the second century at which point it was recorded in the First Apologia of St. Justin, which I quoted in full in Chapter Two. For the first 300 years of Christian history the eucharist was always celebrated in private houses. This would have restricted the maximum number of participants to about seventy, thus assuring a sense of intimacy. Clearly it was the central factor in holding together the local Christian communities.

Constantine gave to Christianity first of all freedom, and later made it the religion of state. Not surprisingly numbers rose dramatically, and the character of the eucharistic liturgy changed. When the celebration moved to the basilicas, it became altogether more elaborate , and processions, choirs and other embellishments followed. The result was a beautiful and dignified ceremony, which had been thought out carefully on theological principles. It set the pattern of the mass which has lasted until the present day, about which I will have more to say in the chapter on Prayer. Although the intimacy of the house masses could not be sustained there is no reason to suppose that a sense of community was lost. Even the largest of the Roman towns did not have the anonymity of modern cities.

More important for the quality of the liturgy was the fact that it was still fully participated by the laity who understood the language in which it was conducted. The importance of this aspect can be judged by the fact that in the pontificate of Pope Damasus (fourth century) the Roman community dropped Greek and adopted Latin for the liturgy because only then, somewhat surprisingly, did the majority of the Christians in Rome speak Latin. Hitherto their majority language had been Greek.

For reasons which I will not go into here, the Council of Trent dealt with the Eucharist in two sessions separated, regrettably, by a period of eleven years. The doctrine of the real presence

---

[7] Benedict XVI , proposition 11 in his statement at the conclusion of the Synod in Rome , October 2005, available on the Vatican web site, www.vatican.va

was promulgated at the end of Session 13 on 11th October 1551, whereas the sacrifice of the mass had to wait until Session 22 on 17th September 1562. This has set a pattern, largely in response to Protestant disagreements, which is hard to break out of. The doctrine of the real presence which has been held since antiquity, is profoundly mysterious, and no theological

explanations have ever improved upon the clarity of the fourth gospel. I will quote verbatim from the last section of the long speech of Jesus in chapter six, although I recommend the reader to read the whole of that chapter, slowly and thoughtfully. "The Jews then disputed among themselves, saying ' How can this man give us his flesh to eat ? ' So Jesus said to them, 'Truly, truly I say to you , unless you eat the flesh of the Son of man and drink his blood, you have no life in you; he who eats my flesh and drinks my blood has eternal life and I will raise him up at the last day. For my flesh is food indeed, and my blood is drink indeed. He who eats my flesh and drinks my blood abides in me, and I in him. As the living Father sent me, and I live because of the Father, so he who eats me will live because of me. This is the bread which came down from heaven, not such as the fathers ate and died; he who eats this bread will live for ever."(John 6: 52 - 58).

The message is so stark and unambiguous that it is not surprising that many people have been tempted to dismiss it as merely poetic symbolism. The very first audience listening to those words evidently felt unsettled by their uncompromising realism. After all, it could be construed as cannibalism, which was even more repellent to the Jews than to a modern reader, since all blood was regarded by them as sacred. The idea of eating flesh was equally repugnant; it also occurs in the bible as a metaphor for slander (Psalm 27:2). Jesus insisted on the literal meaning of what he had said, and had to endure the departure of many of his followers on that account (John 6: 66).

The practical relevance of this sacrament is obvious. Since the central business of Christianity, at the personal level, focusses upon a relationship of intimacy with Christ, it means that Christians of the twenty first century have access to him as a person just as closely as did his first followers who walked with him in the roads and towns of Palestine. Relationships cannot be sustained just by thoughts about our friends, but we need real meetings in person, at social gatherings, visits, meals together and many other such points of contact. However I will not attempt to improve upon the many writers who have commented upon the extraordinary privilege given to Christians in this sacrament. In spite of all its theoretical difficulties the doctrine of the real presence has been held unswervingly since earliest times. Various philosophically minded theologians have offered elucidations of greater or lesser usefulness. The most famous has been transubstantiation, which explains the complete change of bread and wine in the eucharist in terms derived from the metaphysics of the Greeks, as developed by mediaeval theologians. It was approved by the Council of Trent but I will devote no more space to it here, because of its extensive dependence on philosophical presuppositions which lie outside the scope of this book.

Whereas the doctrine of the real presence entails intellectual difficulties arising out of philosophical problems of space, distance, and extension, the sacrifice of the mass has even more complicated problems because of the additional factor of time. It was this aspect of the eucharist which was most strongly attacked by all Protestants.They insisted (rightly) that the sacrifice of Calvary took place once only, and they accused the Catholics of attempting to multiply that event by teaching that the mass was a sacrifice. Protestant opinion held generally that the celebration of the eucharist should be regarded as a memorial, rather like a wedding anniversary, for example, though of much deeper significance of course.

A careful reading of late mediaeval theologians makes it clear that they were well aware of the danger of seeming to multiply the sacrifice of the Cross. Whatever account they gave of

the matter they were always careful to speak of sacrificial aspect of the eucharist in the singular, (as did the Council of Trent). Intellectually the theological position entails much the same difficulties as the doctrine of the real presence, and the solution of these problems is also arrived at on the same lines. (One must always bear in mind that this sacrament is a profound supernatural mystery, which cannot be explained totally, and for which theology can merely supply answers to the various objections and difficulties). In the most general terms one can say that just as the doctrine of the real presence accounts for the believers' being in contact with the body of Christ, despite the problems of distance, the same real presence of the body and blood of Christ link up the believer with Calvary across the time gap of centuries. The double consecration of bread and wine symbolising the separation of his body and blood in a violent death, was Christ's way of indicating that his impending execution was also contained in this sacramental ritual. This understanding of the event is confirmed by the words of Jesus over the wine, which he declared was his blood "poured out for many for the remission of sins" (Matthew 26:28). The other synoptics have similar phrases which indicate a sacrificial death. St. Paul takes up the same idea in slightly different words, saying that "as often as you eat this bread and drink this cup, you proclaim the Lord's death until he comes". (I Cor. 11: 26)

It is difficult to think out examples from everyday life to supply some sort of analogy for so profound an event and its being recaptured in a sacrament. Years ago when I was teaching undergraduates I used to present them with a parallel which some of them found helpful. Let us begin with the coronation of Queen Elizabeth II in Westminster Abbey in 1953. A long and dignified ceremony was being performed inside the church. Let us again suppose that there were security guards placed on the roof of the abbey for the protection of the important people inside. It is not too fanciful to imagine that those guards would walk around the flat places of the vast roof and look in through the windows to see what was going on inside. The analogy is not perfect, but it means that those men at different places on the roof , and at different times looked in and made some kind of personal contact with the important ceremony being enacted below. The fact that different men saw it, at different times, and in different places did not mean that the one and only coronation was in any way split up. They had devised different ways of linking up with it at different times and places. I offer this somewhat homely example to the reader for what it's worth.

Matrimony

Among the seven sacraments matrimony was the last to have its sacramental status formally acknowledged by the Church. It usually surprises people to realise that the process took about a thousand years. In the earliest period of its history the Church accepted the rightfulness of marriage as enshrined in the customs and laws of the societies into which its mission penetrated. Its first moral task was to try to put an end to divorce which was a practice tolerated in all those societies. For that high standard they had the explicit command of Jesus "What therefore God has joined together, let not man put asunder" (Mark 10:9).

Before the fourth and fifth centuries the marriages of Christians were accompanied by no prayers or blessings. A priest was not present as a witness, nor did the Church as a community claim any jurisdiction over the institution of marriage or its derivatives, like inheritance. Up to the eleventh century religious ceremonial began to make an appearance, the ceremony was

Sometimes accompanied by prayers, a priest might be present to give a blessing, but this was given initially outside the church in the porch.

During the eleventh and twelfth centuries canon law underwent a spectacular development, and in that period the Church acquired complete jurisdiction over the institution of marriage. This legal development preceded its being recognised as a sacrament.[8] For the modern mind it is difficult to understand why it should have taken so long for the sacramental status of marriage to be acknowledged. Several powerful factors contributed to this situation. In the New Testament St. Paul recommended virginity as preferable to marriage. There is also the incredible personal influence of St. Augustine. He in turn seems to have been influenced permanently by his earlier period in Manichaeism. At the risk of some over-simplicification one can say that their system taught that spirit was good and matter was bad. The connection between marriage and the joys of the body is obvious. St.Augustine's position is also complicated by the fact that his experience of sex was outside marriage. At the age of thirty one, and two years before his baptism, he repudiated his mistress whose name remains unknown, and their son Adeodatus.

In reality the acknowledgement of the sacramental status of marriage came about in the context of Western theologians seeking a precise answer to the question as to how many sacraments there were. The yard-stick which was tacitly agreed upon was that they would look for a transaction of grace to an individual, which was accompanied by a symbolic ceremony. When they applied this criterion they excluded ceremonies like the consecration of a church. A wide ranging agreement appeared in the second half of the twelfth century when Peter Lombard and his contemporaries put the number at precisely seven, and matrimony was among them. The positive factors leading to its inclusion among the sacraments were Jesus's statement that the spouses were joined together by God (cf. Mark 10:9 above), and St. Paul's using the relationship between Christ and the Church (Ephesians 5: 23 - 33) as the image of Christian marriage.

Since that period the Church's teaching has upheld the dignity and importance of marriage. This support has become increasingly important since the latter part of the twentieth century when increasing numbers of people chose to live together without any formalities from State or Church. Significantly those people who are involved in marriage guidance and help with relationship problems strongly support the institution of regularised marriage. It seems that the public commitment to lifelong fidelity constitutes a powerful psychological strength to the couple. The results are positive and in some cased unexpected. Married people, as opposed to those merely cohabiting, have better health and live longer, they are far more likely to provide care for ill or disabled relatives, and their children are far more likely to be in

---

[8] Schillebeeckx, E.(1965), *Marriage: Secular Reality and Saving Mystery.* London: Sheed & Ward, vol. 2, p.60. I have made use of that work extensively in this section.

full -time education at the age of 17.[9]

Despite its being acknowledged as a sacrament the disputes about its nature and ramifications did not cease.

The debates which took place in the middle ages seem bizarre to the modern mind. Was sexual pleasure always sinful even when it accompanied the desire to produce a child ? Did sex constitute a barrier to receiving Holy Communion on the following day ? Was intercourse permitted during pregnancy ? Amid this welter of uncertainties one thread was constant and at a later period it led to clarification on several disputed points. The constant factor in question was the moral acceptability of non-reproductive sex. Unlike many aspects of matrimony, this principle is firmly grounded in the New Testament. The words of Jesus that they are two in one flesh (Matthew 19:5) concerns only their union and says nothing about reproduction. In fact the passage in Genesis (2: 18 - 24) to which he was alluding was concerned specifically with the problem that it was not good for man to be alone. St. Paul told his readers in Corinth that they should not abstain from sex in case they might be tempted infidelity (I Cor. 7: 4 - 7). He made no mention of their intentions about procreation. St. Paul also permitted the remarriage of widows. There must have been some uncertainty about its rightfulness, but St. Paul allowed it (I Cor. 7: 8 & 9). For many of them conceiving a child would have been impossible for reasons of age. For the same reason the Church eventually removed all opposition to intercourse during pregnancy. Most of the opposition to that practice arose from the fear that intercourse during pregnancy might induce an abortion of the already developing foetus. The marriages too of those who after years remained childless were held to be valid.

The debates of the modern period really begin with biology. The ancients had considered that the male semen contained the whole future embryo, and ascribed to the mother nothing more creative than supplying the appropriate environment in which it could develop. Early in the nineteenth century the discovery of the female ovum overturned the ancient theories. It also overturned most of what the ancient Christian writers had said about the limiting of births. Their opposition to what we would call birth control was basically because they viewed it as a form of abortion.

Coupled with the discovery of the ovum was the realisation that it was released from the ovaries once in approximately twenty eight days, which meant that the time when conception was possible could be predicted. Understandably this led to speculation about the morality of sex during a time when pregnancy was known to be impossible. Rome was asked whether it was permitted, and a favourable answer was given by the Sacred Penitentiary (an administrative department in the Vatican and not a prison). On the 16th June 1880 the reply was that there was no moral obstacle.[10] This was in keeping with the consistently held principle namely the moral acceptability of non - reproductive sex. In the twentieth century the predictability of the infertile period became more accurate the was adopted as a method of family planning by many Catholics because it received the explicit approval of the Church

---

[9] Curtis, Polly, writing in *The Guardian* 5th October 2007.

[10] Denziger - Shönmetzer, op.cit. n. 3148.

authorities.[11] Contraception was widely practised and discussed in the Western word in the twentieth century. In 1930 the Lambeth Conference gave its approval to the responsible use of the practice. In the following year Pope Pius XI condemned the practice in his encyclical entitled "Casti Connubii"[12]. The principles on which he based his negative stance were the

sin of Onan (Genesis 38: 9), and the subordination of purposes, i.e. firstly procreation and secondly the enjoyment. He maintained that the latter should not be obtained to the exclusion of the former. Both of those were shortly to be seen as flawed. Biblical scholars agreed that the sin of Onan was an offence against generosity and not about sexual purity, when he refused his duty to beget sons in the name of his dead brother. The subordination of purposes was officially dropped by the Second Vatican Council, when it enumerated the purposes of marriage in such a way as deliberately to remove any prioritising of one above another. [13]

The statement about marriage in that Council is so positive and affirmative that it deserves to be read in full. There is just one section to which I would draw the readers attention, it is the statement that sex in marriage is honourable and morally good. This may seem a superfluous observation in the modern world, but in view of the past pessimism of so many theologians and official documents it was extremely important that a line should be drawn under that negative trend .[14] Before that statement from the Second Vatican Council much of the writing in the Church about marriage, and the decisions of the rule makers, were pessimistic about the whole institution. They seem to have been unaware of the great opportunities for generous love within marriage. Indeed one of the joys of starting a family is that the helpless infants provide the most natural occasion for the bestowal of unconditional love. Another opportunity for that degree of generosity occurs in old age, if one of the spouses should become ill. In that situation too, one sees extraordinary examples of devotion and care which attain the highest levels of selfless generosity.

It is in the context of the positive outlook of Vatican II that the basic definition of matrimony has been modified. Half a century ago it was common for text books of sacramental theology to define marriage (as if that were possible !) as a contract between a man and a woman giving them the right to sexual intercourse. It is difficult to envisage anything more drab and minimalist. Such text books overlooked the fact that the words of the marriage ceremony gave the lie to any such glib definition. The crucial words of consent have been for centuries:-" I, X take thee Y to be my truly wedded wife, to have and to hold from this day forward, for better for worse for richer for poorer, in sickness and in health till death do us part". They pledged themselves to an unknown future which might bring totally unforeseeable situations, like becoming an invalid. It is common knowledge that a contract requires that all the facts are known in advance and are unalterable.

---

[11] Pope Pius XII in an address to Italian midwives on October 29th, 1951. Pope Paul VI, Encyclical *Humanae Vitae,* section 11.

[12] Denziger - Schönmetzer, op.cit. n. 3716.

[13] Vatican II, Pastoral Constitution, *Gaudium et Spes,* section 48, ed. Abbott, p.250.

[14] Vatican II , *Gaudium et Spes,* sections 47 - 52, with special reference to section 49.ed. Abbott, pp. 249 - 258.

It is helpful to consider marriage as a covenant, which precisely admits of unknown developments in the future. In this convenant husband and wife promise to share their lives in a permanent relationship of love, and in which they hope to produce children.

Despite the positive presentation of Christian marriage in the Second Vatican Council, the problem of birth control was not finally resolved. Pope Paul VI kept the matter off the agenda of the council and appointed a special commission (including married men and women) to study it. After months of free discussion the vast majority (more than 60) came to the

conclusion that the arguments against contraception were theologically unsustainable. They were opposed by a minority of four who admitted that they could not maintain their case theologically. Eventually conservatives within the Roman Curia persuaded Pope Paul VI that he should uphold the ban on contraception, otherwise papal authority would be weakened if he reversed the decisions of his immediate predecessors.[15]

The condemnation of artificial birth control was upheld in the encyclical *Humanae Vitae* which Paul VI promulgated in July 1968. In retrospect one can see that its authors had an impossible task. The bible is silent on the matter. The patristic tradition could not distinguish between abortion and contraception, and the subordination of purposes had been ruled out by Vatican II, as I stated above. With so little room for manoeuvre the awkwardness of the central argument should not surprise us. The exact wording is :- " The Church calling men back to the observance of the norms of natural law, as interpreted by her constant doctrine, teaches that each and every marriage act (*quilibet matrimonii usus*) must remain open to the transmission of life."[16] The expression "open to the transmission of life" is ambiguous but in the context it can only mean that the transmission must not be prevented artificially. The reason for that injunction is given supposedly in the next section (12) of the encyclical :- "That teaching, often set forth by the magisterium, is grounded upon the inseparable connection, willed by God and unable to be broken by man on his own initiative, between the two meanings of the conjugal act: the the unitive meaning and the procreative meaning". That statement is ambiguous because its simple wording rules out the use of the infertile period, which was permitted by Vatican II, several popes and also by *Humanae Vitae* (in section 11). The opaque language masks a simple tautology, which can be paraphrased as follows: "artificial birth control is wrong because the sexual act must be open to the transmission of life. What does the word 'open' mean in this context ? It means not impeded artificially".

When the encyclical was published, the Vatican's spokesman Mgr. Lambruschini stated more than once that the pope had not claimed his infallible teaching authority for the document. This opened the door for legitimate dissent. It is useful to reflect that it is by no means the only papal statement which subsequent generations have rejected as mistaken. Pope Leo X declared against Luther that the burning of heretics was perfectly in accord with the will of the Holy Spirit. Clement VIII condemned the notion of freedom of conscience. Pius VI rejected the Civil Constitution in France in 1791 and condemned in particular the "abominable philosophy of human rights". Gregory XVI and Pius IX both condemned

---

[15] The whole disedifying story is related in Robert Blair -Kaiser's *The Encyclical that Never Was.* London , Sheed & Ward 1995. especially pp.175, 176.

[16] Encyclical letter *Humanae Vitae* section 11.

freedom of conscience as "sheer madness".[17]

Within a few days of the encyclical's publication the inadequacy of its argumentation was apparent, and a mass of protests appeared all over the world. A number of dissenting theologians were summarily dismissed from their posts in Catholic teaching establishments, and the rest kept quiet. No respectable theologian then or since has produced a convincing justification of the prohibition of contraception. The laity simply ignored it and eventually

when surveys were conducted it became apparent that in places like Western Europe and America more than 90% of practising Catholics disobeyed the encyclical in good conscience.[18] All of this should have been foreseen. I recall a conversation in the early 1960's with one of the theology professors at the University of Fribourg. He said that once the principle of family planning by the safe period had been conceded by the Church authorities, it was impossible to try and forbid other methods. After all the concept of artificiality is morally neutral.

The dismal postscript to this unhappy incident was the Church authorities' official attitude to the Aids crisis. Being consistent with the principles of the birth control encyclical condoms for Aids victims were forbidden.

It is sad for me to have to record the whole sorry episode, but those who are seeking belief in Jesus, must fortify themselves against disincentives arising out of ill thought-out policies by the Church authorities both in past history and in the present.

Holy Order

The word order comes straight out of Roman law. After Christianity had become the religion of state the ministers serving the Christian community received the social and legal status of other orders in the empire. Their status was something like the modern civil service in England. This evolution was complete by the end of the fourth century. They were being turned into a privileged class.[19]

This was a long way from the picture of the Church leaders as revealed in the New Testament. The most significant feature of the epistles and other documents of the first generation of Christians is the sedulous avoidance of the word "priest". They were making a conscious separation from the liturgy of the Jerusalem temple, and its priests descended from the tribe of Levi. They were equally careful to distinguish themselves from the temples and priests of the pagans who were numerous all over the empire. The Letter to the Hebrews deals extensively with the priesthood of Christ, which came to him automatically with the incarnation, and not by birth in the tribe of Levi. The union of divine and human in his person made him the

---

[17] The list was published by Rev.S. Fagan in *The Tablet* of 16/23 December 2006.

[18] Even in Italy family size has contracted since 1968. In 2007 it was reported that on average Italian woman now had only 1.3 children. Reported in the newspaper *Die Welt* 9 August 2007.

[19] Enshrined in the *Codex Theodosianus, 16: 26.* quoted in *Études sur le Sacrement de l'Ordre*, eds. B. Botte, A. Gelin, J. Danielou and others, (1957), Paris: Éditions du Cerf, p.127, n.4.

perfect mediator between God and humanity. His liberating sacrifice was accomplished once and for all, and never repeated like the Jewish sacrifices. The First Letter of Peter and the Apocalypse make five references to Christians' sharing in that priesthood by their baptism. I Peter 2:5 describes the baptised people as a "holy priesthood, to offer spiritual sacrifices acceptable to God through Jesus Christ" , and in 2:9 they are described as " a chosen race, a royal priesthood, a holy nation, God's own people". The same ideas are present in Apocalypse 1:6, 5:10, and 20:6.

As I stated in the chapter on the Church, the communities of Christians were led by a threefold ministry of overseers, elders and servants, which are the modern equivalents of the

ancient terms episcopoi, presbyteroi, and diakonoi. Significantly they were never called priests: that was the unique role of Jesus.

From the third century onwards, when the break with Judaism and paganism had been achieved definitively there was a tendency to apply to the Christian ministries some of the ideas which the Old Testament applied to the Levitical priests. It was not a particularly happy evolution, since it came at a time when Roman law was making them a privileged class.

In 1123 and 1139 the First and Second Lateran Councils passed regulations by which major orders became a nullifying impediment to marriage, and marriage was an invalidating impediment to priestly ordination. As there is no intrinsic connection between the sacrament of Order and the obligation to life - long celibacy, I am relegating the question to a post script at the end of this chapter.[20]

Although the lay administration of baptism in an emergency was always recognised as valid, the celebration of other sacraments passed exclusively into the hands of bishops and presbyters, except for matrimony whose ministers are the husband and wife. The Fourth Lateran Council of 1215 declared that only priests could celebrate the eucharist .[21]

The Council of Trent dealt with what we now call priesthood in two parts. Doctrinally it adopted a defensive position against the Protestants and upheld that the sacrament had been instituted by Christ, in the context of conferring on the apostles the competence to celebrate the eucharist and other sacraments. [22] The pastoral reform which Trent initiated was much more positive and creative, namely he institution of seminaries, promulgated in 15 th July 1563. This was one of the most far sighted and positive reforms of the Council. In the modern world we take it for granted that professional people receive a specific education for their work. That was not so in past centuries. Many occupations were learnt on the job, like an apprenticeship, and that extended even to surgeons. As late as 1870 commissions in the British army and navy could be obtained by purchase rather than by training.

The Council decreed that a special college should be established in each diocese precisely for

---

[20] The absence of an intrinsic link was duly noted by Vatican II, *Presbyterorum Ordinis,* section 16.

[21] IV Lateran Council, chapter 1, Denziger - Schönmetzer, op.cit. n. 802.

[22] Council of Trent, Session 23, July 1563, Chapter 1, Denziger - Schönmetzer,op.cit. n. 1764.

the training of the clergy. Candidates were accepted at an early age before they were seduced by the "cares of the world", and provided that they knew how to read and write. At that time admission to seminaries of boys between 12 and 14 was almost inevitable in the absence of universal schooling. They had to be taught Latin and ordinary school subjects before they could proceed to theology. Although the system was not taken up immediately by the whole Church, it meant that eventually the Church had a professionally educated body of parochial clergy.

An equally important decision of the Council, which is frequently overlooked, was the injunction on bishops that they were not to ordain any one to the priesthood unless there was a specific vacant parish to which he could be appointed forthwith. At one stroke the Council

solved the root cause of so much slackness in clerical life. Prior to the Council too many men had been ordained. For example the city of Rome was swarming with unemployed priests desperately looking for salaried posts either in parish work or in the Curia, or as domestic chaplains to titled families. Their lives were idle and disedifying.

An important matter which was not settled by Trent or any other Council was the nature of vocation to the priesthood. There was a certain amount of debate about it in the 18th and 19th centuries, whose details need not detain us here. A remarkably succinct formulation of the matter was supplied in recent years by Prof. N. Lash. He enunciated his proposition in the context of the so-called shortage of priestly vocations at the end of the 20th century. The authorities' responded to this situation by amalgamating parishes and inviting lay people to new forms of ministry. In that context Prof. Lash declared: " There is no shortage of vocations. Men and women have vocations when the Church invites them to undertake some office. All talk of lay people taking on "new forms of ministry" is so much persiflage until the ecclesiastical authorities bite the bullet and invite sufficient men (married or celibate) and women (ditto) to be ordained to the presbyterate. Without the Eucharist, the Church perishes." [23]

The Second Vatican Council studied the notion of priesthood with some care, and also facilitated a wide ranging debate on the matter within the Church. Whereas in the past the clergy had been viewed almost like functionaries in an organisation dispensing sacraments and sermons to those who sought them, it was clear in the period after the Second World War that the clergy would have to be facilitators giving supportive leadership to lay people in the joint mission to a de-Christianised society. There was no longer any place for the paternalistic and sometimes autocratic clergy of previous epochs. Far sighted theologians envisaged that in many parts of the world the pattern of priestly life which could best profit the Church was that of a part - time priest who earned his own living, and whose immersion in the ordinary world of work would help him to conduct a realistic role as leader. Such a role could well be discharged by a retired family man with a pension. Thanks to modern medicine many retired people can look forward to about twenty years of reasonably good health. Their experience of work and bringing up a family would be a spiritual enrichment. In fact that scenario is almost exactly the job-description which we read in the Epistles to Timothy and Titus where St. Paul advises them on who to select as presbyters.

[23] Reported in *The Tablet,* 18 th August 2007.

Admittedly the documents of Vatican II did not go quite as far as that, but they redressed the balance of the over-clericalised pattern of priestly life inherited from the mediaeval period. The Decree on the "Life and Ministry of Presbyters"made a deliberate choice of vocabulary, employing the Latin words "presbyter" and "presbyteratus" deliberately. It is unfortunate that the standard English translation renders them as priest and priesthood, which is misleading. The Council had indicated that it was separating its message from the imagery of the mediaeval functionaries, and returning to the New Testament usages.

One very important aspect of a presbyter's life was the affirmation of the role of worker priests. As it is often, but falsely, assumed that the worker priest movement had been officially condemned by the Vatican, it is worth quoting the passage from the Council

verbatim :- "All presbyters are sent forth as co-workers in the same undertaking, whether they are engaged in a parochial or supra-parochial ministry, whether they devote their efforts to scientific research or teaching, whether by manual labour they share in the lot of the workers themselves - if there seems to be need for this and competent authority approves - or whether they fulfil any other apostolic tasks or labours related to the apostolate. All indeed are united in the singe goal of building up Christ's' Body, a work requiring manifold roles and new adjustments, especially nowadays."[24]

Although the Council document did not say so, the approval of manual work connects with the most ancient practice of the lives of the parochial clergy. Records have survived of about half a dozen provincial councils held in France and Spain in the fourth and fifth centuries which laid down rules about the wage earning occupations of the clergy. The fact that they worked for their own living is taken for granted in the texts. The decisions gave directions about what occupations were most suitable. The decrees favoured what we would call self employed work, usually skilled manual work, which would leave the presbyter free to stop whenever he chose, so that he could attend to Church business if and when required, such as joining the community to sing vespers (about which I will have more to say in the chapter on Prayer).[25]

Sadly the seminaries in the 1960's were not in any way geared up to implementing such a vision of the ministry.

Seminary Training in the Centuries after the Council of Trent.

At their best the Tridentine seminaries trained clergy who were the maintenance men for the parishes of Catholic Europe. By the twentieth century the Church needed clergy who were missionary leaders. That is to say spiritual guides who could animate a Christian community for the complexities of mission to a de-christianised soceity.

---

[24] Second Vatican Council, Decree *Presbyterorum Ordinis,* section 8, ed. Abbott, p. 550.

[25] Details of these councils and their decisions can be found in my modest volume, (2002) *Misguided Morality: Catholic Moral Teaching in the Contemporary Church.* Aldershot: Ashgate Publishing Limited, p.212.

By the twentieth century three factors had combined to make the clergy ineffectual . Firstly the specialist education in seminaries had the effect of separating their students from the intellectual and general cultural life of the soceity which they were to evangelise. This was reinforced by the fact that the clergy has become a privileged class since before the middle ages. They did not have to earn their living in the normal fashion; no matter how infficient their work was, they would not be threatened with dismissal. Thirdly was the effect of celibacy, which without a supportive community, cut them off emotionally and psychologically from yet another dimension of real life. They would never know the anguish of a married man, at the beside of his sick child, hearing his wife's dreaded question " Can we afford the doctor ?" In short they were trained and deployed in an atmosphere of which the kindest thing one can say is that it was artificial. This accounts for indicators which otherwise suggest that they were totally unfeeling. No clergy joined the hunger marches to London from Glasgow in 1929 and Jarrow in 1932. In 1926 Cardinal Bourne declared in a pastoral letter

that it would be a sin to take part in the general strike. After the war, in 1956 Cardinal Griffin led the English hierarchy in opposing the creation of the National Health Service. At heart they were not bad men. They has simply been removed from reality by the system in which they had been trained and deployed.

Although some improvement of the seminaries' programmes has taken place in the wake of the Second Vatican Council, the pre-cociliar regime of training and organisation meant that the young priests formed in that traditiion were working as the parish priests in the period after Vatican II, and who should have implemented the Council's decisions with gratitude and enthusiasm. Yet most of them had been rendered virtually incapable of doing so by the regime in which they had been schooled as students. In the simplest terms one can say that the priests of the latter part of the twentieth century had been trained for a maintenance operation rather than for mission, or the renewal of the Church. The shortcomings of the training system is one of the most powerful forces making the institutional Church ineffectual in its mission, and hence an obstacle to faith.

The Sacrament of Anointing of the Sick

Of all the sacraments this has had the least complicated history. Its understanding has been blessed with a simple but comprehensive introduction in the New Testament. The Letter of James describes it quite simply :- "Is any among you sick ? Let him call for the presbyters of the church, and let them pray over him, anointing him with oil in the name of the Lord; and the prayer of faith will save the sick man, and the Lord will raise him up; and if he has committed sins, he will be forgiven". (James 4: 14, 15). In St. Mark's gospel there is also mention of anointing the sick, but in the context it is not clear that it was connected with the forgiveness of sins. The blessing of the oil for this anointing is contained in the third century Apostolic Tradition of Hippolytus. Other information about its employment in the patristic period show that it was performed regularly and did not give rise to any controversy.

Although there has been no real controversy about the sacrament, (apart from its rejection by the early Protestants), there has been a shift of emphasis. In the middle ages it was reserved for the hour of death, and was classified as one of the three last sacraments together with confession and communion (in that instance called viaticum, as I noted above). It was at that time that the sacrament acquired the name Extreme Unction, emphasising that it was the last anointing that the Church could give to a person. Other anointings had been given earlier at baptism, confirmation, and for some, at ordination. The anointing at ordination was given on the palm of the new priest's hand, so by custom a dying priest was anointed on the upper side of his hand. (It is reported of the famous Bishop Talleyrand that after apostatising, and joining the revolutionary government of France, he finally made an edifying repentance on his death bed. The last exquisite gesture was when he laid his hands palm downwards on the bed clothes so that his hands could be anointed correctly for a dying priest.[26])

Since the middle ages five anointings had been given in this sacrament, on the five senses which might have been the channels for sin. After the Second Vatican Council the ritual was simplified and the anointing was simply performed on the person's forehead. The emphasis was removed from the occasion of imminent death, and people were encouraged to receive the sacrament in a case of serious illness also.

The special relevance of this sacrament is that is forgives the sins of a well disposed recipient, even if he or she is incapable of speech. In other words it is a safety net for those who cannot make the self accusation of sin, which is a condition for valid absolution in the sacrament of penance . This is extremely important for those who are incapable of speech, after a stroke for example, or sufferers from an illness like motor neurone disease . It conveys to them, and their families, peace of mind in the knowledge that they have received the forgiveness of God, even if they may be unablel to speak and therefore confess.

POST SCRIPT : THE ORIGIN AND RATIONALE OF CLERICAL CELIBACY

The preceding chapter has shown, I trust, the importance of Mass and the sacraments in the life of the Church. At the beginning of the twenty first century the whole system is at risk because of an acute shortage of priests in the vast majority of countries. Except for matrimony and emergency baptism, the administration of all sacraments is restricted to bishops and priests, and obligatory celibacy is the most prominent obstacle to recruiting clergy. The situation is complex, and there are other more fundamental reasons which deter young men from coming forward. Yet paradoxically celibacy is the main deterrent, and its remedy is the simplest, namely an administrative decision by the Pope.

As far as the theme of this book is concerned the matter is one of merely indirect interest. However it constitutes a disincentive to an aspirant to Catholicism, so I will describe the main outlines of the problem, so that he or she can evaluate it in its proper context, and I refer readers to another book for a fuller treatment and further elucidation .[27]

---

[26] It seems that Talleyrand's Catholicism never really left him. While he was in the revolutionary government a colleague, the minister for public cult, is said to have sought his advice with the words "Monsieur de Talleyrand, I am informed that you have some experience of matters religious. I am having some difficulty in promoting the cult of Reason. Could you perhaps give me some advice ?" Talleyrand reflected for a few moments, and then replied . " Contrive to get yourself crucified, and then come to life three days later !"

[27] The matter is expounded in detail, with references to the sources in my study (2002) *Misguided Morality: Catholic Moral Teaching in the Contemporary Church,* Aldershot: Ashgate Publishing Limited, 2002, pp. 91 - 96 and 107 - 114.

118

Jesus made no restriction about marriage among his apostles and disciples, nor did he give any instruction for the future which touched upon the matter. The Epistles to Timothy and Titus envisage married men as bishops and presbyters (I Tim. 3: 1 - 7. Titus 1: 5 - 9). The Jewish tradition did not place any moral value on the single life, but parenthood was highly prized. The sources are then completely silent on the matter until the beginning of the fourth century, when the council of Elvira (in Spain) contained some restrictions on the sexual relations of priests, within its list of rules. The only reasonable deduction from those two standpoints is that in the first few centuries generally the clergy were married. Between the fourth and sixth centuries there are a small number of patristic opinions, and rules from popes and local councils which limit the exercise of sex by the married clergy. They are not particularly edifying, Pope Damasus likened it to the conduct of animals. The reason stated in all such instances is quite simply the concept of ritual purity. That was an attitude which established incompatibility between the sacred and certain bodily conditions. If he was

involved in sacred duties a priest could not have contact with disease, corpses, nor make love with his wife. It was a purely pagan notion, which entered the Old Testament from the earliest period of Judaism, and it was the attitude of all their pagan contemporaries. It is significant that this pernicious notion entered Christian thinking at the time that ideas were being taken from the Old Testament and applied to the Christian ministers.

By an extraordinary paradox of history, the Greek speaking part of the Church adopted a different practice although they too had accepted the pagan notion of ritual purity. This arose by the simple accident that the Greek Church followed the older practice of celebrating the eucharist only once a week, on Sundays. The Greek priests therefore continued normal marriage relations with their wives except on Saturday nights! The Catholic Eastern rites follow the ancient Greek custom which is why secular priests in those rites are, and always have been, married.

During the middle ages when the Church became a wealthy landowner there was an added motive, namely the reluctance of the authorities to see ecclesiastical property pass into the clerical families by inheritance. Nevertheless the old attitudes of cultic purity persisted. In 1130 Pope Innocent II addressed the Synod of Clermont with the words "Since priests are supposed to be God's temples, vessels of the Lord, and sanctuaries of the Holy Spirit - - -it offends their dignity to lie in the conjugal bed and live in impurity". Significantly that statement was pronounced midway between the First and Second Lateran Councils of 1123 and 1139, which enacted the laws making marriage an impediment to ordination, and vice versa, ordination was a barrier to a valid marriage. Only the decisions of those councils have survived, not the discussions, but one can be in doubt about the motivation, in view of what Pope Innocent stated.

The Second Vatican Council destroyed the foundations of the law by two pronouncements. In the decree on the Life and Ministry of Presbyters (section 16) the Council stated that there was no intrinsic connection between presbyterate and celibacy. In the constitution Gaudium et Spes (the Church in the Modern World, section 49) the Council declared that sex between husband and wife was morally good. This may seem glaringly obvious to most people, but in view of the pessimism on the matter in many ecclesiastical pronouncements in the past, it was important for the Council to make the point explicitly.

Pope Paul VI prevented the matter from being discussed at the Second Vatican Council. In 1967 he issued an encyclical letter on Priestly Celibacy, in which he upheld the current law, but gave no reason to justify it. In the course of the letter he was careful not to denigrate the rule in force in the Eastern Churches (Catholic and Orthodox). His words (in section 38 of the encyclical) deserve to be quoted verbatim :- " If the legislation of the Eastern Churches is different in the matter of discipline with regard to clerical celibacy, as was finally established by the Council of Trullo held in the year 692, and which has been clearly recognised by the Second Vatican Council, this is due to the different historical background of that most noble part of the Church, a situation which the Holy Spirit has providentially and supernaturally influenced." One is tempted ask if this is the extreme form of theological suicide: is it conceivable that the Holy Spirit would inspire contradictory laws in the two halves of the Church ? i.e. marriage is good for the Greek clergy, but bad for the Latin priests? To put it more courteously, the Pope was clearly at a loss to find a satisfactory principle by which he could justify the retention of obligatory celibacy for the Latin Church.

In 1983 another inconsistency in the law occurred when the English bishops under the leadership of Cardinal Hume, obtained permission from Pope John Paul II to ordain convert clergy from the Church of England even if they were married.

In 1992 a German theologian, H.J.Vogels published a study (*Celibacy - Gift or Law*) which completely demolished the theological rationale of the law. He began with a principle , accepted by all moral theologians, and affirmed by Pope John Paul II in his encyclical *Evangelium Vitae,* namely that no merely human law can invalidate a divine law. He then cited various popes including Leo XIII and Pius XI who had declared that marriage was a fundamental human right by divine natural law, which no human law could abrogate. The inalienable right to marry was also affirmed in Vatican II.[28] This means that the prohibition against priests marrying has no rational or theological foundation. This was bound to lead to demoralisation among the clergy, and may be the principal reason why so many priests resigned to get married. It has been estimated that in the years after the Second Vatican Council one hundred thousand priests resigned, most of them subsequently married.

In 1994 the Vatican took a retrograde step. The Congregation for the Clergy published a document entitled *Directory on the Ministry and Life of Priests* which upheld the mediaeval law, and justified it by the ancient concept of cultic purity. During the post-Conciliar period no scholar had produced a satisfactory case to justify the mediaeval ban either on theological or rational grounds. The intellectual bankruptcy of the official position was confirmed in the last decade of the twentieth century, when Pope John Paul II forbade bishops' conferences to discuss the question except to reaffirm the existing law.

---

[28] Vogels, H.J. (1992) *Celibacy – Gift or Law* ,Tunbridge Wells: Burns & Oates, p. 98.

CHAPTER EIGHT : CHRISTIAN MORAL LIFE

SECTION 1 : A SIMPLE STARTING POINT

Having seen how the human race has been reconciled to God and liberated from evil by the work of Jesus, we can now turn to the most practical expression of that liberation, namely the Christian moral life. The bestowal of grace through the sacraments and other channels empowers those who have committed themselves to Christ in faith and baptism to lead a life of fulfilment by directing their activity in accordance with his ideals. If properly pursued this will be positive, joyful, creative, and at times heroic.

Having stated the basic scenario I must begin with an apparent disclaimer. For Christians there is no law or set of rules in the sense of the Pentateuch and its attendant clarifications. These latter in the time of Jesus amounted to 613 precise rules devised by the rabbis to safeguard the integral observation of the regulations in the bible. St. Paul told them bluntly that it was all finished (Ephesians 2:15 for example). The Old Covenant of Sinai had served its purpose. It had been fulfilled in the work of Jesus, and his New Covenant had replaced it, not in the sense that it had been of no value, but it was now superseded by the definitive system for which it had been the preparation and education. There are times in an individual's life when he must move forward, and in the collective life of God's People that time was Pentecost. In the ancient Jewish liturgy the festival of Pentecost commemorated the giving of the first Covenant to Moses on Mount Sinai. The bestowal of the Holy Spirit on the occasion of that festival was to show the early Christians that the Holy Spirit would do for them what the Law had done for their ancestors. Henceforth morality would be guided by a person whose influence could not be encapsulated in any rules or regulations.

Lest it should seem that the appeal to the Holy Spirit is too imprecise, let me remind the reader that it was the apex of the moral teaching of the most orthodox of theologians, St. Thomas Aquinas. The Jesuit theologian John Mahoney, expressed it thus :- (after describing St.Thomas's discussion of various kinds of law) "Aquinas came finally, in a totally original treatment, to what he termed the evangelical law, which is called the New Law. In this new law he posited a fundamental and radical distinction between what he called its primary and secondary elements. The secondary element comprises all the teaching of Scripture, the documents of faith and the precepts which put order into human reactions and human behaviour . . . . .all of which have one simple function, either to dispose man to receive the primary element of the new law or to help man express that primary element. And the primary element of the Gospel law is nothing other than the presence of the Holy Spirit within man".[1]

The very simplicity of this moral programme has left many Christians feeling somewhat without bearings and in need of some supplementary guidance, without wishing to return to a set of rules like the Jewish system. St. Paul has given us in effect four over - arching principles to set us in the right direction. Firstly there is the love of God and our neighbour. Secondly he draws attention to the basic message of Genesis that man had been created in the image of God. This means that our conduct must be creative. This in turn gives rise of a pair

---

[1] Mahoney, J.(1987) *The Making of Moral Theology,* Oxford:O. U.P., pp. 254, 255, referring to Aquinas S.T. I - II q. 106.

of complimentary principles, namely that we must not be ruled or enslaved by our relationships to creation. That is to say, in the most general terms, not to be dominated by material pleasures or comforts and the desires which arise in the pursuit of them. The other aspect of creative behaviour concerns personal relationships which must be creative and not exploitative. We must relate to other people to enhance them and not to enslave them. Fourthly St. Paul urges his readers to live their lives so as to build up the Christian community. This has several consequences some of which I have discussed already. [2]

Whether we like it or not, Christian experience has not been content to live within such simple moral frameworks as I have described above, but other more precise patterns of behaviour have been sought but which were not the adoption of another set of rules. Natural law proved to be greatly attractive to Christian thinkers in the days of the Roman Empire. Theologians of that period discerned intellectual and moral allies in the ethical writers such as Aristotle, Plato and the school of the Stoics. The world vision of the latter group was attractive to Christian sentiment on account of its picture of a purposeful universe within which man ought to collaborate by harmonising his behaviour with the overall orientation revealed by the harmony of the natural world. In other words, the concept of natural law had entered the programme of the Church. It was a helpful ancillary source of guidance, provided that it did not become tyrannical in the light of its alleged precise demands, which was to happen at a later stage of the Church's history.

Baroness Warnock has pointed out that the long tradition of natural law in European philosophy has done little to motivate the human heart. In that context she drew attention to the contribution of David Hume who showed how the ideals could appeal to the whole person:- "What is honourable, what is fair, what is becoming, what is noble, what is generous, takes possession of the heart, and animates us to embrace and maintain it". [3]

It is important to remember that no amount of regulation of human conduct by detailed rules based on divine authority, or insights of natural law can cater for the exact circumstances of individual human predicaments. For example in ordinary business activities, at what point does a persuasive advertisement become a lie deceiving the potential purchasers ? Only the individual responsible for the activity can make the decision. Utilising the guiding principles which I have outlined above he or she must make a practical judgement which is the exercise of the individual's conscience. This is the final arbiter in all moral decisions, and conscience must always be obeyed.

SECTION 2 : AQUINAS AND THE VIRTUES.

A few lines above I drew the reader's attention to St. Thomas's remarkable claim that the Holy Spirit is our guide in making life's moral choices. Yet, wearing his other hat, St. Thomas

---

[2] For the discussion of St. Paul's moral theology, I am indebted to the indispensable study of Jerome Murphy O'Connor, (1978) *Becoming Human Together,* Dublin: Veritas Publications, especially pp. 215 - 229.

[3] Hume, D. *An Enquiry Concerning the Principles of Morals,* Book 1, section 1, para. 136, quoted in Warnock, M. (2001), *An Intelligent Person's Guide to Ethics.* London: Duckworth, p.120.

the teacher divides human moral conduct systematically into seven areas for the sake

of clarity when explaining the whole vast field to his students and subsequent readers. As a pedagogical method he adopted the classical Greek system of four moral virtues, prudence, justice, fortitude and temperance. To these he added, in the first place, the three Christian theological virtues of faith, hope and charity.

Faith as the Foundation of the Moral Life

Before Vatican II faith was usually presented as the intellectual assent to information about God, expressed in clear propositions, and presented to us by the Church authorities. At the time of the Council a more satisfactory understanding of it gained currency, namely that it is a commitment of the whole person to Christ in a relationship of life - long loyalty. The intellectual component is not absent, but it is a subordinate element. It gives the believer a new vision of life and the world, within which he or she will pursue life's journey expressing the loyal commitment to Christ in the moral choices presented by every major practical decision.

This perspective contrasts sharply with the older vision of life, where morality was based on obedience to rules presented by the Church authorities. Apart from its pragmatic failings, the old system of obedience did not do justice to the real moral responsibility of adult committed Christians. They had never been encouraged to take real responsibility for their own moral choices. Fortunately in the post conciliar period that has all changed and convinced Catholics now make their decisions in the light of their commitment to Christ, their religious vision of the world and their responsibility for it. Morality has become an expression of faith. (I can only speak with confidence about the change of attitude of Catholics. Other Churches have had different histories in this matter. The Quakers deserve the respect of all other Christians for their independence of mind and action.)

Hope Keeps us Going.

The difference between the commonplace understanding of the word 'hope' and its meaning in the New Testament is that the former connects it with something that is a possibility but in the bible it designates something already achieved in principle. The example of the lottery will make this clear. Every week millions of people buy lottery tickets in the hope that they might win a large prize. It is only a possibility in their minds, and a pretty remote one at that, probably a chance of about one in fourteen million. In the Christian understanding of hope the prize has already been won, and the only element not fixed is the situation in which we will receive it. By this I mean that the victory of good over evil has already been achieved by the liberating work of Christ's crucifixion and resurrection.

The full extent of his victory will become apparent only at the end of time, when Christ will return to earth in glory and gather to himself all those individuals who have accepted his gift of salvation. This future event is named as the *parousia* in the language of the New Testament, and it is the goal to which human history is moving purposefully, not in an aimless succession of events just randomly unfolding one after another. [4] The resurrection of

---

[4] cf. Jurgen Moltmann, (1967) *Theology of Hope,* London : S.C.M. Press, pp. 224 - 9.

Jesus is the sign for the encouragement of Christians, indicating to us that the victory of Christ has already been achieved. Unlike the devotees of the lottery, the prize has already been won for the Christians. In the life of grace the believer enjoys its benefits in this life.

Because of the prevalence of evil in the human race which is dominated by original sin, the virtue of hope is supplemented by a subsidiary virtue which in the New Testament is named as *hupomone*. To translate this word as 'patience' does not do justice to it on account of the passive overtones of that English word. A better translation would be 'patient endurance'. It is the virtue which sustains us against all the negative pressures which tend to discourage us from the pursuit of morally worthy objectives. Its highest expression is martyrdom when heroic Christians endure every privation including death, but do not abandon their loyalty to Christ. Its application in life can be seen for example in the campaign to abolish the slave trade. Men like Wilberforce and his associates were vilified, ridiculed, menaced, even with death threats, and some of them saw the wrecking of their political careers. Nevertheless they persevered against all obstacles until their moral objective had been achieved.

If hope is described as our confidence in God, then confidence in our fellow men can be designated as trust. This too is a subsidiary virtue allied to hope. It operates at the domestic level in family life. Small children must be given increasingly difficult tasks for the development of their personalities. Parents must trust their small children to carry a plate or cup from the table to the kitchen sink without dropping them. As they grow older they should be trusted to do adequate revision for important exams without draconian pressure. In the adult world of work it applies to industrial relations. If the management trusts the employees and organises the work accordingly, the outcome is seen in efficiency. If this trust is patently absent the result is disputes, strikes and endemic inefficiency.

The concept of trust received a very important clarification in the 1930's in the Principle of Subsidiarity. This was first enunciated by Pope Pius XI. Briefly it means that in the operation of large institutions practical decision making should be made at the lowest feasible level of management, and not at the highest possible point. For example, in a supermarket, the location of the pool of customers' trolleys should be decided by the branch manager and not by head office. It depends on the lay-out of the building and other factors of which the manager on the spot is better equipped to decide. Although the principle had a pope for its author, and it was endorsed by the Second Vatican Council, it is badly observed within the Church's organisational structures. [5]

Charity as the Mainstream of Christian Moral Life.

The love of God and our neighbour was first announced to the Israelite people in the Pentateuch (Deuteronomy 6:5 and Leviticus 19:18) and it received frequent confirmation in the exhortations of the prophets. In the teaching of Jesus it moved into the absolute centre of his moral programme, and has remained so ever since. Comparisons are odious, but one cannot help noticing that profound generosity is to be seen in the lives of people with strong

---

[5] Abbot . W. (ed.) *The Documents of Vatican II* , page 300, where other references are cited concerning its use in papal encyclicals.

religious commitment. In view of its importance in the Old Testament it should not surprise us that our spiritual cousins the Jews are famous for their generous philanthropy. To cite but one example: Benzion Dunner who lived in north London in 2008, gave away two million pounds in one day, to celebrate the Jewish festival of Purim. Knowing his generosity, people who had fallen on hard times queued up outside his house all night. In the morning he started interviewing them one by one, and went on writing out cheques until 4.am on the following morning. Two days later he was killed in a car crash. One cannot think of a better way of a rich man preparing to meet his Maker.[6]

Another example of the religious motivation for loving one's neighbour was in the life of a retired Anglican priest and his wife. It concerns Natasha who is now a talented and successful artist, but her life was not always a success. When she was 16 her father committed suicide, and two years later her stepfather stabbed her mother to death, in the family home. She had three siblings. All four of them were taken in and brought up by the local vicar and his wife, Barry and Mary Kissell, whose grown up children had left home. "It was what made me a Christian," says Natasha. "I was struck by the kindness and love of strangers. I'm still bowled over by their selflessness".[7]

The central place accorded to the love of God and neighbour derives from the long discourses of Jesus like the Sermon on the Mount (Matthew chapters 5, 6, and 7, with parallels in the other synoptics) and the discourse on the Last Judgement in Matthew chapter 25: 31 - 46 . Having illustrated the practicalities in giving food to the hungry, a lodging to the homeless, and care to prisoners and the sick, Jesus sums it up in the well known words " When you did it to the least of these my brethren your did it to me" (Matt. 25:40). In fact, as is well known, in all the gospels and epistles there are countless examples illustrating the love of God and neighbour.

The biblical examples are for the most part illustrations of spontaneous reactions to individuals in hardship (like the parable of the Good Samaritan), yet it does not detract from the moral generosity if the activity is organised to some extent. I mention this because some people feel uneasy if charity is institutionalised or even provided with a legal framework. In the course of the Church's long history religious orders have institutionalised some aspects of Christian life. Care for the poor and homeless was also a by-product of their life of prayer. At a later stage in the Church's history religious orders were founded specifically to promote works of charity, such as care for the sick. It is significant that in the later middle ages all the hospitals were religious foundations. The achievement was remarkable. At the end of the fourteenth century England had 470 hospitals. This pattern was repeated all over Europe, Italy having perhaps the best provision. In the fifteenth century, in Florence alone there were 33 hospitals, which was approximately one hospital for every 1000 inhabitants. But disaster was in store for England. When King Henry VIII shut down all religious houses, one of the unintended results was the closure of the hospitals. England was left with just three in London, and possibly a fourth in Norwich, which had been re-started by the local citizens. By

---

[6] Reported in *The Observer,* 30 March 2008.

[7] Reported in *The Observer*, (Womens' Supplement) January 2008.

the year 1700 the three in London were open. The rest of the country had no hospitals at all.[8]

St. Vincent de Paul , in 17th century France, is probably the best know organiser of practical charity. He founded religious orders, raised large sums of money, and organised a superb network of hospitals and orphanages. This kind of systematic institutionalisation has become traditional in the Church. Catholics are sometimes shy about a more modern manifestation of the same principle. I will justify it by a case study, namely the abolition of slavery, which was achieved in the English speaking world thanks to Christian initiatives. There are four stages which have to be gone through if the betterment of peoples lives is to be achieved successfully. They are amelioration, protest, enablement, and institutional change.

In relation to the slave trade, the first stage, amelioration, can be seen in the work of St. Peter Claver. He was a Spanish Jesuit, born in 1581, who went to Colombia in 1610. He was ordained priest in 1615, and spent the rest of his life in the sea port of Cartagena, working for the welfare of the slaves. At the end of their horrific transatlantic journeys he provided them with food and medical care for a start. He also saw to their spiritual welfare, shirking nothing in the course of duty, so that he even accompanied convicted criminals to the gallows. On his death in 1654 he was canonised by popular acclamation, such was the strength of his reputation. It does not belittle his heroic generosity if one should reflect on the limitations of his confining his activities to the corporal works of mercy.

The role of protest in the exercise of charity can be seen, in this context, in the life and work of another Spaniard, the Dominican Bartolomé de las Casas. His involvement with the slave trade goes back almost to the beginnings of the Spanish empire. He was born in Seville in 1484 and a few years later his father and one of his uncles accompanied Columbus in his second voyage to the Caribbean. In 1502 Bartolomé himself went to Haiti as a soldier, and also served in the invasion of Cuba. Like so many other soldiers he was rewarded with a grant of land in a system known as the *encomienda* . The natives who lived on the land were obliged to work for their Spanish masters without payment. The system was not quite as bad as outright slavery, because the natives were not reduced to the status of merchandise. Eventually Bartolomé became a priest (incidentally the first European to be ordained in America), and in 1514 he freed his Indian workers. Thereafter he resolved to try to end the system. Between 1515 and 1543 his life was extraordinarily busy. He made several crossings of the Atlantic. He spent years in Europe writing about the situation in the Caribbean and lobbying the king and his ministers about the conditions of the native Indians in the Spanish possessions in America. His specific objective was to persuade the authorities to enact new laws to protect the rights of the natives, so that they should not be exploited by compulsory unpaid work. He also undertook missionary work in Nicaragua and Mexico. He entered the Dominican order in 1524. Eventually the Spanish Government passed laws to free the natives from the constraints of the *encomienda* system, and required that they should be paid wages for any work done.

On becoming a bishop in Mexico he initiated the policy of refusing the sacraments to Spanish colonial farmers who did not free their native workers under the terms of the new laws. At this time of his life he also condemned the trade in African slaves. Hitherto he had assumed that they were condemned criminals.

---

[8] Porter,R. (1996), *The Cambridge Illustrated History of Medicine,* Cambridge: C.U.P. pp. 211, 212.

The third element in the exercise of charity is enablement. The principle was exemplified in

the twentieth century by a South American bishop who said " If I give a fish to a poor man he can feed himself and his family for a day. If I give him a rod and teach him how to fish, he can feed himself and his family for the rest of his life." That is something of an over simplification, but it illustrate the principle. In the 18th century this principle was put into effect by an American Quaker named John Woolman. As a young man he tried his hand at a number of careers, including tailor, surveyor, and school teacher, but at the age of 23 he gave up work and toured the Quaker communities of North America writing and preaching against the slave trade. The year 1758 marked a singular success in his work: he persuaded the Quaker community of Philadelphia to liberate all their slaves. Many other Quaker communities were persuaded to do the same.

The fourth and final component in the institutionalising of charity is structural change. In the case of the slave trade it meant entering the political arena to bring about changes to the legal system which would make it a criminal offence. The best known activist in the movement, in England was William Wilberforce, his hard working and close collaborator was Thomas Clarkson who deserves to be better known. Their lives followed remarkably close parallel courscs. Wilberforce was born in 1759 and Clarkson a year later. Both men studied at Cambridge. The difference was one of wealth. Wilberforce was born into an exceedingly rich family, whose wealth ensured his election to Parliament as M.P. for Hull in 1780. Clarkson was the son of a country clergyman of modest means, who was also the headmaster of Wisbeach grammar school. Initially he intended to follow his father into the ranks of the clergy, but significant events re-shaped his life in 1785. In that year (in addition to a first class degree in mathematics) he also won a university prize for an essay entitled "Is it Right to Enslave Men against their Will?" Shortly after gaining that prize he travelled to London to arrange for it to be published. In the course of the journey, near the town of Ware in Hertfordshire, he underwent a transforming spiritual experience. He thereupon decided against ordination, and resolved to spend the rest of his life campaigning for the abolition of slavery.

In the same year Wilberforce too underwent a conversion experience while on holiday in France. Thereafter he changed his manner of life, devoting the early hours of each day to prayer and study, and consciously sought a good cause to which he could purposefully devote his life. The purpose was presented to him providentially when he was approached by the Committee for the Effecting of the Abolition of the Slave Trade. They invited him to become their representative in parliament.

The combination of generous love of neighbour and hard headed realism is to be seen in the work of both men. Clarkson sought out the facts. He toured the sea ports of England interviewing sailors who had worked on slave ships. Eventually hc interviewed 20,000 sailors. Wilberforce persuaded his collaborators to make a severely practical decision, namely to limit themselves to just one objective, namely to make the trade illegal. He realised that slavery itself was too diffuse an institution to be eradicated by one single measure. Yet he calculated that if the trade in slaves was abolished, the rest of the system would collapse inevitably.

Thus the scene was set for more than twenty years of hard work, lobbying, writing, and negotiating. Its darker side was the unscrupulous opposition of the commercial vested interests, who saw how much money they might loose. The campaigners suffered vilification,

hostility, death threats , and in the case of Wilberforce, the loss of any prospect of advancement in parliament. But for espousing the cause of the slaves, he might well have become prime minister. After several unsuccessful attempts, a bill to abolish the slave trade was passed in parliament in 1807. In 1833 slavery as such was outlawed in Great Britain and its colonies. The whole operation is a classical example of the virtue of Christian charity pursuing the path of institutionalisation, or structural change, in order to make its philanthropy more effective and permanent.[9]

For Prudence read Politics.

As the traditional order of the moral virtues, prudence, justice, fortitude and temperance, is so well established, I will follow it in this chapter. But as the word prudence has become distorted in general usage, I prefer to introduce it the context of politics. It is on the path of political life that human moral conduct requires prudence as its guide. Let me explain.

In 1926 Cardinal Bourne, then the leader of the English Catholics, declared that it would be sinful for Catholic to take part in the General Strike. In 1938 in Austria Cardinal Innitzer welcomed the take over of their nation by the Nazis. Both those decisions were disastrously wrong, and it is not just with the wisdom of hindsight that we can see it. If the leaders in question had been guided by the virtue of prudence they would surely have acted differently. Aquinas defines this virtue as *recta ratio agibilium* which could best be translated as 'the right plan for activity'.[10] In that context the word 'right' refers to moral rightfulness and not to the practical matter of having devised the correct practical course to bring the activity to a successful conclusion.

In the second half of the twentieth century Liberation theologians devised a tool of great value for the exercise of this virtue : it is called Conscientization. It operates in two stages. The first stage is the exercise of discernment and awareness in confronting any practical problem. For example, let us consider infant mortality, which in many parts of Africa and Latin America is as serious as it was in mediaeval Europe. Conscientization requires that they examine the problem in the light of experience, faith, and science. Is it one of life's hazards like M.S. and other incurable diseases ? No, clearly it is a simple matter. Most of the young lives could be saved by providing pure drinking water.

The second stage of conscientization is more specific. If it has become apparent that the problem is not inevitable, one must ask, what is the appropriate moral course of action. Is it a protest against the local government for failing in its duty to provide the most basic requirement of life, namely clean drinking water?

---

[9] At roughly the same time the revolutionary government of France abolished slavery on the basis of the principle of human equality. However, this does not invalidate the role of Christian charity in the parallel process which took place in England.

[10] Aquinas S.T. I - II q. 47. a.2, following Aristotle, *Ethics* Book 6, chapter 5.

A wide range of complex commercial and political problems almost always contain a moral component which is sometimes the key to the whole operation, and the solution to its problems. For example, in the 1970's a certain Swiss company made great efforts with

persuasive advertisements to sell its brand of powdered milk in Africa. Women who were misled by the advertisements gave up breast feeding and gave their babies the alleged more sophisticated powdered milk. As a result large numbers of infants died of dysentery or other enteric diseases. Without absolutely pure drinking water and the ability to sterilise the bottles, the use of the powdered milk was literally lethal. Conscientization indicated that their failure to make allowance for this was morally culpable. It is to the credit of several Christian pressure groups that large scale pressure was put upon the manufacturing company in Switzerland, and they were forced to curtail their sales promotion in the developing countries.

Justice

The virtue of justice is something of an anomaly. Whereas the bulk of the Christian moral programme concerns my obligations to other people, justice also includes obligations to myself. It is concerned with the reciprocal upholding of rights. It is the concept of right which gives rise to the "two way traffic". A right can be defined as a relationship between myself and the outside world of people and objects which gives rise to obligations towards me, in addition to my obligations to others. For example if I purchase a car for £ 18,000 or whatever sum, other people have an obligation not to steal it from me. (It is too obvious to spell out that I must not take other peoples' cars). Furthermore if I work for eight hours picking grapes in a vineyard, this activity gives rise to an obligation by the owner of the vineyard to pay me for eight hours' work.

At the level of private ownership of property the principles of justice were fully worked out by the ethical philosophers and jurists of antiquity. Right up to the middle ages the concept of rights was largely connected with those which accrued to property. The concept of human rights came later. It was expounded influentially in 18th century Europe by the thinkers of the Enlightenment. However its origins may go back further. Cromwell's soldiers were debating the issues in the famous meetings in Putney parish church in 1647 during a lull in the Civil war.

The Second Vatican Council embraced the concept enthusiastically.[11] In the aftermath of the Council the Vatican took a step backwards, and the concept was conspicuously absent from the revised Code of Canon Law promulgated in 1983. In spite of this regrettable lacuna over human rights, the popes in the latter part of the 20th century, following the lead of the Second Vatican Council, made some extremely positive statements about world poverty and the distribution of wealth. One important idea which was made explicit in the post - conciliar encyclicals was the concept of structured injustice. This is a situation where economic or political power has been institutionalised in such a way that wealth or freedom automatically move away from the poor and into the hands of those who are already rich. Pope Paul VI wrote about this in the context of capitalism, and he declared that a just economic order could

---

[11] Vatican II, document *Gaudium et Spes,* section 41, ed. Abbott p. 241.

not be built on liberal capitalism. [12] It was emphasised again in Pope John Paul II's encyclical *Sollicitudo Rei Socialis* of 1987. Their warnings received depressing confirmation in the financial crises of international capitalism after 2008. In 1994 Pope John Paul II was unambiguous in his encyclical *Tertio Millennio Adveniente,* in urging that Third World debt

should not be simply alleviated, but cancelled altogether .

Obedience as a Subsidiary part of Justice

As a component of the Christian moral programme obedience is definitely an anomaly. In its widest usage it is nothing more than a pragmatic arrangement to get things done. In the life of the Church it has acquired a more dignified role thanks to the community life of monasteries and other religious orders. Experience shows that a group of enthusiasts living in community must have some kind of rule to live by and some one who is entitled to co-ordinate their living according to that rule or custom. Otherwise the result is chaos. A community like a monastery is too large for the operations of the informal dialogues which keep family life running smoothly at the domestic level. In his famous rule St. Benedict stressed the importance of obedience to the abbot as an expression of doing the will of God.

As a basic principle no adult should hand over to another the responsibility for his or her moral choices. The practical exigencies of daily work , as outlined above, do not really amount to a surrender of personal moral responsibility. This principle must be borne in mind in serious issues like carrying out military orders to kill civilians in time of war. Aquinas prepared his readers for this by classifying obedience with justice. This means that individuals can offend against it, as in other matters of justice, by giving too little obedience or too much. It was this latter area which caused a complete revolution in the perception of obedience in the context of Nazism in Germany and the Second World War in particular.

In principle citizens have a moral obligation to obey the just laws of a legitimate government. However if the laws are not just a moral conflict arises. In the Nazi period in Germany in the 1930's and 40's the government enacted measures against Jews and other racial minorities in the pursuit of so called racial purity. This led to systematic persecution of the Jews , and ultimately their extermination, as well as medical experiments and clinical killing of psychiatric patients.[13] In that period of institutionalised wickedness the medical profession, the army, and the Churches acquiesced deliberately or at least tacitly.[14]

The Christian Churches of Germany cannot escape responsibility for preparing the ground for that kind of atrocity. The laity had been conditioned to obedience towards their religious superiors, and political rulers, and as far as the Catholics were concerned independent

---

[12] Encyclical Letter *Populorum Progressio ,* section 26.

[13] Platen - Hallermund, A.(1948) *Die Totung Geisteskranker in Deutschland,* Frankfurt am Main: Verlag der Frankfurter Hefte, passim ,esp. pp. 63, 81,& 91. Engl translation, *The Killing of the Mentally Ill in Germany.* London 1948.

[14] The events have been researched carefully in well known studies, i.e. Goldhagen, D.J. (1996), *Hitler's Willing Executioners,* London: Abacus. Spicer, K. P. (2008) *Hitler's Priests: Catholic Clergy and National Socialism,* DeKalb, Illinois: Northern Illinois University Press,

judgement in moral questions was totally discouraged.

It is to the credit of one Christian Church, the Quakers, that they have consistently encouraged independent moral decision making including positive defiance of laws and commands which they perceive to be at variance with the New Testament ideals. During the 17th century Civil War their founder, George Fox was in prison. He was offered his freedom if he would accept

the post of a captaincy in the Parliamentary army. He refused because he would not kill his fellow human beings. His followers have been consistent in their refusal of military service. They have been equally independent in many other areas too, thereby giving witness to authentic Christian values which other Churches would have done well to imitate.

Truthfulness as a Component of Justice

Truthfulness, unlike obedience, is a virtue which is totally positive. It is so central to Christianity that in the perspectives of the fourth gospel it was the way in which Jesus defined his mission. When he was questioned by Pilate about his alleged political activities, he replied: "I was born for this, I came into the word for this: to bear witness to the truth" (John 18: 37). Earlier in his public life John reports his applying the virtue to the lives of his followers:- "If you make my word your home, you will indeed be my disciples, you will learn the truth, and the truth will make you free". (John 8:32).

Truth combined with practical activity really does give people freedom from immoral compromises which simply diminish them as human beings. Habitual practice of this kind of truthfulness is described as integrity. Its highest expression, as witness to truth, is martyrdom. In the life of a saint like Thomas More all these qualities can be seen. In the entourage of the tyrannical king Henry VIII, More was the only one who had real freedom. He made it clear to the king and others that he did not seek political advancement. Men like Wolsey and Cromwell were compromised on account of their ambition. In the final analysis they could not tell the king unwelcome truths.

Apart from the moral beauty of heroic integrity, the practical realities of everyday life depend on its more pedestrian performance. If people generally told lies to one another instead of truth, commerce, education, social life and other human activities would grind to a halt. This has been illustrated recently by the publication of detailed biographies of the French philosopher Jean - Paul Sartre. His attitude to truthfulness was epitomised in a remark to a friend "There are some people one simply had to lie to".[15] Some years later he was on holiday in Rome with his mistress Michelle Vian . He lost interest in her, prompting her to write in distress to her own secret lover named Reweliotty, threatening suicide. Reweliotty hastened to Rome to console her. Concealment was impossible. The reality of the situation was clear to all three. Michelle and her lover left Rome secretly. Sartre realised that she had been unfaithful to him for the whole nine years of their relationship, and he felt grieved and morally outraged by her lies. He seems not to have appreciated that he had done just the same to her.[16] That painful incident did nothing to alter Sartre's conduct. Toward the end of his life

---

[15] Rowley, H. (2006) *Téte à Téte : The Lives and Loves of Simone de Beauvoir and Jean-Paul Sartre.* London: Chatto & Windus, p.84.

[16] Rowley, op. cit. p.250.

another friend asked him how he coped with all his women, some of whom were notoriously jealous. He replied "I lie to them. It is easier and more decent." "Do you lie to all of them?" his friend asked. Sartre smiled " To all of them". "Even to the Beaver (his nickname for Simone de Beauvoir) ?" "Particularly to the Beaver", was his reply.[17] Clearly his systematic

lying totally exploited and wrecked the lives of a number of individuals around him. If that pattern of conduct were pursued by too many people the normalities of life simply could not survive in society as a whole.

Society in England has benefited greatly from the truthful exactitude of the Methodists and members of other free Churches in everyday life, which had given rise to the famous non-conformist conscience. One may smile at their moral preciseness, but societies which do not have such a sensitive moral code suffer innumerable injustices and inefficiencies, for example with town hall bureaucracies which must be bribed at every stage, and with whom the citizens can never feel secure.

The enemies of truth are numerous. Apart from the basic offence of telling lies, they comprise the various ways in which truth is imprisoned. The first of these is concealment. For example the danger of working with asbestos was known as early as the 1950's. By that time it had been clear to scientists that even slight exposure to the fibres could cause incurable damage to the lungs resulting in a painful death. Only slowly did government agencies take the necessary precautions for their workers, and some commercial organisations ignored it until near the end of the century. They realised that providing the protective clothing and other safeguards would cost money and lessen their profits.

Another enemy is the habit of politicians and governments of concealing policies and decisions which show that they have made unwise or immoral decisions. Shortly after the Falklands War a civil servant, Clive Ponting was present at a meeting where a number of ministers worked out a systematic plan to conceal the truth about the unlawful sinking of the Argentinian warship the *General Belgrano*. His sense of moral revulsion was so strong that he disclosed the whole matter to the press.

By the same token the silencing of scholars by politicians or Church censors is an extremely delicate matter. In purely secular matters scholars and writers can be left to correct one another's mistakes in the free debates of academic life. In extreme cases, like the condemnation of Arianism, the Church in a general council for example, is entitled to declare that a given theory is at variance with the traditional revealed doctrine. However it is illegitimate to extrapolate from that situation to the repressive control of all new ideas which are being floated among theologians.

The period after the Second World War saw a regrettable surge in that kind of pressure against innovative theologians. A classical case was the fate of the famous Dominican theologian Yves Congar. After the publication in 1953 of his ground breaking book *Vrai et Fausse Reforme dans l'Église* (True and False Reform in the Church), he came under suspicion at the Vatican. As a punishment he was removed from his teaching post, exiled

---

[17] Rowley, op.cit. p. 335.

from France and sent to the Dominican house in Cambridge. Furthermore he was forbidden to write any more books in the future. The summary dismissal from his teaching post was bad enough, but the prohibition against future writing was totally unjust. It was equivalent to punishing a man in advance for crimes which he had not yet committed. When the enlightened pope John XXIII was elected Father Congar was exonerated and was made one of the expert theological advisors to the Second Vatican Council.

The most discreditable offence against truth in the recent history of the Church was the

official attempts to cover up the scandals of sex abuse of children by priests. The events have been so widely publicised in the press that it is necessary only to recall the salient points here. In the 1990's allegations began to appear before the law courts and in the press of massive abuse of children (sexually and by physical cruelty) by Catholic priests, and by members of religious orders of men and women who were running childrens' homes. These scandals have been widely publicised in Great Britain, Ireland, U.S.A., Australia and Canada. The numbers involved are massive. In the U.S.A. the church commissioned a study which found that 10,667 people accused 4,392 priests of child sex abuse from 1950 until 2002. [18] Those facts are bad enough. What has compounded the whole tragedy morally has been the attempt by the authorities to hush up everything. Originally the offending priests were simply moved swiftly to other parishes or dioceses, and secrecy was imposed so that the reputation of the institution should not be tarnished.

The Virtue of Fortitude

Undeniably the worst evil which one human being can inflict upon another is killing, because of its finality. Every sin can be repented, but this one must always remain without restitution. To face suffering and death for a noble cause has always been admired and the moral strength to do so has been called fortitude since the time of the ancient Greeks.

Christianity entered a world whose culture placed a high value on military courage. Homer's epic poems, the Iliad and the Odyssey had set the tone, which was followed in the Roman sphere by Virgil's Aeneid. All those epics and others like them extolled courage in battle. It is worth noting that the brutal cruelties of war were effectively concealed by the poets, and by glorious uniforms, theatrical- style parades, and military bands. In many countries too a career as an officer in the armed forces was socially acceptable in middle class and aristocratic families.

What was the Christian reaction to that mind-set ? Initially it was extremely hostile . The earliest official document indicating the Church's attitude is the third century *Apostolic Tradition* of Hippolytus of Rome. As I have noted earlier in this book, the document records the liturgical practices of the Roman community, which is a representative guide to what Christians thought and did elsewhere. In the section on baptism he lists a number of occupations which are incompatible with Christianity, and which have to be abandoned by candidates for baptism. The list of forbidden occupations begins with brothel keepers, and includes gladiators and their trainers, actors and prostitutes and also soldiers. The actual wording of the prohibition is instructive and deserves to be quoted verbatim:- " A soldier

[18] Reported in *The Observer*, 13 th April 2008.

under authority shall not kill a man. If he is ordered to he shall not carry out the order; nor shall he take the oath. If he is unwilling let him be rejected. He who has the power of the sword, or is a magistrate of a city who wears the purple, let his cease or be rejected. A catechumen or believer who want to become soldiers should be rejected, because they have despised God".[19] Clearly the underlying principle is the sacredness of life, because the ban applies to magistrates who can exercise the death penalty. The outlook reflected in Hippolytus

was also embraced by the Council of Nicaea in 325. Canon 12 decreed that if a soldier had left the army, become a Christian and then returned to the army he was required to do penance for thirteen years before being re-admitted to the eucharist.

Many soldier martyrs are honoured in the Church's liturgy, who were executed because they obeyed those injunctions and refused to kill. In presenting martyrdom as a high moral ideal, the infant Church proposed to its followers a form of courage which was more valiant than that of the military heroes. The martyr's triumph over fear was so complete that he or she did not offer resistance, or make an attempt to escape. It is significant that in the church's liturgy the martyrs were the first saints to be honoured in public worship after the apostles.

After the time of Constantine the Church had to make difficult choices. By the time that Christians were a majority in the empire, it became clear that they must take up some responsibility for the defence of that empire, whose stable society provided the peaceful environment for the Christian religion to flourish. In that context St. Augustine, in the fifth century produced the first formulation of the theory of a just war. It was refined in the middle ages by St. Thomas Aquinas, and has remained substantially unchanged since then. Basically it is an extrapolation to the national level of the personal right of self defence, if an individual is attacked by a violent criminal. The conditions for a Christian to join the armed forces in a just war are that the cause must be just, all peaceful methods of resolving the dispute have been exhausted, and that in the course of the conflict there must be a proportionality between the violence and the result which is being pursued. It is difficult to think of any instances when these considerations have influenced the military adventures of Christian nations. Nuclear weapons and other technical advances in weaponry in the 20th century has made the concept of proportionality almost meaningless.

The abandonment of the restraint of proportionality was exemplified in a terrifying manner in the high altitude air raids on Germany by British and American aircraft in the Second World War. They were totally indiscriminate. Even in daylight they could not see their targets with sufficient clarity to pinpoint them. At night time the bombers could not be sure that their bombs would land any closer than four miles from a given target, so they resorted to carpet bombing, which had been authorised by Winston Churchill on July 8th 1940, just two days after he became Prime Minister. [20] The policy was re-affirmed in February 1942 when the really large four engined bombers came into service.[21]

---

[19] Hippolytus, *Apostolic Tradition,* section 16, ed. Cummings,G.J. (1984) Nottingham: Grove Books, p.16.

[20] Johnson, P. (1995) *The Withered Garland: Reflections and Doubts of a Bomber,* London: New European Publications Ltd., p. 318.

[21] Johnson, P. op.cit. p.320. In his directive to Bomber Command, Air chief Marshal Portal stressed

What is depressing is that this indiscriminate cruelty met with no Christian protest . In particular the military chaplains in the R.A.F. seem to have made no attempt to encourage any such moral independence in the airmen for whom they were responsible. Gordon Zahn researched the matter thoroughly after the war, and in particular reference to the bombing of Dresden in February 1945.[22] The city of Dresden had no munitions factories, it was not a

military base.When questioned carefully after the war chaplains of all Christian Churches disavowed any obligation to protest.[23] The concept of the "prophetic role" of a Christian, and in particular of a military chaplain, was simply not regarded as part of their job.[24]

Despite having a theology of the just war, it was ignored in practice, of which the worst example was the Crusades. The first Crusade was initiated by Pope Urban II and proclaimed by him at the Council of Clermont in 1095. The objective was to regain possession of the holy places in Palestine by military force. It would be difficult to think of a more complete reversal of the principles of the New Testament.

During and after the First World War public opinion in Europe underwent a complete change in its attitude to war, and the same thing happened in the United States in the course of the Vietnam War in the 1960's. The change of attitude owed little to Christianity. The era of free speech, public criticism of democratic governments, and much wider education rendered the myths of nobility in warfare untenable. For the United States the activities of T.V. journalists exposed the myths during the Vietnam War. In England we are greatly indebted to a remarkable group of war poets like Robert Graves, Siegfried Sassoon, Wilfred Owen, Isaac Rosenberg and others. Having lived through front line trench warfare they could not be contradicted when they exposed its utter inhumanity. In all fairness to an earlier poet, Shakespeare, one must remember that although he is best remembered for the patriotic speeches put into the mouth of King Henry V, there is another side to his perception of war. In Henry VI, part 3, there is a remarkable scene in the aftermath of the Battle of Towton, in which battle more Englishmen were killed in one day than in any other one day in our history.[25] Two soldiers enter the stage each one carrying over his shoulder the dead body of the opponent whom he has killed. They start pulling off the armour of their victims in the quest for plunder. As they remove the helmets of the dead men, one soldier realises that he has killed his son, and the other sees that he has killed his father. Their lamentations which follow are among the most noble and tragic in our nation's poetry, and constitute a remarkable insight into the very nature of warfare.

Not long after the Second World War, Vatican II dealt realistically with the issues of war and

---

that the targets should be cities rather than dockyards or aircraft factories.

[22] Zahn, G. C. (1969), *Chaplains in the R A F,* Manchester: Manchester University Press, .

[23] Zahn, G. op.cit. p. 185.

[24] Zahn, G. op.cit. p. 262.

[25] Between 20,000 or 28,000 dead: this astounding fact was published by Martin Kettle in *The Guardian* , 25 th August 2007.

peace in the document on The Church in the Modern World (*Gaudium et Spes*). Concerning the modern concept of total war the Council proclaimed the following remarkable statement:-
"This Holy Synod makes its own the condemnations of total war already announced by recent Popes, and issues the following declaration: Any act of war aimed indiscriminately at the destruction of entire cities of of extensive areas along with their population is a crime against God and man himself. It merits unequivocal and unhesitating condemnation." [26]

It is reassuring that after so many centuries of confusion in which the principles of the New

Testament were totally obscured, the Catholic Church's supreme authority has made such a clear pronouncement about the morality of warfare. The council's stance undoubtedly assisted the development of peace movements, such as Pax Christi, the international Catholic peace movement. As a post script to this section on the virtue of fortitude, I would like to quote the famous saying the the non-Christian pacifist Mahatma Gandhi " I am prepared to die for my convictions, but not to kill for them".

Healthy Restraint a k a Temperance.

This appears to be the least attractive of virtues because it has so often been portrayed as the denial of enjoyable and legitimate pleasures.

However in another context the start of the twenty first century saw temperance move into centre stage as the most reliable remedy for five interrelated crises whose mutual interaction threatens not just the well being, but the very survival of life and civilisation as we know it. The crises in question are so serious that it is difficult to write about them without adopting a hyperbole which sound like hysteria. Yet in all sobriety the crises in question speak for themselves if we have patience to sit down and reflect upon them rationally. The five crises are the world population explosion, the fuel shortage, the food crisis, climate change and the financial turbulence. Individually all five of them reached their own crisis points in the first decade of the new millennium, and since they are all causally interrelated, their exponential advance threatens the human race. This is the perception of all serious minded people, particularly scientists. Yet many people who lack education, especially in the developing world cannot see it on the global scale. In the democracies most of the politicians lack the moral courage to face it, and are even more reluctant to initiate policies to counteract the menace. These would entail drastic curtailment of the comforts of life to which we have grown accustomed in advanced societies, and the politicians know that the majority of their electors would never forgive them for such hardships, and vote them out of office at the next election.

What the scientists perceive clearly and what the politicians dare not act upon creates a vacuum of practical measures which Christianity alone call fill. Common sense and scientific research are not strong enough to motivate whole societies to adopt the stringent measures which are now needed literally to save the planet. Only Christianity has the capacity for this massive change of attitude towards the world's resources, thanks to its overall perception of the universe as God's creation, and with the motivation drawn from the virtue of healthy restraint, otherwise known as temperance. Although I make this claim for Christianity, I am

---

[26] Vatican II ,*Gaudium et Spes* section 80, ed. Abbott, p. 294.

well aware that the leaders of the Catholic and other Churches may yet lack the single-mindedness to espouse the cause, and remain obsessed with trivialities like the morality of different methods of birth control.

Temperance as understood by Christianity is the determination to use the world's resources of food, drink, minerals, materials and energy in a manner which is sufficient to sustain one's own life and that of the community, and not to use up unwarrantable quantities of resources. In the past it was not always easy to determine the quantifiable aspects of this orientation of life. Now the practical problem has been solved for us. At the end of a long history of human development homo sapiens has occupied the whole planet, canalised every known form of energy and learnt how to utilise virtually all minerals and other resources. The only answer is

for all of us to aim for the sustainable basics of life rather than the maximisation of our pleasures. And that sentence is an alternative description of the virtue of temperance.

Taking the crises separately the basic one is the increase in the world's population. Some facts strike home alarmingly. In the course of my own life, I became aware of the fact that the world's population had doubled some time between the year of my birth and my sixtieth birthday. This is an unsustainable rate of growth. In 2008 the world's population reached approximately 6.2 billion and it is expected to rise to 9.5 billion in less than 50 years. How are they all to be fed ? This rapid increase in population is partly due to advances in science, and technology notably in the widespread provision of clean drinking water. Medicine too has played its part in eliminating a number of killer diseases. An increasing population requires more food, which in turn means more agricultural land. In fact though we have just about utilised all land which is fit for agriculture, and supplies of fresh water are diminishing as one of the indirect consequences of climate change. It is one of the anomalies of this problem (population growth) that some societies still have powerful motives for large families. In the past, for most societies survival of the family, clan, and tribe was the first priority in the face of the ravages of diseases which they simply could not cure. Even after the advances in medicine a large family is the only source of security in illness, old age, or unemployment, in societies whose governments are not sufficiently rich or sophisticated to have provided state-funded pensions, health care, and unemployment benefit. This is just one indication of the complexities of these interrelated crises. When a primitive society does manage to lift itself out of poverty, their aspirations for a better diet are one of the first signs of their new found prosperity. The government's chief scientific adviser, Professor John Beddington has declared "Once you move to an income of between £1 a day and £5 a day, you get an increase in demand for meat and dairy products . . . .and that generates a demand for additional grain".[27] This entails either finding more arable land, or using grain to feed animals, that would have been destined for human consumption. The professor was also scathing in his remarks about setting aside land for growing biofuels so that rich countries could have cheaper fuel for their cars. Temperance would indicate simply less use of cars.

These consideration lead naturally to the consideration of the second crisis, namely the shortage of food. Shortages, and therefore price rises in basic foods, occurred suddenly in 2008. In less than a year the price of wheat had risen by 130%, that of soya by 87%, and rice by 74%. These are the basics for the majority of the human race. According to the United

---

[27] Reported in *The Guardian* 7 th March, 2008.

Nations' Food and Agriculture Organisation, in April 2008 there were only eight to twelve weeks stocks of cereals in the world, while grain supplies were at their lowest since the 1980's.[28] A number of causes were working conjointly to produce this shortage, such as the increase in population, noted above, and the increase in prosperity in some nations, particularly in China. But the single most powerful cause which triggered the immediate crisis was the decision of the United States Government to give subsidies to American farmers so that they could grow corn that can be converted into ethanol as fuel for cars.

The search for more fuel leads one naturally to consider the world's third major crisis, namely the diminishing supplies of minerals which can serve as fuel and produce energy. Coal, oil,

and natural gas resources have been explored and exploited with increasing thoroughness since the nineteenth century. During the twentieth century demand for them increased steadily on account of technological advances and prosperity in the developed world. Car ownership and holidays abroad by flying increased the demand for oil based fuels at an exponential rate. In 2005 the last coal mine in France closed. In England too coal mining is coming to an end for all practical purposes because the richest seams have long ago been worked out.

In the first decade of the new millennium geologists, with no commercial interest in the matter, were investigating whether the world's production of crude oil had reached its peak, and whether production would henceforth diminish steadily. The literature on this matter is extensive. One example selected more or less at random is the report of the German based Energy Watch Group whose report was published in London in October 2007. They concluded that the world production of oil peaked in 2006 , and that it will decline by 7% per year thence forward. On that basis production will have halved from the 2006 figure by the year 2030.[29]

In this period the nations which posses the oil wells were very secretive about their reserves. In 2006, in an unprecedented step, the Royal Society publicly reproved the oil giant ExxonMobil for distributing 2.9 million dollars in 2005 to 39 groups which seek to misrepresent the scientific facts about climate change.[30] In other words they were trying to bend public opinion lest a growing universal consensus, as to the connection between fossil fuels and global warming, should lessen the consumption of oil, and thereby reduce their profits.

Even more alarming is the possibility that the scramble for the diminishing supplies of oil and gas could lead to war. Back in 2003 it was clear to many people that the American and British invasion of Iraq was basically to try and secure control of the oil supplies there. Subsequent developments have confirmed this interpretation despite the disavowals of politicians. One hopes that the ghastly aftermath of that invasion, which for years reduced Iraq to chaos, might

[28] Reported in *The Observer*, 13 th April 2008.

[29] Reported in *The Guardian* 22 nd. Oct. 2007.

[30] Reported in *The Guardian* 20th Sep. 2006.

serve as a warning against further military adventures to seize the resources.[31]

The fourth of the interrelated crises for the world is the fact of climate change. As with the other crises which I have been describing in this section, climate change is causally interrelated to the others, and they reinforce one another in an accelerating spiral. To put it simply, a rapidly increasing world population is making ever greater demands on energy supplies. Currently the most widespread production of energy is by burning fossil fuels, coal, gas and oil. The end product of all of them is carbon dioxide, whose presence in the atmosphere causes the so - called greenhouse effect which is heating the planet to dangerous temperatures. The natural balance of interacting forces of nature can no longer produce the universal equilibrium which protected living things on the planet for the previous millions of years. Human beings who have created the crisis must now plan and act deliberately to stop it from getting out of hand.

What is depressing for the politicians is the fact that their best intentions seem to be made obsolete by each new development of scientific investigation. For example, the European Union agreed upon a target of limiting carbon dioxide to 550 parts per million in the atmosphere. This was the most stringent target in the world. In 2008 a reliable group of scientists in the U.S.A. (whose national record is not reassuring) calculated that this limit was much too generous. Even if the whole world succeeded in bringing the levels to 550 parts per million this would lead eventually to an increase of six degrees in overall temperature. The authors conclude, that in the present state of knowledge, the safe limit must be 350 parts per million.[32] Research in this field is constantly producing new evidence. Each new revelation seems more pessimistic than the previous conclusions. One respected expert in the field declared that if the average global temperature is to be held at 1.5 degrees above the pre-industrial level, it will be necessary to decarbonise the global economy totally. [33]

The fifth of the interlocking crises is the turbulence in the money markets which hit England in the autumn of 2007 with the collapse of the Northern Rock bank. Turbulence is the euphemism which the financial columnists employ when what they really mean is the consequences of the greed of decision makers in large corporations who take unwarrantable risks to secure exorbitant profits, and earn enormous bonuses for themselves. When the bubbles of deceit burst and confidence evaporates the collapse of giant enterprises is delicately described as turbulence.

 Acquisitive greed is as old as the human race. The Old Testament forbade usury, which is the ancient term for charging interest on a loan. It was forbidden to the ancient Israelites because they perceived that the lender in such a transaction was simply taking advantage of the weaker party's misfortune. In those days people went into debt only if they had fallen on hard times; raising capital for creative investment was then unknown. The situation changed in the time of the maritime discoveries of the 16th century. To his credit Calvin realised that the situation of loans had change totally. By his time it was not a question of taking advantage of one

---

[31] cf. the study of John Gray published in *The Guardian* 30th March 2008.

[32] Reported in *The Guardian* , 7 th April 2008.

[33] George Monbiot writing in *The Guardian* , 4 th December 2007.

person's misfortune, but taking advantage of opportunities for trading. For example if ten men lent money to an eleventh so that he could buy a ship and meet the expenses of a voyage to buy spices in Indonesia, then they could legitimately ask for one eleventh of the profits.

Thus was capitalism born, and it remained to be seen whether the profits would be reasonable or exorbitant. R.H. Tawney had pointed out in his influential book *Religion and the Rise of Capitalism* that what the mediaeval theologians had condemned was the unfettered quest for unlimited profits.[34] This was an almost prophetic description of what took place at the end of the twentieth century in the money markets.

Admittedly free competition is essential for commerce: it engenders efficiency. The strict communist alternative to what they regarded as exploitation, was for the State to control all economic activity in the nation. History has shown this to be unworkably inefficient. In the

latter days of the U.S.S.R the economy was in chaos. In 1991 at the time of the Soviet system's collapse nearly every kind of food was rationed, although it was a nation which could produce all its own food without needing to import anything.

In the financial chaos of the first decade of the new millenium it was difficult to decide which was the most pernicious influence, greed or deception. In any case, the only fundamental remedy is the well tried virtue of Christian temperance, which restrains the desires of excessive appetites.

At the end of this chapter on morality, I remind the reader that the systematic divisions into virtues was St. Thomas's method for study. In real life he insisted that the Christian's guide is the Holy Spirit. In the real world, the different circumstances of peoples' lives are so diverse that no preconceived system of rules or virtues can supply guidance for every eventuality. Sensitivity to the guidance of the Holy Spirit alone is adequate.

---

[34] Tawney,R.H. (1972) *Religion and the Rise of Capitalism,* Harmondsworth: Penguin, p.48.

CHAPTER NINE :   PRAYER   AND   CHRISTIAN CULTURE.

Earlier in this book I described theology as the articulation of the basic act of faith, in the direction of greater intellectual understanding of God and his dealings with us and the whole universe. In a similar way prayer is another articulation of that basic personal commitment, but in this case it is the relationship itself which is developed consciously. This may sound rather clinical and detached, like a psychological definitions of love, which reduces the description to a dry caricature of the reality. In prayer we reflect on, develop, exercise and consciously refine the original loving commitment in life, which being dedicated to God is the basic orientation of our existence. It fills out our realisation that our life is on a meaningful course in a purposeful universe. Prayer makes us constantly aware of our conscious orientation towards God in the choices of daily life, in its joys and sorrows, its achievements and frustrations. All of them contribute to the enriching of our relationship of loyalty and commitment to our creator, in a manner similar to the enrichment of a marriage relationship which thrives on the humdrum details of ordinary life like buying new shoes for the children, and countless other small but purposeful activities.

SECTION 1 : PRAYER AS A REQUEST

The best known exercise of prayer is that of petition, or asking God for favours.The pre-Christian Greeks did it, and asked their gods for success in battle, business or romance. This immediately raises he question for a serious minded Christian: does this form of prayer have any place in the elevated monotheism of Christianity and the kind of relationship which we have with Jesus and the Father. From one point of view it appears almost as a trivialisation of the deep commitment of faith.

However, when we turn to the pages of the New Testament we see that it is urged upon us constantly. A few examples will make this clear. The exercise is recommended in the Sermon on the Mount:- "Ask and it will be given to you; seek and you will find; knock and it will be opened. For everyone who asks receives, and he who seeks finds, and to him who knocks it will be opened. Or what man of you, if his son asks for bread, will give him a stone? Or if he asks for a fish will he give him a serpent? If you then, who are evil, know how to give good gifts to your children, how much more will your Father who is in heaven give good things to those who ask him!" (Matthew 7: 7 - 11). There are several other injunctions to constant petition in the gospels and letters of the New Testament. In short it is the constant message.

If prayer is not answered, it may well be because the petitioners have asked for stones and serpents instead of good things. People have been known to pray for fine weather, or winning a tennis match. In the perspectives of eternity one must seriously ask whether such objectives are really worthy of divine intervention. The insistence that God will give good things to those who ask prompts serious consideration. In Matthew chapter seven we read of good things. When the same speech occurs in the gospel of Luke, written some years later, there is a slight but significant change in the wording. What is obviously the same parable has its ending recorded thus in Luke :- "What father among you, if his son asks for a fish, will instead of a fish give him a serpent; or if he asks for an egg will give him a scorpion ? If you then who are evil, know how to give good gifts to your children, how much more will the heavenly Father give the Holy Spirit to those who ask him"(Luke 11: 11-13). It is possible that in the years intervening between the writing of the two gospels the early Church had

come to the conclusion that the only good gift worth asking for was the gift of the Holy Spirit.

Although many people find it somewhat immature that Christians should ask for favours in this apparently infantile fashion, it is worth remembering that it is totally consistent with the theology of grace. The destiny to which Christians are called, namely a relationship of intimacy with the God who is infinite, is by definition beyond the reach of merely human capabilities and efforts. It is rightly described as a favour or gift from God, to which we have no claim, right, or ability to secure it by our own endeavours. Petitionary prayer is an authentic path which gives the believer a deliberate part in the process, it shows his appreciation of its importance, but it does not conflict with its totally gratuitous character. Moreover there is no question of laying claim to any sort of right with God, or bargaining with him.

There is a connection between petitionary prayer and the all important response of gratitude. If one were to speculate on the best gifts which God might bestow, it is clear with hindsight that the greatest gift exceeds the imagination of the petitioner. It is unlikely that any one could have had the foresight to ask for the Incarnation. Nevertheless this event has been realised, unasked, and the Christians' reponse can only be one of incessant gratitude. This attitude must influence our whole prayer life. It is not an accident that the central act of worship is named as the Eucharist, which is a Greek word meaning thanksgiving. This perspective should govern the whole prayer life of the Church.

For the sake of clarity I will divide the practice of prayer into three categories, prayer which employs other peoples' words, prayer which consists of my own words, and finally prayer which uses no words at all.

SECTION 2 : PRAYER IN SET FORMS OF WORDS

In the category of using other peoples' forms of words I include the liturgy of the Eucharist and the other sacraments. However the basic ideas are perhaps more clearly seen in the prayers which we can recite alone. In this category I have in mind primarily those prayers which are presented to us in the bible, namely the Lord's prayer, the Magnificat, the Benedictus etc. Every Christian knows the Our Father by heart, but it is surprising how few Catholics could recite the Magnificat, in spite of the emphasis given to Our Lady in Catholic piety. The sentiments enshrined in these prayers from the gospels are so important that it is imperative that they should form the substance of the prayer life of all Christians. The sentiments expressed in the Psalms are not always so obviously conducive to the love of God and neighbour.

The element of revenge in several psalms has been a constant problem for Christians. I knew of one monk in a famous English monastery who simply kept his mouth closed as the monastic choir came to the words of Psalm 137: 8 , 9.
　　　　　"O daughter of Babylon you devastator,
　　　　　　Happy shall be he who requites you
　　　　　　With what you have done to us.
　　　　　　Happy shall be he who takes your little ones

And dashes them against the rocks."

This is not the only psalm which asks God for revenge on Israel's enemies, and that sentiment has been a problem for many believers. The solution to this difficulty is, I think, to situate the psalms in the overall context of Israelite religious evolution from a primitive theology when God adopted them in the time of Abraham, until the establishment of the refined monotheism on the eve of the Incarnation. This evolution was not a steady education in correct ideas. It was an untidy and sometimes unpredictable journey through history, in which the fortunes of the Israelites, their kingdom, and their religion were caught up in the political and cultural changes of that region of the near East. One of the most important elements in that process was the defeat at the hands of the Babylonians in the sixth century B.C, which entailed the loss of political independence, destruction of Jerusalem and its temple, and exile for a large segment of the population. To appreciate the significance of all that , it is instructive for Catholics to reflect on how they would have felt if the Vatican buildings including St. Peter's basilica had all been destroyed in an air raid in the Second World War. During the exile the Israelites were forcibly deprived of everything which was not essential to the true faith, such as political independence and their own king. During the intense sufferings of that period their monotheistic faith was matured, under the guidance of prophets of remarkable spiritual stature like Jeremiah and Ezekiel. If we are to appreciate the true worth of Israelite monotheism, we must re-live that formative journey with them in some way. Poetry is the most appropriate literary vehicle for entering into the sentiments of our spiritual ancestors. Singing and meditating on their psalms is the most effective way of doing it.

This general context does not quite answer the problem of the vengeful psalms. I would like to   suggest that all generations of Christians must endeavour to go through the Israelite experience in in all its salient features, if we are to have a proper appreciation of the magnificent monotheistic vision of God which came at the end of the process. The most effective way to do this is to read, and meditate constantly upon the psalms. In those poems we will see every sentiment that a believer experiences in his or her relationship with God. All these sentiments are still relevant today, because they are literally timeless situations. There are the lamentations of good people who feel abandoned by God. They see wicked people prosper while honest men are persecuted. Why does a benevolent God allow all this to happen? Some psalms express the aridity of soul in the quest for conscious intimacy with God. Many psalms deal with serious illness, and the fear of a premature death. These psalms were written at a time when the Israelites had no clear ideas about a rewards in the afterlife, and when illness and an early death could be interpreted as a punishment for sins. Many psalms speak with joy and admiration as the poet contemplates the beauty of the created world, its mountains and stars, and understands it all as a sign of God's power and benevolence. Other psalms reflect a background of political instability and violence in the villages, where criminals like the mafia were operating. The citizens could not count upon judges who had integrity and the threats of the gangsters disturbed their religion. There are still many regions of the world where that kind of situation is rampant. As I noted above, all these sentiments are timeless, and have repercussions on the spiritual life of the believer. Above all, we must remember that those spiritual turmoils and joys, and specially their national calamities were the matrix in which Israel evolved to a pure and profound belief in the one true God. It is a path which we must all tread with them in spirit.

There is one final consideration about the psalms which is of supreme importance. It is the simple fact that they are poems, and not prose descriptions. The deepest sentiments of the

human heart cannot be expressed in plain prose: the idiom must be poetry. For example in the first World War the cruelty and pathos of the slaughter was conveyed to the public, not by the columns of the newspapers, but by the poets. As I noted above, the remarkable group of war poets (Isaac Rosenberg, Siegfried Sassoon, Wilfred Owen and others) brought about a change in the public perception of war. From that time onwards it was no longer regarded as something noble or beautiful. It was thenceforward perceived as something bestial. After the Second World War public opinion was horrified by the revelations about Nazi concentration camps, and particularly the systematic extermination of the Jews. In the 1970's there was an attempt to portray the Holocaust by a television serial. One perceptive TV critic declared that it was a failure, that it trivialised the horror by making it look like a soap opera. He concluded that the only adequate medium to describe a tragedy of that proportion would have to be poetry. For the appreciation of the Israelite experience in its agonies and in its spiritual achievements, only poetry can suffice, and that is why the Christians have made the psalms the staple constituent of their prayer life since Apostolic times.

The Church's Public Prayer: The Divine Office

In the third and fourth centuries this form of prayer assumed a carefully structured form .[1] Several times a day, and at night, the whole Christian community in any given city would assemble with its bishop and clergy to sing the psalms, read passages from the bible, and offer informal prayers too. The underlying principle was that the community would dedicate the different sections of the day to God, at dawn for example, and midday. Their work and other activities would be deliberately sanctified. Admittedly obligations of work, or the care of small children would prevent literally everyone from being present, but those who did attend were conscious that they were representing the whole community for whom public prayer was a corporate responsibility.

It was a remarkably well thought out form of prayer, and it could be re-introduced in the contemporary Church without delay. Sadly it seems to lie outside the perspectives of many of the clergy because it did not form part of the training, certainly in the seminary days of the older priests. In the fourth century mass was celebrated for the most part only on Sundays. For the other days of the week the community assembled several times a day for what we would now describe as the divine office. The possibility of re-introducing this form of corporate prayer should be considered very carefully at the present time. I have indicated earlier in this book that the eucharist should be celebrated in small communities of no more than seventy or a hundred. The recital of the divine office does not require such a small or coherent community. It could easily take place in the existing parish churches. It does not require the presence of a priest. Any lay person could lead the prayers. The modern breviary, rightly named as *The Prayer of the Church* is admirably designed for communal use. With the advance of medical science, many retired people are living healthy lives for up to twenty years after they retire from work. When their children leave home elderly people have plenty

---

[1] For this section I am greatly indebted to the seminal study of Dom Pierre Salmon, (1959), *L'Office Divine,* Paris: Éditions du Cerf.

of time on their hands, and it would be a genuine enrichment of life for them to attend the corporate prayer once or twice every day. Some people with that amount of disposable time attend daily mass. It is difficult to decide between the merits of different kinds of prayer, but

it is instructive to remind ourselves that in the early Church mass was celebrated once a week, and the divine office took place several times each day.

One final practical detail must be borne in mind. The psalms must be chanted and not recited. It is difficult to give convincing reasons why this must be so, but anyone who has experienced the two possible forms of articulating them will have appreciated that spoken recitation is not the appropriate way to do it. When I say that they must be chanted, I include the simple monotone. It does not have to be the more elaborate singing like plainsong or the modern melodies of Père Gelinot for example. Any form of singing will suffice to give this corporate prayer its proper form. This recommendation is confirmed by the fact that in antiquity the Israelites did not recite them, but chanted them.

In the fourth century two developments occurred which were destined to modify the pattern of public prayer. The first was the establishment of monastic communities. Groups of men, and later of women, left the normal life of the cities and went out into deserts and remote rural areas (to secure silence) and they took with them the pattern of daily prayer, which was then commonplace for the bishop's community. With the passage of time the monastic office became more sophisticated, but it is important to realise that at its origin it was the ordinary prayer of the laity. The second development was the multiplication of city and rural parishes, which arose as a consequence of the numerical increase in Christians after Constantine's edict of toleration early in the fourth century. These smaller communities did not maintain the complete cycle of public prayer, but adopted parts of it, vespers for example. Those who lived close enough to the bishop's church would also attend parts of the complete cycle of prayer which continued at the main church. The traditional pattern of reciting the divine office in parish churches survived vestigially until the start of the twentieth century when many parishes still sung vespers on Sunday evenings. Its demise later in that century would seem to be connected to the problem of the incomprehensibility of Latin which could not be ignored in Europe and north America with the advent of universal literacy.

It is arguable that the retention of Latin for public worship was one of the worst self-inflicted wounds that the Catholic Church imposed upon itself. It arose quite simply from a series of historical accidents and not as a result of any deliberate policy. Christianity has never espoused the concept of a sacred language. In the earliest days of the Church the missionaries translated the bible and liturgy into the living languages of the converts within one or two generations of their adopting Christianity. All the surviving evidence shows that this was the case in Egypt, Ethiopia, Syria, Armenia, Georgia and all the cultural centres of early Christian expansion. In the western part of the Roman empire the situation was more uniform because Greek was spoken as the general language of everyday life as far away as Rome itself. It is significant that in the fourth century when the majority of the Roman community was speaking Latin rather than Greek, the liturgy was translated into Latin. The bible had already been translated into that language, and St. Jerome made a completely new translation known ever since as the Vulgate version.

The next wave of evangelisation saw an unplanned development. After the collapse of the

Roman empire in the west the Latin speaking missionaries like St. Augustine in England, St. Patrick in Ireland, and St. Boniface in Germany all retained Latin for the liturgy and bibles which they brought to their converts. It is difficult to know why. Possibly it was because the countries from which they came still used Latin, and spoke it too. Moreover the societies

which they evangelised did not then have writing. Furthermore, in Italy, Spain and France the evolution from Latin to the modern romance languages was so slow as to be imperceptible. There was no point in history right up to the renaissance period when the older people could look back on their childhood and realise that the language had changed unrecognisably, and therefore the next generation would need a vernacular liturgy. By contrast when the eastern part of Europe was being evangelised the missionaries invented alphabets for their illiterate neophytes. The best known case was the work of the Greek monks St. Cyril and St. Methodius who evangelised the Slavs. With great brilliance they invented an alphabet which corresponded to the Old Slavonic language, and the Christians of the Balkans and Russia had bibles and liturgy in their own language. Why a similar undertaking did not take place in western Europe is hard to say. Be that as it may, Western Europe was subjected to a Latin liturgy and bible for centuries. It was not the result of deliberate planning but historical accidents and its disadvantages are now obvious. Inevitably the laity became spectators at the liturgy and not active participants. Admittedly there were some ameliorations such as walking in religious processions, but the actual words of the liturgy were incomprehensible to them. Most probably this accounts for the fact that the mass became the private preserve of the priest who celebrated it with his back to the people and the most solemn prayers were recited silently.

Reform was slow to come and this may have had something to do with Protestantism. From the start of his reform movement Luther realised that public worship should be understood and the laity should have an active part. Vernacular liturgies and bibles were produced in the first generation of every society which adopted Protestantism. The fact that it was championed by the Protestants may well have persuaded Catholic sentiment to oppose it, such was the hostility between the two camps at the period of the Reformation.

Within the Catholic Church public opinion was slow to demand worship in modern languages. In the nineteenth century various public prayers were popularised in spoken languages such as the Stations of the Cross (whose origin is much older) and the October devotions, consisting of the rosary and litany of the saints. These exercises were no substitute for the official liturgy, and they were unsatisfactory because they were basically meditations and hence unsuitable for corporate recitation. Towards the end of the nineteenth century scholarly research into the origins of Christian liturgy made it clear that in antiquity the laity shared actively in the whole liturgy and it was always conducted in the spoken languages of the people. Half measures like the publication of bi-lingual missals were unsatisfactory. In many parts of the world, especially the poorer parts of Africa and Asia, people were illiterate, and even if they could read they were too poor to purchase such a book. It took more than half a century of enlightened scholarship and pressure on the authorities in Rome to effect the change. It must rank as one of the supreme achievements of the Second Vatican Council that the Church's liturgy was once again presented in the spoken languages of the people.

The Eucharist

Having dealt with the divine office in the preceding section, it is now time to say more about the Mass. By the twentieth century it was clear from the consensus of scholarly research that the Latin mass, as reformed and fixed by the Council of Trent, was seriously distorted by a large number of historical accidents. Looking back on it now, after forty years, it is clear that it was a formalised and frankly, fossilised ceremonial. Fortunately the reform initiated by the

Second Vatican Council was not just a superficial modernising on the surface, but it went back to the roots. We now enjoy a eucharist in which every element is purposefully planned as a component in this sacred drama. First of all it is an exercise of the whole community for which the celebrant faces the people and addresses them in their spoken language. The first part of the celebration consists of readings from the bible which have been selected on a cycle which enables Sunday mass goers to hear effectively the whole of the gospels in three years, and the major parts of the apostles' letters. The most significant parts of the Old Testament also occur on the three year Sunday cycle, and those people who attend daily mass are enabled to hear approximately half of the Old Testament, in the cycle of readings designed for week-day masses. That systematic planning of the readings is a remarkable achievement. The role of laity as participants and not just as spectators has been ensured by authorising lay men and women to read the scriptures publicly during Mass. This has been a development of extraordinary value. Their presentation has been arranged to maximise their effect, namely there should be a silent pause after each reading and a corporate response has been introduced. After the first reading the community sings a psalm and after the second the gospel is greeted with the alleluia prayer. If the celebrant lacks liturgical sensitivity these simple devices can be reduced to formalism. The ideal pattern is for a cantor to sing the verses of the psalm and the congregation can sing the response. Prose recitation of that particular prayer simply falls flat. The same applies to the gospel acclamation which also should be sung.

After the gospel a homily on the scriptures is recommended. This presents an almost insoluble problem. Modern educational research shows that of all forms of communication, the least effective in conveying conviction is the situation where the audience is silent and has no sort of dialogue with the speaker. Political parties discovered this years ago when they dropped the kind of TV political broadcasts which had the monologue form of almost a secular sermon. For the present the only solution would seem to be that of keeping the homily as short as possible, rather like the three minute slot of the the radio's Thought for the Day just before the breakfast time news. If it is to be within three minutes it must be written and not spoken spontaneously, which presents too tempting and invitation for "rambling".

The participation of the laity is again emphasised by the presentation of gifts at the offertory procession. The central prayer of thanksgiving (in Greek, Eucharist) varies throughout the year as the community reflects upon the key elements of salvation history for which we express gratitude to the Father, such as the birth of his son, the resurrection, and the bestowal of the Holy Spirit at Pentecost. Although it is thoroughly formalised the image of a commemorative meal is perfectly clear. This aspect is even more deliberately expressed in small group masses where for example the bread assumes a more realistic form. Instead of the small white circles which look like paper (and taste like it), a real home-baked loaf can be used. It can then be broken into parts just before communion as was done in St. Paul's day. It is difficult to convey the gratitude which the older generation experienced when the chalice was offered to us at Holy Communion after centuries of being denied it. It is equally hard to understand how this element of the sacrament, explicitly commanded by Jesus, should have been omitted in the Western European (Latin) rite. Probably it had something to do with the low ebb of spiritual life in the middle ages. The Fourth Lateran Council of 1215 had to command people to receive Holy Communion once a year as a minimum. The fact that the authorities were content with giving only the consecrated bread may have had something to do with the general minimalist attitude to sacraments. Furthermore as I noted in the chapter

on the sacraments, in the face of Donatism the Church had felt obliged to make clear that the sacraments achieve their effects regardless of the spiritual limitations of the minister bestowing them. Regrettably this lead to a minimalist attitude among many of the clergy in which they felt justified in presenting a liturgy which was merely valid, rather than seeking the best possible presentation of the sacraments. Sadly the denial of the chalice to the laity fits disconcertingly well into the parameters of those two depressing tendencies.

After the distribution of Holy Communion the new liturgy recommends a pause for silent recollection. This is important because many churches have noticed that when the mass is over, conversations begin spontaneously among the congregation. The performance of a community activity has set the tone and it is natural for them to speak with the people with whom they have shared the liturgy.

After centuries of formalised ceremonies the Catholic Church now has a liturgy in which we can place complete confidence. The quality of the celebrations vary from place to place, and further improvements can be envisaged, but the essentials of our public worship have been established, and safeguarded from interference thanks to the authority of a General Council.

SECTION 3 : PRAYER USING OUR OWN WORDS AND THOUGHTS

The next kind of prayer which I wish to consider is that in which we use our own words and thoughts. It was described with great clarity and simplicity by a Dominican priest whose at whose retreat I assisted more than fifty years ago, but whose message is still clear in my memory. He recommended that we should transport ourselves in imagination back to Palestine two thousand years ago, and envisage what it would be like, had we been in the crowds who heard Jesus speak. He suggested that we should picture ourselves present at one of the miracles, such as the healing of the paralytic who was lowered through the roof so that he could be placed close to Jesus. What would be our reaction to such an event, and, more to the point, if we had the opportunity to speak with Jesus then, what would we have said to him. What we would have said to him then, could be spoken at any time in the present, and in doing so we will strengthen the living relationship with our Saviour. Sometimes this kind of prayer is called meditation, and many authors have suggested systematised forms to discipline our thoughts towards Jesus and ward off distractions. These systematic frameworks may be more or less helpful depending on such factors as peoples' different temperaments. Many authors have written admirable books on the subject, to which I refer my readers.

The miracles of Jesus have another symbolic message which is important in the Christian's practice of prayer. When confronted with sickness, Jesus did not decree that paralysis should be cured miraculously throughout the whole of Galilee. The miracles were for specific individuals and were in response specific requests which indicated the petitioner's faith. The symbolic message is that the individual human being is important in the eyes of the infinite God. This is something which Christians could easily take for granted. The authors of the

Psalms were well aware that it was an act of divine graciousness that the infinite Being should bother about the cares of such incomparably small creatures. Not only does God care for his creatures, but Christians are invited to a relationship of intimacy with the infinite God. This is the constant message of the New Testament where we are invited to address God as Father, and with whom we have the status of adopted children. It is important to emphasise the extraordinary privilege offered to Christians, namely that our relationship with the Father is

one of intimacy. We have been accustomed to it for so long that we might easily take it for granted, or fail to appreciate its importance. None of the other monotheistic faiths in the world aspire to such a close relationship with God. It is an important presupposition underlying all forms of Christian prayer.

For this meditative kind of prayer, two sorts of background preparation are essential. The first is that we must read the gospels regularly. Without this constant familiarisation with the life and teachings of Jesus, his personality would be almost that of a stranger. The second requirement is the absolute necessity of silence. This is the prayer for which Jesus recommended :- "But when you pray, go into your own room and shut the door and pray to your Father who is in secret ; and your Father who sees in secret will reward you." (Matthew 6:6). It is significant that in his own prayers Jesus always sought solitude. At the start of his public life, after the cure of Peter's mother in law, and many other people in the locality, it is recorded :- "And in the morning a great while before day, he rose and went out to a lonely place, and there he prayed."(Mark 1:35). Later in his public life, after the miracle of the multiplication of the loaves and fishes Jesus retires to pray :- "Directly after this he made the disciples get into the boat and go on ahead to the other side while he would send the crowds away. After sending the crowds away he went up into the hills by himself to pray."(Matthew 14: 22, 23). Other instances are recorded in the gospels of his seeking solitude for prayer, and it is reasonable to assume that it was his constant practice.

In the situation of the modern world, especially town life, it is not easy to create the conditions of silence and recollection for meditative types of prayer, but it is essential. Quite simply it has to be planned with considerable care. We have to avoid the radio, TV and mobile phones, not to mention the talking of other people in the house. Probably the most practical course for people who wish to practice this kind of prayer, is to ensure that they wake up early in the morning and set aside time and place when they can be alone and in silence. Admittedly it is difficult when the children are young, but it is not beyond the capabilities of a resourceful adult to devise a time and place for recollected prayer. Some noise is not intrusive, such as the sound of raindrops on the roof, or birdsong, or the wind blowing through the trees. What is really distracting is other peoples' voices, particularly if they should want to speak with the person who is trying to pray. As the children grow up it is easier to organise the time of silence, and later in life, in the years of retirement it should present hardly any problem. Those are the years in which a person's prayer life should come to occupy a more and more central place in life, as we approach closer to the time of our entry into eternity, when the kind of communication which we practised in prayer will become our principal occupation.

It may be helpful at this point to say a word about distractions in prayer. A former Archbishop of Canterbury was once asked how long he devoted to prayer each day. He replied, " One minute", and then added, but it takes me fifty nine minutes to clear my mind of worries, anxieties, problems, plans and other distractions. That is why it is best to set aside a specific time early in the morning before the day's business has made the mind more active, and brought the plans and problems into the mainstream of consciousness. In a sense the distractions can be brought into the substance of the prayer. There is a beautiful image of this in the Book of Genesis. God is planning the first covenant with Abraham concerning the promised land, and according to tradition it had to be solemnised by a sacrifice. Several animals were commanded by God. They were killed, cut in half and then laid on the ground in

pairs in a straight line. Abraham stood on guard and chased off the birds of prey. These predators can be regarded as the distractions. Eventually, in his own good time, God appeared in a flame of fire passing between the two lines of divided carcasses. God had accepted the sacrifice. (Gen. 15: 7 - 21).

SECTION 4 : PRAYER WITHOUT ANY WORDS

A touching incident is recorded in the life of St. John Vianney, (a famous parish priest in rural France in the 19th century). He had observed that an elderly peasant spent a considerable time each evening in the church without using a prayer book or rosary, or any other visible adjunct for prayers. Vianney asked him how he prayed. The man replied " I look at the good Lord, and the good Lord looks at me". That form of loving awareness is not unlike the experience of many parents. As they gaze on their sleeping infants they experience and awareness of unconditional love towards their children which requires neither words nor demonstrative gestures. It is utterly simple.

Prayer in this wordless form is contemplation of God, or more precisely an intuitive reflection upon our relationship with Him. The basis of this prayer is the realisation that we are invited to a relationship of intimacy with the infinite God, whom we are urged to address as Father, and from whom we have received (at baptism) the status of adopted children. I emphasise the factor of intimacy, because we too readily take if for granted. Among the Muslims who also appreciate the infinity of God, the basis of their relationship to him is one of submission. [2] No words, thoughts or ideas can do justice to this profound relationship, and we rely on the wordless guidance of the Holy Spirit. People pursuing this manner of prayer may find that an occasional phrase or sentence may help to keep the mind free of distractions. Classical works of spirituality provide a number of examples. In his *Confessions* St.Augustine wrote a famous sentence which has been repeated endlessly. "Thou hast made us for thyself O Lord, and our heart is restless until it repose in thee." In the middle ages an anonymous English mystic the author of *The Cloud of Unknowing* epitomised his message with the injunction " Strike that thick cloud of unknowing with the sharp dart of longing love". In the nineteenth century Cardinal Newman, in *The Dream of Gerontius,* records his hero's simple request to his guardian angel, " I would have conscious communion". These three quotations from the mystics epitomise something of the wordless articulation of the soul's intimate relationship with the Father.

The point of transition to this kind of prayer has been indicated clearly in three places by St. John of the Cross. [3] In practice it is the point at which discursive meditation becomes

---

[2] According to the Muslim scholar Ayaan Hirsi Ali, reported in *The Guardian* , 17th May 2005.

[3] The three places where he describe the indicators are *The Ascent of Mount Carmel,* Book 2,

impossible, yet the soul ardently desires a deep prayerful union with God. However it lies outside the scope of a book of this kind to pursue the matter further. I recommend to my readers the numerous books on the matter written by authors more experienced than I am. In

practice too, one should seek a competent spiritual guide at that point.

POST SCRIPT : PRAYER AND CHRISTIAN CULTURE

This brief overview of Christian prayer is the most appropriate point at which to introduce the subject of Christian art. It is a well known fact that in the past all great art was inspired by religion. This applies to architecture, painting, sculpture, music and poetry. The Parthenon in Athens being a temple was obviously religious in inspiration, but so too were the famous Greek dramas which were composed for performance at religious festivals. The list could be pursued endlessly, but a detailed account lies outside the scope of this book which is a presentation of the essentials of Christianity to a sympathetic enquirer. Yet a few words must be said about the specific dynamism of Christian art.

The underlying cause of the richness of Christian art was the conviction, largely taken for granted, that the material world is good. That simple judgement is expressed repeatedly in the account of creation in the first chapter of Genesis. Thanks to the power of a Christian past we take that for granted, but it was not always so. There have been religions and philosophical systems which have categorised spirit as good, and matter as bad. The author of Genesis may have had something like that in mind, when he kept repeating that God saw his creation and it was good. Other religions, notably in Asia , have had doubts about the importance, or indeed the reality of the material world. Is it something insubstantial and inconsequential compared with the values of the spiritual world? Such attitudes are bound to undermine both the pursuit of art, and in a wider context, the pursuit of scientific research and technology. Christianity has given a powerful impetus to art and science thanks to its conviction that the material world is good. Indeed Christianity had gone further in proclaiming the material world as the vehicle for holiness, notably in the Incarnation of Jesus, and in the sacraments understood as channels of grace.

At the institutional level Christianity has safeguarded the development of art and culture, because unlike all its predecessors, the religious community was distinct from and independent of the political organisation notably the apparatus of State. That meant that the religion was not tied to the fortunes of the State, and in an extreme situation it could survive the demise of the latter. This indeed is what happened when the Roman Empire in the West collapsed in the fifth and sixth centuries.[4]

---

chapter 13, *The Dark Night of the Soul* , Book 1, chapter 9, and *The Living Flame of Love,* Section 34 and following. The matter has been summarised with great clarity in an article by Abbot John Chapman O.S.B. entitled *Contemplative Prayer: A Few Simple Rules.* in the journal *Pax,* Vol.5, no. 36. Aug. 1913, pp.339 - 44.

[4] For these considerations I am dependent on the writings of Christopher Dawson, who in the 1940's and 1950's wrote extensively on the subject. See for example his books *Progess and Religion, The Historic Reality of Christian Culture, Christianity and the Rise of Western Culture* . etc.

The immediate cause for the beginnings of Christian art were the requirements of the liturgy. As I have stated elsewhere in this book, the first large buildings in which Christians conducted their liturgy were the basilicas, whose basic style influenced the first specifically church buildings constructed by the Christians themselves. After the establishment of the churches, came the decoration of them, and this gave rise to the development of painting, sculpture, and the invention of stained glass windows. In this development Christianity benefited from the fact that it suffered from no inhibitions about plastic or painted images, which has curtailed the religious art of Judaism and Islam. Music however did not come

under that ban, and its place in worship is common to the three great monotheistic faiths. Indeed there are reasons to believe that plainsong may have been derived from Jewish religious music. There are records of a number of Jewish cantors in the city of Rome who converted to Christianity in antiquity.

The spiritual motivation of this great artistic movement was not simply to encourage the attention of the congregations during the liturgy, but also to give glory to God through the beauty of material artefacts. In the high middle ages when the towering gothic cathedrals were constructed, detailed carvings were carried out high up on parts of the stonework which were invisible to the viewers at ground level. It was all done for the glory of God. In keeping with that motivation was the fact that the cultivation of beauty extended beyond the churches to all the other buildings which were connected to the Church's mission, namely hospitals, schools, and university buildings. One of the most remarkable examples of this development is the chapel of King's College in Cambridge. It is hard to appreciate that this enormous and beautiful building was conceived as the domestic chapel for one of the colleges of the university. (Its beauty today is enhanced by its having preserved its complete set of stained glass windows, which survived the ravages of the reformation. It is one of only two churches in the entire country whose complete set has been preserved whole and intact.)

Whereas the mediaeval achievement in the arts was purely a Christian creation, the next phase, the Renaissance, was a creative interaction between Christian inspiration and the genius of the ancient world of Greece and Rome. A remarkable balance was achieved between those two cultural influences. Works of art like the frescoes on the walls and ceiling of the Sistine chapel in Rome indicate the continuing dynamism of the Christian inspiration of art.

Christianity's contribution to the wider intellectual culture of Europe after the collapse of the Roman empire is such a vast field that it would be impossible to do justice to it in a book of this scope. However it is profitable to reflect that in the area of pure intellectual development and science, Christianity was once again the driving force. It is not a coincidence that science and technology made their real impact in the culture which had been created by Christianity, which accorded such intrinsic value to the material world. It did not occur in the much older cultures of Asia.

CHAPTER TEN

ETERNITY : IMMORTALITY , HEAVEN AND RESURRECTION

SECTION 1 : ENTERING ETERNITY

In the month of April 2008 I attended the funeral of an elderly relative. The aunt in question had died at the age of one hundred and three, so the family gathering was not dominated by an atmosphere of tragic grief. Our thoughts reflected on her active and fulfilled life, and one's mind turned naturally to the well known sentence in the Book of Qoheleth, "For everything there is a season, and a time for every matter under heaven: a time to be born and a time to die." (3:1 & 2). Without being unfeeling, one could say that in that instance everyone felt that death was the appropriate transition to the after life. It so happened that in the same month one of our sons was making his final preparations for going to university. He was revising for A levels, negotiating a student loan, applying for accommodation in one of the university's halls of residence, and many other practical details. The two events had much in common. My wife and I were somewhat saddened at the prospect of his leaving home, yet we realised that it was a supremely appropriate way for him to move on. His normal development indicated that childhood should be left behind, and he was then taking his place in the adult world, for which our upbringing had been preparing him.

In a similar way believers should regard death as the appropriate transition to the next stage of our existence for which the earthly course of life has been the preparation. English literature has two remarkable descriptions of death, firstly Bunyan's towards the end of *Pilgrim's Progress*, and later in J.H. Newman's poem *The Dream of Gerontius.*[1] Both writers chose the experience of unconsciousness as the basis of their descriptions, and the person in question wakes up in eternity. The transition is painless and both Christian and Gerontius awake with great happiness in the realm of eternity. Bunyan the Protestant takes Christian through a river where he undergoes a painless drowning experience, and then he situates him in heaven right away. Newman the Catholic leads Gerontius via a painless sleep and then initially to purgatory. Both accounts take for granted what one might call the continuity of the conscious self, although neither author uses that precise form of words. The two narratives deserve to be read in their own right, so I will say no more about them for the present.

The various states after death present considerable problems to the imagination and to the intellect of the believer, because they take place in realm of which we have no direct experience. The first factor to note is that we will be outside the world of time, and situated in eternity. This concept is viewed by some people as a rather frightening prospect, mainly because they have not understood it. Years ago an atheist acquaintance of mine told me that he would be bored in eternity. The comedian Woody Allen expressed the same perception when he declared that "Eternity is very long, especially towards the end."[2] The Hebrew bible does not have the concept of eternity, and expressions which are translated as " for ever ", or

---

[1] Bunyan, J. *Pilgrim's Progress,* Harmondsworth: Penguin edition (1987), pp.136 -38. Newman, J.H. *The Dream of Gerontius,* in "Verses on Various Occasions", London, (ed. of 1912) Longmans Green, pp.234 -38.

[2] quoted in Rees,M.(2000), *Just Six Numbers,* London: Orion Books (Phoenix), p. 80.

other similar phrases, strictly indicate a very long time of indeterminate duration. It was the

Greek philosophers who gave the world the concept of literal eternity, meaning outside time.

It is perhaps helpful to try and conceptualise the notion by analogy with extended space. With this concept we do have experience of being present within it and also being outside it. Our spiritual soul enables us to envisage ideas like position or location, without being confined within precise dimensions. The experience of my thought processes is as real to me as the awareness of my body. The latter is intrinsically connected with space, dimensions, and distances from other material objects, but the thought processes are totally outside the spatial parameters, thanks to my spiritual soul. Similarly that which occurs in eternity is simply outside time: it is not to be envisaged as events taking place in a sequence of very long duration. A simple example from everyday life may help. Two people who are in love will always enjoy being alone together. At times or great emotional intensity they may say to themselves: "I wish that this moment did not have to end". That is a glimpse of the richness of eternity understood as a present experience of hightened awareness. Their feelings would not be so well captured if they said : "I wish this could go on for ever".

It may also help us to understand eternity, if we reflect upon the fact that time is not an absolute entity in its own right. It is merely a function of things that change. One can compare it to temperature which is a function of material bodies, and has no independent existence. Time is a similar function, and does not exist independently of the measurement of changes, any more than temperature does. Hence it is absent from a realm of unchanging stability.

SECTION 2 : THE IMMORTAL SOUL

In the transition from the world of time to the realm of eternity, the constant element in the journey is the human immortal soul. This entity which is central to traditional Christian anthropology presents a problem to many people in modern times, because the intellectual outlook is so powerfully influenced by science. Radio telescopes have enable us to see the most distant stars, electron microscopes have made visible the tiniest particles of matter, and even the trajectories of molecules can be detected with certain very sophisticated instruments. All of this seems to imply that anything which is real can be measured and weighed. Since no such measurements are possible for a spiritual entity, people feel slightly ill at ease with the notion of a soul. In some quarters there is the widespread optimism that one day computers will be able to do all that the human psyche is capable of. In other words, if the present generation of computers can play chess, there would seem to be no limit to what the next batch of even better designed computers might do.

So it is useful to start by reflecting on the limitations of computers, because to some people they seem like magic. In reality their internal workings are basically simple mathematical additions and subtractions. The complexity of their programmes are completely dependent upon their human designers, who set them up to cope with a very large range of alternative responses. Admittedly there is a superficial resemblance between a computer and the human brain.The brain consists of some hundred billion nerve cells, joined by approximately one hundred trillion connections. As such it is a very well designed instrument for some of the soul's operations. At this point it is important to remember the distinction between the soul and the brain. The latter is the instrument for some of the soul's operations, those of the mind

154

or intellect to be precise. As an instrument it warrants our respect, and care. The number of cells in the brain is so large that it defies the imagination. Even this vast array of cells cannot

convert it into a self conscious free spirit. There is an unbridgeable qualitative difference between the two. In a normally functioning nervous system the neural activity of the brain is a necessary, but not a sufficient condition of ordinary human consciousness.[3] Studies in the functions of the brain and the workings of computers have not rendered the spiritual soul superfluous. One recent writer has summed it up succinctly in the words: "Thinking is done *with* the brain, because we need images, but not *by* the brain".[4]

Basically a computer can do no more than it is "instructed " to do by the person (i.e. a spiritually directed intelligence) who designs the programme. Once the programme is settled the computer has absolutely no ability to deviate from it. Obviously it cannot exercise freedom or originality, by the same token it cannot make mistakes, which is why it is so valuable to us. They work much faster than our brains, hence their value to us, but they have no possible ability to innovate, or perform tasks of originality or creativity.

A more technical demonstration of the limitations of computers has been produced by two scientists, John Barrow and Frank Tippler, it is based upon the pioneering work of a brilliant mathematician, Alan Turing and involves what is known as the Halting Theorem.[5] It is best to start with a specific example. The ratio between the circumference of a circle and its diameter is the number designated by the Greek letter *pi*. It cannot be calculated exactly because its refinement, getting ever more exact is unlimited. It is no use turning to mechanical or electronic machines for help. They may take the solution further or more quickly, but they are limited to a finite number of actions. Since computers fall into this category of machines it follows that they are incapable of solving what is known as a non-terminating problem. Barrow and Tippler have extended these considerations to point out that a computer could never fully understand itself. This in turn means that it can never discharge the role of a soul in the human person. For a fuller treatment of this abstruse matter, I must refer the reader to the book of Barrow and Tippler.

The strongest basis for our conviction that we do have spiritual souls is the direct experience of the total transparency of our self consciousness. Not only are we aware of our mental states, but we have clear knowledge of ourselves in the act of introspection. We can examine our thoughts, ideas and free decisions. In the latter area we know that we are free, and that we can change our minds right up to the last moment before we take the practical steps entailed in the choice. Furthermore we know that we can initiate intellectual activity in any field which we choose to select, even if it is only to ponder upon our limitations in technical subjects upon which we have not been educated. Like my speculations, for example, about the Chinese language (about which I am totally ignorant). Equally powerful indicators of the spiritual nature of the soul and its activities are the judgements which we make about moral issues, about aesthetic evaluations, about theoretical components of the intellectual life. These extend

---

[3] cf. Tallis, R, (2004) *Why the Mind is not a Computer.* Exeter: Imprint Academic, p.29.

[4] Selman, Francis, (2004), *The Soul - An Inquiry,* London, St.Paul's Publishing, p. 65.

[5] Barrow, J. & Tippler, F.J.(1988), *The Anthropic Cosmological Principle,* Oxford, O.U.P.1988, p. 4 ff.

to very abstract concepts of mathematics and philosophy, coming back again to self consciousness like speculating on the meaning of meaning. None of this could be done by any computer which could be envisaged.

These basic experiences of the capabilities of my spiritual soul are rather like the axioms of geometry. They are at the fundamental level of intellectual activity and have nothing deeper to refer to, in an attempt to prove them. But like the axioms of geometry they do have one additional guarantee of their correctness, namely if we reverse the inferences and contradict those basic insights we find ourselves in the realm of absurdities. For example if I were to declare that I am not free, nor do I have reliable knowledge of the world around me, then I would not be able to carry out even the simplest activities of everyday life, if I were to act consistently with those allegations.

Christian writers since the patristic period have been deeply influenced by the Greek philosophers' studies on the spiritual nature of the soul. The more ascetically minded saw an ally in Plato who regarded the pure spirit as being imprisoned in a material body, from which it longed to be set free. Aquinas was more strongly influenced by Aristotle and taught that soul and body were natural companions, or components of the human entity. In his technical terminology he declared it to be the form of the body, which imparted to the body its distinctive characteristics as human. The Greek philosophers considered that the soul was immortal, since being a spirit, there was nothing in it which could suffer decomposition. This notion was well received by the Christians, who saw therein a confirmation of the explicit teaching of the New Testament that the individual person survives death.

Whereas Christians agree that life in eternity is the ultimate destiny of the soul, its origin at the beginning of a person's life has not had the same measure of agreement. Some Christian writers in antiquity and in the middle ages, following the Greeks, suggested that it might enter the body several days or even weeks after the foetus had been conceived. Modern developments in biology would suggest strongly that it is present from the moment of conception. The DNA equipment is complete from that point onwards, and there is embryological evidence of differentiation as early as the two cell stage. This is a clear indication of the unity and integrity of the conceptus shortly after fertilisation.[6] Moreover provided that implantation takes place, and the mother's maternal organs are functioning normally, there is no further significant intrinsic change to the foetus which would suggest that the human soul had entered it. All the changes which take place gradually are the unfolding of the programmed development which began at conception and which attain their term at the birth of the infant.

SECTION 3 : BODILY RESURRECTION

Whereas the ancient Greeks' understanding of the soul provided the Christians with support for their belief in immortality, the same cannot be said for their attitude to the destiny of the body. Greek thought was totally opposed to the Hebrew view of personal resurrection, but in opposing it they did a long term service to that doctrine which was clarified by the early Christians. St. Paul was forced to refine his theology of personal resurrection in an intellectual

---

[6] Meyer, John. R. "Embryonic Personhood and Rational Ensoulment" , in *Heythrop Journal* , (XLVII) April 2006, p. 219.

climate which was as hostile to it as are many modern scientists. Modern science takes for granted that the chemical components of the body cannot last for ever. It is also accepted that the cells of the body undergo complete replacement every seven years or so. For their part the

Greeks, without knowing the details about cells and their chemistry, were equally certain from philosophical considerations that the human body could not survive death and defy decomposition.

St. Paul's starting point was the Jewish belief in personal resurrection which is illustrated by the dialogue between Jesus and Martha by the tomb of Lazarus:- "Jesus said to her 'Your brother will rise again.' Martha said to him ' I know that he will rise again in the resurrection at the last day' ". (John 11: 23,24). This general background belief had been made more real for St. Paul by the resurrection of Jesus, whom he had seen. When he came to Athens in his second missionary journey, he was listened to respectfully by the pagan audience until he spoke of the resurrection of Jesus, at which point they laughed at him, and fobbed him off saying that they would listen to him on some other day. He was forced to rethink the whole matter, in the light of the scepticism of the Greek philosophers, and when he came to write the his first Letter to the Corinthians, we see the results of that theological reflection.

He treats of the whole question in the fifteenth chapter of that letter, and his words warrant careful consideration. The first part of the chapter deals with the resurrection of Christ, then he turns his attention to the resurrection of Christians, which leads on to his supplying answers to some of the questions which his converts had asked him : " But some one will ask, 'How are the dead raised ? With what kind of body do they come ?' You foolish man! What you sow does not come to life unless it dies. And what you sow is not the body which is to be, but a bare kernel, perhaps of wheat or of some other grain. But God gives it a body as he has chosen, and to each kind of seed its own body for not all flesh is alike, but there is one kind for men, another for animals, another for birds and another for fish. There are celestial bodies and there are terrestrial bodies; but the glory of the celestial is one, and the glory of the terrestrial is another. There is one glory of the sun, and another glory of the moon, and another glory of the stars; for star differs from star in glory. So it is with the resurrection of the dead. What is sown is perishable, what is raised is imperishable. It is sown in dishonour, it is raised in glory. It is sown in weakness, it is raised in power. It is sown a physical body it is raised a spiritual body. If there is a physical body, there is also a spiritual body." (I Cor. 15: 35 - 44).

He was teaching his non - Jewish converts that in eternity the human body will be transformed and glorified like that of the risen Christ, so that it will no longer be subject to any kind of change, including chemical decomposition and decay. Paradoxically he was helped in the formulation of that idea by the Greek conviction that the stars and planets were of a different constitution to the material bodies on earth. For them they were extended and visible, but their substance was not subject to change or decomposition. In short, they were what could be described as eternal bodies. That gave St. Paul a concept with which to illustrate his teaching on the incorruptible state of the glorified body of Christ, which was also the destiny for his followers. St. Paul's line of thought is not invalidated by the fact that modern science has discovered that the material composition of the planets and stars is the same as matter on our planet. He has used the currently accepted notion by way of an illustration: his argument did not depend upon its scientific accuracy.

The doctrine of personal resurrection entered main stream Christian belief. The doctrine of resurrection has featured in all the baptismal creeds from the earliest formulations right up to and including the more detailed creeds of the Councils of Nicea and Constantinople, which we recite at mass every Sunday.

SECTION 4 : HEAVEN

All the creeds conclude with an attestation to "Life everlasting", which is the state of the individual whose soul and glorified body live in eternity. The New Testament also teaches that it is the reward of a good life, and not surprisingly the nature of the happiness in that state has given rise to considerable speculation.

The scenario is so rich and profound that it should not surprise us that the New Testament has provided many images which emphasise one or other aspect of this mysterious state of happiness to which human experiences and language cannot really do justice. Theology too has definite limitations: the quest for intellectual precision carries with it the danger of diminishing the beauty of the mysterious reality which is being investigated, rather like psychological definitions of love.

The basic element is the joyful union with Christ which cannot thenceforth be lost. St. Paul states it very simply in the letter to the Philippians (1: 21, 22) :- "For to me to live is Christ, and to die is gain. If it is to be life in the flesh, that means fruitful labour for me. Yet which I shall choose I cannot tell. I am hard pressed between the two. My desire is to depart and be with Christ, for that is far better."

The fundamental characteristic of that future life with Christ is its permanence, which theology later elaborated as its being eternal. The fourth gospel states it thus."For God so loved the world that he gave his only son, so that whoever believes in him should not perish, but have eternal life". (John 3:13). And in the same gospel, speaking of the Bread of Life, Jesus said "For this is the will of my Father, that everyone who sees the Son and believes in him should have eternal life; and I will raise him up at the last day." (6: 40). It will be an inclusive life, with room for everyone, if one may speak informally :-"Let not your hearts be troubled; believe in God, believe also in me. In my Father's house are many rooms; if it were not so, would I have told you that I go to prepare a place for you ? And when I go and prepare a place for you, I will come again and will take you to myself, that where I am you may be also." (John 14: 1 - 3).

The homely image of a large house with many rooms, has overtones of conviviality, as does the biblical image of heaven as a banquet or family party. The way in which it is mentioned in St.Matthew's gospel seems to imply that the Jewish audience was familiar with the concept. One example is the brief speech of Jesus after curing the centurion's servant at Capernaum. After praising the faith of the pagan centurion, which was stronger than that of many Jews, Jesus stated: "I tell you, many will come from east and west and sit at table with Abraham, Isaac, and Jacob in the kingdom of heaven, while the sons of the kingdom will be thrown into the outer darkness;" (Matt. 8: 11, 12). The image of a banquet occurs again in Matthew's gospel, clearly indicating the reward after death. "The kingdom of heaven may be compared to a king who gave a marriage feast for his son, and sent his servants to call those who were invited to the marriage feast;" (Matt. 22: 2, 3).

The image of a celebratory meal is implied in Luke's parable of the rich man and Lazarus the pauper. The rich man feasts sumptuously every day, and Lazarus would have been content with scraps which fell from his table. After the deaths of both of them we read : "The poor

man died and was carried by the angels to Abraham's bosom." (Luke 16:22) The precise wording has caused some puzzlement. It only makes sense if it is understood as a formal banquet. In Palestine at the time of Jesus the guests did not sit on chairs, they reclined on couches, with their heads close to the table, and feet far from it, supporting themselves on the left elbow, and eating with the right hand. The host would be at the centre of a horseshoe shaped table, giving the servants access in the middle. The most honoured guest would be close to the host, but strangely for our way of thinking, he would have his back to the host. In this position the host could pay him the supreme courtesy of using his right hand to place pieces of food in the mouth of the favoured guest. That is the meaning of Lazarus being in the bosom of Abraham, and it implies a formal banquet, which is the image Luke had chosen to describe the reward of heaven. The imagery only makes sense if we take account of a cultural setting very different from that of modern Western society.

What I have described as overtones of conviviality in the biblical imagery is consistent with the traditional Christian conviction that in addition to the joy of the presence of God, one component of the happiness will be re-union with those whom the blessed ones have loved while on earth. This human component has been a constant element in the traditional doctrine of heaven and has been commonplace in standard text books of theology. [7] One way of reflecting on this is to look upon it as the perfection of the union of Christians which begins on earth in the community which St. Paul describes as the Body of Christ. It is inconceivable that this profound supernatural bond of unity in charity should be dissolved on death. In heaven it receives its perfection. The manner in which those souls communicate with one another is difficult to speculate about, because we have no experience in this life of conscious beings effecting immediate conscious communication with one another.[8]

It is sometimes stated, incorrectly, that marriage will be no more. This is based on a misunderstanding of a sentence in St. Luke. The context is the question from the Sadducees about the woman who had been married to seven brothers, all of whom died, and whose wife would she be at the general resurrection ? The reply of Jesus needs to be read very carefully. "Jesus said to them, The sons of this age marry and are given in marriage; but those who are accounted worthy to attain to that age and to the resurrection from the dead neither marry nor are given in marriage."(Luke 20: 34, 35). The particular Greek word employed by St. Luke designates not the permanent state of the marriage bond, but the ceremony (or contract, perhaps we should say) in which the woman's father gives her to the man, and the bridegroom accepts her.[9] In other words no new marriages will be initiated. It should not be

[7] For example, Schmaus, M (1959). *Katholische Dogmatik* Munich: Max Heuber Verlag, Vol 4 (ii), pp.632 - 36.

[8] Mersch,E. *The Theology of the Mystical Body,* English trans. Cyril Vollert, (1951), St. Louis & London: Herder Book Co. pp.126,127.

[9] cf. Bauer,W.(1979), *A Greek - English Lexicon of the New Testament and Other Early Christian*

understood as signifying the end of all marriages which had been entered into on earth.

The images of house, or banquet are complemented by another metaphor of community and

security, namely a city. The author of the Hebrews sets the scene, saying "For here we have no lasting city, but we seek the city which is to come"(13: 14). The author of the Apocalypse identifies the city as the heavenly Jerusalem, which he depicts with extravagant imagery. Extravagant cosmic imagery is one of the characteristics of the apocalyptic literary idiom. It was a vehicle to convey the greatness and transcendence of God. The author also describes with great delicacy the happiness which is promised to those who are present there. For instance, the heavenly Jerusalem is depicted in the following manner:- "And I saw the holy city, new Jerusalem, coming down out of heaven from God, prepared as a bride adorned for her husband; and I heard a great voice from the throne of God saying, 'Behold the dwelling of God is with men. He will dwell with them, and they shall be his people, and God himself will be with them; he will wipe away every tear from their eyes, and death shall be no more, neither shall there be mourning nor crying nor pain any more, for the former things have passed away.' " (21: 2-4).

Since the middle ages the conscious loving union with God has been designated as the beatific vision. It is the achievement of life's overall purpose and the culmination of of a loving and intimate relationship which began with the first act of faith, and was developed in prayer. A number of people have glimpses of it in this life and this privilege is not confined to the saints. A well known English art historian has left us a description of one such experience in Rome :- "I had a religious experience. It took place in the church of San Lorenzo, but it did not seem to be connected with the harmonious beauty of the architecture. I can only say that for a few minutes my whole being was irradiated by a kind of heavenly joy, far more intense than anything I had known before. This state of mind lasted for several months, and wonderful though it was, it posed an arkward problem in terms of action. My life was far from blameless: I would have to reform. My family would think I was going mad, and perhaps after all it was a delusion, for I was in every way unworthy of receiving such a flood of grace. Gradually the effect wore off, and I made no effort to retain it. I think I was right: I was too deeply embedded in the world to change course. But that I had 'felt the finger of God' I am quite sure, and   although the memory of this experience has faded, it still helps me to understand the joys of the saints."[10]

The beatific vision is supernatural in character, being the final grace given to a human being. It is superior to Plato's concept of the immortal soul consciously surviving death. Within the limitations of human concepts the New Testament writers have striven to convey its richness. St. Paul and St. John describe it as a sharing in the life of Christ. It is essentially mysterious. One concept from modern psychology is helpful, namely the notion of intimacy. It is an intimate relationship of reciprocal love and knowledge, but as far as knowledge is concerned, ideas, concepts or anything of that kind are totally inadequate, since God is infinite and cannot be enclosed in any human thought pattern. That is why the mediaeval theologians

---

Literature, 2nd. ed. revised by W.F. Arndt and F.W. Gingrich, Chicago & London: University of Chicago Press, p.151.

[10]   Clark, K. (1977) *The Other Half: A Self Portrait,* London, p. 108.

described it as vision, in other words, something like a direct intuitive awareness.

SECTION 5: PURGATORY

I have described the soul's union with God as a form of intimate personal relationship. This

notion of relationship is the most satisfactory approach to the consideration of purgatory. The word purgatory is an anglicisation of the Latin word meaning purification. In the past this gave rise to two considerations, namely that the soul is purified negatively by punishment for sins committed during life, and positively in the sense that the soul is refined so as to remove moral and psychological obstacles which would impede the intimate loving relationship with God. In popular piety it seems that the negative aspect has proved to have the more powerful influence on the collective imagination. Who could forget the graphic images from Dante's *Purgatorio* in the *Divina Commedia* ? Those who on earth were guilty of envy spend their time in purgatory with their eye-lids stitched up with wire, as a punishment for the envious glances which they cast upon other peoples' possessions. The proud walk round their circle bowed down under heavy weights on their necks to punish them for their haughty demeanour while on earth.

Close to the year 200 Tertullian wrote about purgatory basing himself on the words of Jesus in Matthew 5:26 concerning reconciliation. Jesus had used the everyday comparison of a legal dispute about money where the guilty party will not be let out of prison until he has paid the last penny. Tertullian applied the lesson the debt of guilt. Although the background for the patristic writings is frequently that of a period punishment after death, their actual message is much more positive. It concerns what the living can do to help them. The earliest surviving evidence concerns private prayers for the dead . Tertullian is our witness again where he describes a widow who prays for her deceased husband : "To be sure, she prays for his soul. She asks that during the interval, he may find rest and that he may share in the first resurrection. She offers the sacrifice each year on the anniversary of his falling asleep."[11]

The final sentence raises the tantalising possibility that the Church at that early date was already praying for the dead in the public liturgy of the eucharist. No liturgical text containing prayer for the dead has survived from that early period, but a little later is seen to be a common feature of the eucharist. Evidence of the practice has survived in several fourth and fifth century sources, such as the Catechetical Homilies of Theodore of Mopsuestia (16:4), the Mystagogical Catecheses of St. Cyril of Jerusalem, (5: 8 - 10) explaining the eucharistic liturgy, The Apostolic Constitutions (8, 12: 40 - 9), The *Testamentum Domini* (1, 23), and in the liturgy of St. John Chrysostom. [12] Prayers for the dead were incorporated in all eucharistic liturgies, and their presence was probably the most powerful influence consolidating the belief in purgatory in the minds of ordinary believers. At a later stage when the Roman liturgy had

---

[11] Tertullian *De Monogamia* , 10, quoted in Johannes Quasten (1953),*Patrology,* Westminster, Maryland: Newman Press, Vol, 2, p.339.

[12] Analysed in Yarnold, E.(1978) "The Liturgy of the Faithful in the Fourth and Fifth Centuries", in Jones, Cheslyn. Wainwright, Geoffrey. & Yarnold, Edward,(eds.) *The Study of Liturgy,* London: S.P.C.K. , p.196.

given a fixed form to every element in the Mass, one of the readings for the masses for the dead was taken from the Second Book of Maccabees, 12: 43 - 45. When burying the bodies of dead soldiers after battle, Judas Maccabeus and his troops discovered that they had carried idolatrous images under their clothing. To make expiation for that sin the writer narrates "He also took up a collection man by man, to the amount of two thousand drachmas
of silver, and sent it to Jerusalem to provide for a sin offering. In doing this he acted very well and honourably, taking account of the resurrection. For if he were not expecting that those

who had fallen would rise again, it would have been superfluous and foolish to pray for the dead. But if he was looking to the splendid reward that is laid up for those who fall asleep in godliness, it was a holy and pious thought. Therefore he made atonement for the dead, that they might be delivered from their sin."

In addition to the concepts of sin, guilt and reparation, there was always present, at least by implication the notion of the soul's being purified to make it worthy, and indeed capable, of enjoying a relationship of intimacy with God. In modern times the psychologists have drawn attention to this important component of a person's emotional life. In the past, when humanity was concerned more with the hazards of survival, it did not feature so prominently. With the conquest of so many diseases by scientific medicine, we are now in a position to attend more carefully to the quality of life. The refinement of personal relationships is one of the advances in this sphere, and the concept of intimacy has come to the fore. When we consider the arranged marriages in the past, (and not only of royal alliances), we can understand how they were bearable only because the partners did not expect the experience of intimacy.

When we apply this concept to our relationship with God it makes perfect sense. The mystical writers like St. John of the Cross describe the purifications of the soul in this life, precisely as ways of removing the soul's obstacles to intimacy with God. Everyday experience has all too many examples of how necessary it is. Sadly there are some elderly people, who as they approach to death seem to become ever more self centred. They appear to be in varying states of animosity to most of the people around them. One wonders how such personalities could be capable of a loving outgoing, and generous love of God. Purification after death, with a view to intimacy with God would seem to be the perfect remedy.

It has been a constant conviction in Christian piety that the prayers of the living can benefit the souls of the dead. It is just one more aspect of the unity of the Church viewed not as an institutionalised society, but as the close knit community of the Body of Christ. On reflection it is clear that praying for the dead is not essentially different from praying for the living, which is a duty which St. Paul constantly urged upon his readers. In this context we can see how positive is the Christian concept of purgatory and the attendant piety that it has generated.

SECTION 6 : ETERNAL PUNISHMENT

There are so many references in the New Testament to the punishment of hell that its existence has never been doubted by Christian tradition. It is depicted as the state of those who have rejected all invitations of love from a benevolent God. It is noteworthy that the longest description of the final judgement in Matthew chapter 25, consigns to hell those who have ill treated their fellow human beings if they were sick, starving or homeless. Those who are old enough to remember the revelations about extermination camps at the end of the Second World War, will recognise a measure of realism in the assessment of human nature which is implied in the concept of eternal exclusion from God, for those who have so badly mistreated their fellow human beings.

Paradoxically it has not been the theologians, but two novelists who have made the most penetrating observation about Hell. Dostoyevsky asked "What is hell ? I am reasoning thus:

The suffering that comes from the consciousness that one is no longer able to love".[13] G.K. Chesterton is reputed to have described it as God's ultimate compliment to human nature, namely the final respect to the free will which he has bestowed on us. God will not force or compel a totally recalcitrant person to submit to his love. It took many centuries for that insight to come to fruition.

In the middle ages the attitude to hell was determined by the context in which it was discussed, namely the juridical environment. A God of justice was understood to be inflicting well deserved punishment on those who had merited it by clear decisions to commit grave sins. At every point the requirements of justice were scrupulously maintained. It provided a field day for the artists and poets. The main entrances of most of the Gothic cathedrals had graphic carvings over the main doors depicting the last judgement, in which the most vivid images were those of the damned being consigned to hell. Poets like Dante and Milton were equally explicit, and it has been remarked that the imagery of Dante's *Inferno* is considerably more exciting (or should one say, graphic) than the *Paradiso*. A considerable amount of popular preaching orchestrated the pains of damnation, in the well intentioned desire to frighten people into leading a virtuous life. It is surprising how long that tradition of fear - inducing sermons lasted. Well into the twentieth century parish retreats and missions, particularly when conducted by certain religious orders, usually ended with a terrifying sermon on the four last things, death, judgement, heaven and hell.

It is easy for us to smile about such excesses in the twenty first century, after the Second Vatican Council. But it is sobering to reflect that the intention of inducing fear as a pedagogical method was routinely employed with small children. Certainly as late as the 1940's small children, being instructed on the then current catechism, were taught that it was a mortal sin to miss mass on a Sunday, and if they should die in that condition they would be punished in hell for all eternity. At best it was an unhealthy way of educating children and for many it was ultimately ineffectual. As they matured they saw through the threats. Some who were completely traumatised gave up Christianity altogether, and others having received no more inspiring motive, gave up attendance at mass.

The final unhealthy element in the mediaeval juridical attitude to hell was the irresponsible attitude displayed by those who consigned to hell whole classes of people who happened to be outside the ranks of Christianity, such as Muslims and Jews in general. A large swathe of theological opinion assumed that they had heard of Jesus and rejected his teaching and were therefore condemned to eternal punishment. A profound change in theological attitude came

[13] Dostoyevsky, F. *The Brothers Karamazov* (English translation, David Magarshack) 1958, Harmondsworth, Penguin, vol. 1, p. 380.

about slowly after the voyages of Columbus and other explorers who discovered hitherto unknown continents. It became obvious to serious minded theologians that vast sections of the human race, perhaps the majority, could not possibly have heard of the preaching of Jesus. It was beyond the limits of credibility that all those people should be condemned to hell.

It lies outside the scope of this book to trace the long and tortuous debates about the salvation of the so called infidels. For Catholics the matter was effectively settled by a number of factors which came together at the time of the Second Vatican Council. After the Second

Word War the mood of constructive criticism prevalent among the best theologians swept away the attitudes of triumphalism and legalism which had bedevilled the ecclesiastical outlook for so long. Serious minded Catholics no longer took any satisfaction in theological programmes which consigned millions of non-Christians to hell.

In a wider context the Council resolved centuries of confusion by speaking positively about non-Christian religions. The Decree *Nostrae Aetate* speaks in generally favourable terms about non-Christian religions which have in them authentic elements, such as monotheism. Hinduism and Buddhism are named specifically, and the decree enunciated an important general principle with the words:- "The Catholic Church rejects nothing which is true and holy in these religions. She looks with sincere respect upon those ways of conduct and life, those rules and teachings which, though differing in many particulars from what she holds and sets forth, nevertheless often reflect a ray of that Truth which enlightens all men. Indeed she proclaims and must always proclaim Christ, 'the way the truth and the life' (John 14:6), in whom men find the fullness of religious life, and in whom God has reconciled all things to Himself .) (cf. 2 Cor. 5:18 - 19)."[14] In the same decree the positive truths of Islam are commended, and particular praise is given to Judaism. Without going into further detail, the point which I wish to emphasise here is that the Council removed at a stroke the basis upon which many mediaeval theologians had consigned so many people to hell.

In the same period a seismic shift had taken place in believers' attitudes to God. The emphasis was on the quality of the relationship with our heavenly Father, and it was understood that this was a relationship of intimacy. This positive attitude displaced relationship based upon obedience and punishments. In this context the remark of G.K. Chesterton, quoted at the beginning of this section, came into its own. Hell was understood as God's final respecting of human freedom. The shift of emphasis was important, namely it is the human rebel who effectively makes the decision to cut himself off from God, rather than an expulsion by God's decision. This change of attitude concerning our relationship with God, namely that the idea of intimacy has displaced that of justice and obedience as the prime component, has had an important repercussion on another aspect of eternal punishment.

To many good people it seems that we advocate belief in a harsh, angry God if we hold to a belief in hell. I would like to suggest that the objection evaporates when we reflect upon the requirements of a relationship of intimacy. If God invites us to a relationship of intimacy, and also respects our freedom, then a measure of realism must exist between us. Let me give a

---

[14] Vatican II *Nostrae Aetate* , section 2, ed. Abbott p. 662.

couple of examples. If a young man was studying at a university where his father happened to be the president, it is just possible that an indulgent father might show him the examination papers before the final exam. If the young man passed his exams with distinction as a result of that mistaken act of kindness, the awarding of the degree would be meaningless, and an insult to both father and son and all that the university stood for. Similarly it is reported, rightly or wrongly, that the Emperor Nero went to Greece to take part in the Olympic games. He entered himself for the chariot race. The other competitors took the hint, drove their horses slowly, and although the emperor fell out of his chariot twice and had to scramble back in again, he came first in the race. The examples which I have cited could take place only in a society of hypocrites, and the consequences could not be upheld by people who respect one

another. In the context of a relationship of intimacy with God, we can understand that if the recalcitrant human has rejected all the initiatives of divine love, then he must be allowed to exclude himself from the relationship. Any other arrangement would be at best artificial, or in reality it would be hypocritical. It indicates a God offering real mature relationships to his creatures, and not a cruel deity.

As a result of these modern factors the Church now entertains a more healthy attitude to hell. That it exists we know, but whether there is anyone "down there" receiving the torments we cannot tell. It remains a possibility.

SECTION 7 : THE SECOND COMING OF CHRIST

For the first generation of Christians who had known Jesus in his earthly life, and who had been witnesses of his resurrection, the prospect of seeing him again, when he returned in glory, was the most wonderful event that they could envisage. It can be compared with the joyful reunions at the end of the Second World War when servicemen returned to their families after years of service overseas, or in prisoner of war camps. That explains why it is always described in such positive terms in the New Testament. In St. Peter's Second Letter he depicts it thus : "Since all these things are thus to be dissolved, what sort of persons ought you to be in lives of holiness and godliness, waiting for and hastening the coming of the day of God, because of which the heavens will be kindled and dissolved, and the elements will melt with fire. But according to his promise we wait for new heavens and a new earth in which righteousness dwells". (3: 11 - 13). It is worth noting that the Greek word which is translated as 'heavens' means, in this context, the sky and the planets and stars which occupy it. In other words the whole visible universe is destined to be renewed. The apocalypse of St. John offers the same message, and uses the same apocalyptic idiom to stress the magnitude of the divine intervention. In this case, there is a clear parallel to the initial act of creation as recorded in Genesis. "Then I saw a new heaven and a new earth; for the first heaven and the first earth had passed away, and the sea was no more. - - - - - - - - and he who sat upon the throne said, 'Behold I make all things new.' Also he said, 'Write this, for these words are trustworthy and true'. And he said to me, 'It is done! I am the Alpha and Omega, the beginning and the end. To the thirsty I will give water without price from the foundation of the water of life. He who conquers shall have this heritage, and I will be his God and he shall be my son. But as for the cowardly, the faithless, the polluted, as for the murderers, fornicators, sorcerers, idolaters, and all the liars, their lot shall be in the lake that burns with fire and brimstone, which is the second death' ". (Apoc. 21: 1, 2, 5 - 8).

The hoped for second coming did not take place in the life time of the early Christians, and the community settled down to await the event at some indeterminate future date. As was the case with the understanding of purgatory and hell, the collective perception underwent a pessimistic transformation in the middle ages, due to their viewing the event in principally in a juridical context where the severity of the punishments was the element which seems most to have gripped the imagination. In the late middle ages, the masses for the dead acquired as the sequence, (the prayer which introduces the gospel), the famous hymn *Dies Irae* (Day of Wrath). It had been composed in the thirteenth century as a meditation on the last day. It is unbelievably pessimistic in tone, as the following selection of a couple of verses will show :-

"Day of wrath, that day when the world will dissolve into dust, as prophesied by David and the Sibyll. - - - - What shall I then say in my misery? What advocate can I appeal to? When even the just are scarcely secure?"

It was only in the twentieth century that the atmosphere of gloom was lifted thanks to the theology of hope elaborated principally by Jurgen Moltmann. The event is now seen in the overall context of the glorious resurrection of Christ, which signifies the definitive victory of good over evil. His return to the visible world will be the final grace given by God to the human race. The concept of general judgement can best be understood as a universal moral audit when that triumph of goodness will be apparent, and it will be inauguration of the life of eternity and the reward of the saints and the just.

Viewed in this perspective the event can be seen as the culmination of human history uniting the destinies of individuals and the community of mankind in a purposeful forward progress, pursuing justice, art, science and every other area of human creativity, towards the establishment of goodness and happiness. The final stage of that progress will be its transformation by the power of God to the realm of eternity, whose permanence will provide the ultimate security for which all human beings have a profound innate longing.

BIBLIOGRAPHY

Barrow, J. & Tippler, J. (1988), *The Anthropic Cosmological Principle,* Oxford: Oxford University Press.

Bauer , W. (1979), *A Greek – English Lexicon of the New Testament and Other Early Christian Literature.* 2nd. Ed. revised by W.F. Arndt & F.W. Gingrich, Chicago and London: University of Chicago Press.

Blair – Kaiser, Robert. (1995), *The Encyclical that Never Was.* London: Sheed & Ward.

Botte, B. Gelin, A. Danielou, J. et al. (1957), *Études sur le Sacrement de l'Ordre.* Paris: Éditions du Cerf.

Browne, R.E. (1994), *An Introduction to New Testament Christology.* London: Geoffrey Chapman.

Browning, C.R. (1992), *Ordinary Men: Police Reserve Battalion 101 and the Final Solution in Poland.* New York: Harper Collins.

Buckley, Michael J. (1987), *At the Origins of Modern Atheism.* New York: Yale University Press.

Bullough, D. (1973) , *The Age of Charlemagne.*

Bunyan, J. *Pilgrim's Progress.* Harmondsworth: Penguin ed. (1987).

Burtchaell, J.T. (1960), *Catholic Theories of Inspiration since 1810.* Cambridge: Cambridge University Press.

Chadwick, Owen. (1975), *The Secularisation of the European Mind in the Nineteenth Century* . Cambridge: Cambridge University Press.

Chapman, H.J. art. "Contemplative Prayer: A Few Simple Rules", in *Pax,* August 1913.

Chapman, H.J. (1928), *Studies in the Early Papacy.* London: Sheed & Ward.

Chang, J. & Halliday, J. (2006), *Mao: The Unknown Story.* London: Vintage Books.

Clark, K. (1977), *The Other Half: A Self Portrait.* London.

Clifford, C. (2002), *The Asquiths.* London: John Muray.

Congar, Y.M.J. (1950) *Vraie et Fausse Réforme dans l'Église.* Paris: Éditions du Cerf.

Cristiani, L. (1948), *L'Église à l'Époque du Concile de Trente.* (Vol 17, in Fliche, A. & Martin, V. (eds.) (1946 onwards), (*Histoire de l'Église.*) Paris: Bloud & Gay.

Crossan, J.D. (1994), *Who Killed Jesus ? Exposing the Roots of anti-Semitism in the Gospel/Story of the Death of Jesus.* San Francisco: Harper.

Cumming, Geoffrey. (1976), *Hippolytus : A Text for Students.* Nottingham: Grove Books.

Dawson, Christopher. (1960), *The Historic Reality of Christian Culture.* London: Routledge & Kegan Paul Ltd. Also by the same author, *Progress and Religion, Christianity and the Rise of Western Culture.*

D'Costa, Gavin, (ed.) 1996), *Resurrection Reconsidered.* Oxford: One World.

de Vaux, R. (1961), *Ancient Israel, Its Life and Institutions.* London: Darton, Longman, & Todd.

de Vaux, R. (1978), *The Early History of Israel.* London: Darton, Longman, & Todd.

Di Lella, Alexander, A. (2002), "God and Wisdom in the Theology of Ben Sira" in : Egger-Wenzel, Renate (ed.) *Ben Sira's God: Proceedings of the International Ben Sira Conference – Durham, Ushaw College 2001,* Berlin & New York: Walter de Gruyter.

Dostoyevsky, F. *The Brothers Karamazov.* (Eng. trans. David Magarshack, 1958), Harmondsworth: Penguin.

Evans, Craig, A. art. "Life of Jesus Research and the Eclipse of Mythology". in *Theological Studies.* Vol. 54. (1993)

Fichtenau, H. (1968), *The Carolingian Empire.*

Figes, Orlando. (1996), *A People's Tragedy.* London: Pimlico.

Flew, A. (2006), *God and Philosophy.* Amherst, New York: Prometheus Books.

Goldhagen, D.J. (1996), *Hitler's Willing Executioners.* London: Abacus.

Gorman, Peter. (1979), *Pythagoras: A Life.* London: Routledge & Keegan Paul.

Grillmeier, A. (1965), *Christ in Christian Tradition.* (trans. J. S. Bowden). London: Mowbrays.

Hadas, Moses. & Smith, Morton. (1965), *Heroes and Gods: Spiritual Biographies in Antiquity,* London: Routledge & Keegan Paul.

Haldane, John. (2000) art. "Natural Theology", in Adrian Hastings (ed.) *The Oxford Companion to Christian Thought.* Oxford: Oxford University Press.

Häring, B. (1977) *Embattled Witness.* London: Burns & Oates.

Harries, Richard. & Meyr – Harting, Henry. (eds.) (2001), *Christianity : Two Thousand Years.* Oxford: Oxford University Press.

Hastings, Adrian. Art. "The Papacy and Rome's Civil Greatness", in *The Downside Review*. 1957.

Hastings, Adrian. (1977) (ed.) , *Bishops and Writers*. Hertfordshire.

Hawkins, D.J.B. (1949), *The Essentials of Theism*. London: Sheed & Ward.

Hickey, J.V. (1960), *The Irish Rural Immigrant and British Urban Soceity*. London: Newman Demographic Survey Publications.

Hook, S.H. (1963), *Middle Eastern Mythology*. Harmondsworth: Penguin Books.

Jalland, T.G. (1942), *The Church and the Papacy*. London: S.P.C.K.

John of the Cross, Saint. *The Dark Night of the Soul, The Ascent of Mount Carmel, The Living Flame of Love*. In "The Complete Works of Saint John of the Cross", Eng. trans. E. Allison Peers, revised edition 1953, London : Burns & Oates.

Johnson, P. (1995), *The Withered Garland: Reflections and Doubts of a Bomber*. London: New European Publications Ltd.,

Kenny, Anthony, (2006), *What I Believe*. London: Continuum.

Kleist, James. A. (1946) *The Epistles of St. Clement of Rome and St. Ignatius of Antioch*. Wesminster, Maryland: The Newman Press. London: Longmans, Green & Co.

Koncsik, Imre, (2005), "Christologie im 19 und 20 Jahrhundert" being Band III, Faszikel 1 e, of Schmaus, Michael et al. (eds) *Handbuch der Dogmengeschichte*, Freiburg: Herder.

Küng, Hans. (1961), *Konzil und Widervereinigung*, Freiburg: Herder. Eng. Trans. Hastings, Cecily. (1961), *The Council and Reunion*. London: Sheed & Ward.

Lampe, P. (2003), *Christians at Rome in the First Two Centuries*. Trans. M. Steinhauser. London: Continuum.

Lantos, P. (2005), *Parallel Lines*. London: Arcadia Books.

Laurentin, R. (1964) *Structure et Théologie de Luc I – II*. Paris: Gabalda.

Levi, Primo. (1987), *Moments of Reprieve*. London: Abacus.

Longford, E. (1964), *Victoria R.I*. London: Weidenfield & Nicholson.

Mahoney, J. (1987), *The Making of Moral Theology*. Oxford: Oxford University Press.

Marx,K. & Engels, F. (1967), *Manifesto of the Communist Party*. Moscow: Progress Publishers.

McGrath, A. (2005), *Dawkins' God*. Oxford: Basil Blackwell.

McGuckin, John, A. (2000), art. "Quest for the Historical Jesus", in Hastings, Adrian (ed.) *The Oxford Companion to Christian Thought.* Oxford: Oxford University Press.

McKitterick, R. (1983), *The Frankish Kingdoms under the Carolingians.*

Mersch, E. (1951), *The Theology of the Mystical Body.* (Eng. trans. Cyril Vollert) St. Louis and London: Herder Book Co.

Meyer, John, R. "Embryonic Personhood and Rational Ensoulment" in *The Heythrop Journal,* April 2006.

Midgley, M. (1985), *Evolution as a Religion.* London: Routledge.

Mlodinov, Leonard. (2002), *Euclid's Widow.* London: Allen Lane.

Moltmann, J. (1967), *Theology of Hope.* London: S.C.M. Press.

Mommsen, Th. (1872), (ed.) *Digest of Justinian.* Berlin.

Moule, C.F.D. (1977), *The Origin of Christology.* Cambridge: Cambridge University Press.

Murphy O'Connor, Jerome. (1978), *Becoming Human Together.* Dublin: Veritas Publications.

Murray, N. (2002), *Aldous Huxley: An English Intellectual.* London: Abacus.

Murray, R.P.R. (1983), art. "Prophecy", in Richardson, Alan & Bowden, John.(eds.) *A New Dictionary of Christian Theology.* London: S.C.M. Press.

Musurillo, H. (1966), (ed.) *St. Justin: First Apologia.* In *The Fathers of the Primitive Church.* London: New English Library.

Newman, J.H. (1878), *An Essay on the Development of Christian Doctrine.* (2nd. Ed.) London: Longmans Green & Co.

Newman, J.H. "The Dream of Gerontius" in *Verses on Various Occasions.* London: (ed. of 1912) Longmans Green.

O'Loughlin, Thomas. art. "How Many Priests Do We Need?" In *New Blackfriars.* November, 2005.

O'Loughlin, Thomas. art. "The Eucharist as 'The Meal That It Should Be' ". In *Worship,* January 2006.

Platen – Hallermund, A. (1948), *Die Tötung Geisteskranker in Deutschland.* Frankfurt am Main: Verlag der Frankfurter Hefte. Eng. Trans. (1948) *The Killing of the Mentally Ill in Germany.* London.

Polkinghorne, J. (1994), *Quarks, Chaos, and Christianity.* London: S.P.C.K.

Porter, R. (1966), *The Cambridge Illustrated History of Medicine.* Cambridge: Cambridge University Press.

Pounds, N.J.G. (2000), *A History of the English Parish.* Cambridge: Cambridge University Press.

Prat, Ferdinand, (1953), *Jésus Christ, sa vie sa doctrine, son eoevre.* Paris: Beauchesne.

Quasten, Johannes, (1953), *Patrology.* Westminster, Maryland: Newman Press.

Radice, Betty. (1963), (ed.) *The Letters of Pliny the Younger.* Harmsworth: Penguin.

Rahner, K. (1963), *The Church and the Sacraments.* London: Burns & Oates. Freiburg: Herder.

Rahner, K.(1966), *Theological Investigations, Vol. 5.* (trans. K. Smith). London: Darton, Longman, & Todd.

Rees, Martin. (2000), *Just Six Numbers.* London: Phoenix.

Rowley, H. (2006), *Téte à Téte: The Lives and Loves of Simone de Beauvoir and Jean-Paul Sartre.* London: Chatto & Windus.

Salmon, Pierre. (1959), *L'Office Divine.* Paris: Éditions du Cerf.

Schillebeeckx, E. (1965), *Marriage: Secular Reality and Saving Mystery.* London: Sheed & Ward.

Schmaus, Michael. (1959), *Katholische Dogmatik.* Munich: Max Heuber Verlag.

Selman, Francis. (2004), *The Soul – An Enquiry.* London: St.Paul's Publishing.

Spicer, K.P. (2008), *Hitler's Priests: Catholic Clergy and National Socialism.* DeKalb, Illinois: Northern Illinois University Press.

Stutz, U. (1895), *Die Eigenkirche als Element des mittelalterischgermanischen Kirchenrechtes.* Basle. English trans. Barraclough, G. (1938), *Mediaeval Germany .* Oxford: Basil Blackwell.

Swinburne, R. (1977), *The Coherence of Theism.* Oxford: Clarendon Press.

Swinburne, R. (1997), "Evidence for the Resurrection", in (eds.) Davis, S. Kendall, D. & O'Collins, G. *The Resurrection.* Oxford: Oxford University Press.

Synave, P. & Benoit, P. (1947), *La Prophétie,* Paris: Éditions du Cerf.

Tallis, R. (2004), *Why the Mind is not a Computer.* Exeter: Imprint Academic.

Tawney, R.H. (1972), *Religion and the Rise of Capitalism.* Harmondsworth: Penguin.

Teilhard de Chardin, Pierre. (1959), *The Phenomenon of Man.* London: Collins.

Thomas, Hugh. (1966), *The Slave Trade.* London: Picador.

Towey, Anthony. Art. "One Flew Out of the Atheist's Nest", in *The Pastoral Review.* Sept/Oct. 2007.

Vogels, H.J. (1992), *Celibacy – Gift or Law.* Tunbridge Wells: Burns & Oates.

Warner, Marina. (1976), *Alone of All Her Sex.* London: Picador.

Warnock, M. (2001), *An Intelligent Person's Guide to Ethics.* London: Duckworth.

Winter, Michael, M. (1960) *St. Peter and the Popes.* London: Darton, Longman & Todd.

Winter, Michael, M. (1995), *The Atonement,* Collegeville, Minnesota: The Liturgical Press.

Winter, Michael, M. (2002), *Misguided Morality: Catholic Moral Teaching in the Contemporary Church.* Aldershot: Ashgate Publishing Ltd.

Yarnold, Edward. (1978), "The Liturgy of the Faithful in the Fourth and Fifth Centuries", in Jones, C. Wainwright, G. & Yarnold, E. (eds.) *The Study of Liturgy.* London: S.P.C.K.

Zahn, Gordon, C. (1969), *Chaplains in the R.A.F.* Manchester: Manchester University Press.